RED MITTEN NATIONALISM

RED MITTEN NATIONALISM

Sport, Commercialism, and Settler Colonialism in Canada

Estée Fresco

McGill-Queen's University Press
Montreal & Kingston • London • Chicago

ISBN 978-0-2280-1416-4 (cloth)
ISBN 978-0-2280-1417-1 (paper)
ISBN 978-0-2280-1514-7 (ePDF)
ISBN 978-0-2280-1515-4 (ePUB)

Legal deposit fourth quarter 2022
Bibliothèque nationale du Québec

This book has been published with the help of a grant from the Canadian Federation for the Humanities and Social Sciences, through the Awards to Scholarly Publications Program, using funds provided by the Social Sciences and Humanities Research Council of Canada.

Funded by the Government of Canada | Financé par le gouvernement du Canada | Canada

Canada Council for the Arts | Conseil des arts du Canada

We acknowledge the support of the Canada Council for the Arts.

Nous remercions le Conseil des arts du Canada de son soutien.

Library and Archives Canada Cataloguing in Publication

Title: Red mitten nationalism : sport, commercialism, and settler colonialism in Canada / Estée Fresco.

Names: Fresco, Estée, author.

Description: Includes bibliographical references and index.

Identifiers: Canadiana (print) 20220390053 | Canadiana (ebook) 2022039010X | ISBN 9780228014164 (hardcover) | ISBN 9780228014171 (softcover) | ISBN 9780228015147 (PDF) | ISBN 9780228015154 (ePUB)

Subjects: LCSH: Nationalism and sports – Canada. | LCSH: Sports – Social aspects – Canada. | LCSH: Indigenous peoples – Canada.
Classification: LCC GV706.34 .F74 2022 | DDC 306.4/830971 – dc23

This book was designed and typeset by Peggy & Co. Design in 11/14 Minion Pro.

Contents

Figures

Acknowledgments

Funding for this research was generously provided by a Social Sciences and Humanities Research Council Doctoral Award and a Minor Research Grant from York University (Faculty of Liberal Arts & Professional Studies).

I spend many pages of this book discussing how activists are working to decolonize Canada. I hope I have done justice to their courage and vision for a better future.

This book began as a PhD dissertation supervised by Daniel Robinson at Western University, and it would not have come to fruition without his expert guidance. He read every draft with care and supported me as I pursued an academic career after graduation. I admire Janice Forysth's work and have benefited enormously from her advice and encouragement. Many others made valuable contributions to my doctoral research. Amanda Grzyb was supportive and insightful; Sasha Torres welcomed me to her office for encouraging conversations about the progress of my research; Romayne Smith Fullerton asked thought-provoking questions in my thesis defence; Gene Allen gave a fresh perspective on my theoretical approach; and the courses I took with Alison Hearn and Pauline Wakeham helped me develop ideas that eventually made their way into this book.

I completed my dissertation with a cohort of generous and gifted students, many of whom welcomed me into their homes when I commuted from Toronto to London. Special thanks to Andrea Benoit, Zak Bronson, Amy Freier, Atle Kjøsen, Sonya de Laat, Eric Lohman,

Claudie Massicotte, Chris Richardson, Gemma Richardson, Tiara Sukhan, Danielle Taschereau Mamers, Jessica Thom, and Liam Young.

Jonathan Crago at McGill-Queen's University Press worked tirelessly to make this book possible. I am grateful for him and for the efforts of McGill-Queen's hardworking staff. The anonymous reviewers provided comprehensive, constructive, and thoughtful feedback that strengthened my manuscript enormously. I am grateful for the time they invested in developing my work; I have learned a great deal from them. Kate Merriman copy edited the manuscript with a keen eye for detail.

I spent considerable time in Canadian archives and was consistently impressed by the diligence of the archivists who organize, preserve, and provide access to the holdings. They do such important work. The archivists at the Bibliothèque et Archives nationales du Québec and City of Calgary, Edmonton, Vancouver, and Victoria Archives responded graciously and helpfully to my requests, many of which were quite onerous.

I won the colleague lottery when I joined the Department of Communication & Media Studies at York University. My colleagues supported me as I navigated the challenges of revising my dissertation into a book, teaching undergraduate courses, and meeting the numerous demands of a tenure-track position. They were nothing but encouraging when I took parental leave, and I am grateful for their friendship and kindness. In addition to being excellent academics, they are principled people whom I admire. Special thanks to Mary-Louise Craven, Natalie Coulter, Susan Driver, and David Skinner, who took on mentorship roles. Thank you to the hardworking staff who keep everything running and everyone laughing. Thank you as well to the undergraduate students in the Communication & Media Studies program at York University and graduate students in the joint Communication & Culture program at York and Toronto Metropolitan University. They have made teaching a real pleasure.

I am fortunate to have wonderful colleagues from other universities. Nancy Bouchier gave me helpful advice about book publishing and Michael Dawson showed exceptional generosity when he shared material from his own archival research with me. I have benefited from collaborating with, and learning from, Nicole Neverson and hope to continue our collaboration for years to come. Sophy Chan, Vincci Li,

Courtney Szto, and Matt Ventresca continue to inspire me with their dedication to advancing social justice in their research.

My friends found seemingly endless ways of encouraging me as I wrote this book. They sent flowers, read drafts, and continued to show interest in my project as the years added up. I am fortunate to call Danielle Baribeau, Ainsley Goldman, Jessica Herschman, Jessica Howsam, Kevin Keystone, Peter Merriman, and Deborah Schwartz my friends.

To my parents, Berny and Karin Fresco, thank you for your unconditional love. You are models of selfless kindness. My parents-in-law Bob Munroe and Sheila Sammon are extraordinary people; I am lucky to have them in my life. My sister and siblings-in-law, and their partners, are a talented group of people – intelligent, creative, funny – with whom I love spending time: Sophie Blumenthal, Chrissy Munroe, David Munroe, Kathleen Munroe, Adam Taller, and Juline Taller Fresco.

Mike Munroe has been my partner in all senses of the word. He shares in the joys and challenges of the life we have built together with a love that continues to amaze me. Our daughters Evelyn and Anna are testament to that love.

Abbreviations

AFN	The Assembly of First Nations
CBC	The Canadian Broadcasting Corporation
COA	The Canadian Olympic Association (now the COC)
COC	The Canadian Olympic Committee (formerly the COA)
CODA	The Calgary Olympic Development Association
COJO	The Organizing Committee for the 1976 Montreal Olympic Games, known by its French acronym COJO (Comité organisateur des Jeux olympiques de 1976)
FHFN	The Four Host First Nations
FLQ	Front de libération du Québec
HBC	The Hudson's Bay Company
IOC	The International Olympic Committee
NCTR	The National Centre for Truth and Reconciliation
NPC	The Native Participation Committee (1994 Victoria Commonwealth Games)
OCO'88	The XV Olympic Winter Games Organizing Committee (Olympiques Calgary Olympics '88)
ORN	The Olympic Resistance Network
RBC	The Royal Bank of Canada
RCAP	The Royal Commission on Aboriginal Peoples
TOP	The Olympic Partners Programme (formerly called The Olympic Programme)
TRC	The Truth and Reconciliation Commission of Canada

VANOC	The Vancouver Organizing Committee for the 2010 Olympic and Paralympic Winter Games
VBC	The Vancouver Bid Corporation
VCGS	The Victoria Commonwealth Games Society
XICGCF	The XI Commonwealth Games Canada (1978) Foundation Archival Collections

ARCHIVAL COLLECTIONS

BAnQ	Bibliothèque et Archives nationales du Québec
CCA	City of Calgary Archives
CEA	City of Edmonton Archives
CVA	City of Vancouver Archives
CVicA	City of Victoria Archives

List of People

Campbell, Ernest: former chief of the xʷməθkʷəy̓əm (Musqueam) First Nation

Campbell, Larry: former mayor of Vancouver

Cardinal, Harold: former president of the Indian Association of Alberta

de Coubertin, Pierre: French baron who founded the modern Olympic movement

Drapeau, Jean: former mayor of Montreal

Elliott, Charles: Coast Salish artist who designed the Victoria Commonwealth Games' Queen's baton (along with Hunt and Thompson) and Games' gold medal

Furlong, John: VANOC CEO

Harcourt, Mike: former premier of British Columbia

Heller, George: VCGS president

Henry, Danny: NPC co-ordinator

Hunt, Corinne: Kwakwa̱ka̱'wakw (Kwakiutl) and Tlingit artist who designed the Vancouver Olympic Games' medals

Hunt, Richard: Kwakwa̱ka̱'wakw (Kwakiutl) artist who designed the Victoria Commonwealth Games' Queen's baton (along with Elliott and Thompson) and Games' bronze medal

Jacob, Gilbert (Gibby): hereditary chief of the Sḵwx̱wú7mesh (Squamish) First Nation

Joseph, Tewanee: FHFN CEO

King, Frank: CODA chairman and OCO'88 CEO

Klein, Ralph: former mayor of Calgary
Krentz, Richard: Coast Salish artist who carved "The Spirit of the Nations" totem pole associated with the Victoria Commonwealth Games
Lougheed, Peter: former premier of Alberta
Niven, Bob: CODA president and member of OCO'88's Board of Directors
Ominayak, Bernard: chief of the Lubicon Lake Nation at the time of the 1988 Calgary Olympics and current chief of the Muskotew Sakahikan Enowuk, the traditional government of the Lubicon Lake Nation
Poole, Jack: VBC chairman and VANOC Board of Directors chairman until his death in 2009
Pound, Dick: Canadian IOC member
Powderface, Sykes: OCO'88 native liaison coordinator
Rousseau, Roger: COJO president and commissioner
Samaranch, Juan Antonio: former IOC president
Sikkuark, Nick: Inuit artist who carved the Edmonton Commonwealth Games' Queen's baton
Thompson, Art: Nuu-chah-nulth (Nootka) artist who designed the Victoria Commonwealth Games' Queen's baton (along with Elliott and Hunt) and Games' silver medal
Van Vliet, Maury: XICGCF president
Vickers, Roy Henry: First Nations artist who carved "The Legend of the Salmon People" totem pole associated with the Victoria Commonwealth Games

RED MITTEN NATIONALISM

Introduction

Impassioned Objects and Seething Absences

Canadian athletes participating in the opening ceremony of the 2010 Vancouver Winter Olympic Games carried symbols of the nation on their bodies. Speed skater (and cyclist) Clara Hughes led Team Canada in the Parade of Nations holding a large Canadian flag in her hands and wearing a Hudson's Bay Company (HBC) scarf around her shoulders. The scarf featured the company's iconic point blanket pattern, which is cream with green, red, yellow, and navy stripes. The Canadian Olympians following behind Hughes were also dressed in outfits designed by HBC: red jackets, black pants, red and black checkered scarves, toques emblazoned with the word "Canada," and red mittens with white maple leaves on the palms. As they waved to the crowd and cameras capturing the event on live television, the athletes' hands looked like miniature Canadian flags. Literally and metaphorically, they embodied national identity (figure 0.1).

Hughes did not wear an HBC-branded toque. Hers bore the emblem of the Four Host First Nations (FHFN), the collective name of the Lil̓wat (Lil'wat), xʷməθkʷəy̓əm (Musqueam), Sḵwx̱wú7mesh (Squamish), and Tsleil-Waututh First Nations, on whose territory the Vancouver Games were held. Before the Parade of Nations began, FHFN representatives delivered an official welcome to athletes and spectators, and Indigenous youth from across Canada danced wearing what Olympic organizers described as "their own traditional clothing and regalia."[1] The dancers remained on stage during the parade, setting up an unexpected and

0.1 Team Canada marching in the 2010 Vancouver Olympics opening ceremony.

likely unintentional scene: as the Canadian athletes marched toward the Indigenous dancers, they looked like Royal Canadian Mounted Police, whose uniforms are similar to the athletes' outfits (i.e., red on top, black on the bottom). From afar, the Olympians looked like a police force invading the dancers' space.[2]

This image calls attention to the multiple symbolic meanings of the athletes' clothing and apparel. While these objects represent national pride to some, they represent Canada's Settler colonial history to others.

The mittens covering the athletes' hands are a case in point. In the lead-up to the 2010 Vancouver Olympics, HBC sold three and a half million pairs of red mittens, replicas of the ones the company designed for Vancouver Olympic torchbearers and Canadian Olympians.[3] The head of the Vancouver Olympic Organizing Committee (VANOC), John Furlong, encouraged Canadians to demonstrate their patriotism and support for the games by wearing the mittens along the torch relay route. He told a reporter, "We're hoping that everywhere the Olympic flame visits in Canada it will be greeted and cheered on its journey by a sea of red mittens *waved proudly by Canadians* in the crowd."[4] A tag attached to the mittens encouraged consumers to "Show your community and Canadian pride by wearing Red Mittens to cheer on the Vancouver 2010

0.2 Blood on Your Hands pamphlet.

Olympic and Paralympic Torch Relay Torchbearers and our Canadian athletes competing at the 2010 Winter Games."[5]

Members of the anti-Olympic activist group the Olympic Resistance Network (ORN), however, did not associate these objects with national pride. They published a pamphlet showing the mittens dripping with blood under the caption "Blood on Your Hands: Are You Wearing HBC's History of Colonialism?" (figure 0.2).[6] According to the pamphlet, "the corporation took control over several areas of Canada, forcing their rules of trade, immigration, settlement and governance onto Indigenous people." It also notes that HBC "acted as the colonial government" in Canada.[7] King Charles II of England established the company by Royal Charter in 1670 and gave it the authority to trade and negotiate treaties with Indigenous groups and defend territory from them. The king also gave HBC a commercial monopoly over the area then known as Rupert's Land, located in present-day Canada.[8] The company was a central player in the Canadian fur trade. Employees gave point blankets to Indigenous trappers in exchange for beaver pelts and sent the pelts to Europe to be made into felt hats. The HBC History Foundation's website describes wool blankets as "among the most popular trade items in the Canadian fur trade."[9]

By the time Vancouver hosted the 2010 Olympic Games, HBC employees were no longer exchanging blankets for beaver pelts. However, the company still uses the point blanket pattern in its clothing and apparel – including the scarf Hughes wore in the Parade of Nations. Moreover, as the ORN publication demonstrates, HBC's historic contribution to the Canadian fur trade informs the symbolic meaning of the red mittens the company designed for the games. These mittens join other commodities sold through the Canadian-hosted Olympic and Commonwealth games – mascot toys, pins, coins, postage stamps, glassware, and more – that represent national identity, and they serve as material expressions of the fusion of nationalism and commercialism.

In this book, I critically analyze the fusion of nationalism and commercialism in the following sporting events: the 1976 Montreal Summer Olympics, 1978 Edmonton Commonwealth Games, 1988 Calgary Winter Olympics, 1994 Victoria Commonwealth Games, and 2010 Vancouver Winter Olympics. I show that the games' commercial dimensions worked alongside their cultural and educational features to shape dominant ideas about Canadian identity and history. These ideas were conveyed through bid-related documents and performances; opening and closing ceremonies; torch and Queen's baton relays; corporate sponsors' promotional practices; Olympic/Commonwealth games mascots and education resources; and the design, production, and consumption of games-related commodities. Collectively, these practices communicated interconnected narratives about Canadian values, citizenship norms, and history that circulated during the Olympic and Commonwealth games hosted in this country.

Games organizers consistently used symbols of Indigenous peoples' cultures to represent the nation to domestic and international audiences. This representational practice intersected with three commercial activities prevalent in the Olympic and Commonwealth games. First, organizers and sponsors depicted corporate investment in the games and the consumption of specially produced commodities as nationally significant acts. Second, they used mascots and education resources to expose young people to select ideas about Canadian identity – ideas that also circulated through other games-related cultural and commercial practices. Third, they used marketing practices to shape host regions' identities and sold games-related souvenirs that reflected politically charged ideas about provincial-federal relations or reconciliation between

Indigenous peoples and Settlers. These practices were present in the 1976 Montreal Olympics and 1978 Edmonton Commonwealth Games; however, they began intensifying and overlapping in the 1980s and escalated to an unprecedented degree in the 2010 Vancouver Olympics.

This fusion of nationalism and commercialism has significant political consequences. It helps legitimate Settlers' claims to own and derive profit from Indigenous peoples' land; shapes definitions of good citizens, creating a dynamic of inclusion and exclusion based on consumer-driven participation in civic culture; and influences public perception of who has jurisdiction over natural resources in Canada. Taken together, the representational and commercial practices I analyze are features of a larger Settler colonial structure in Canada – one that, as Patrick Wolfe notes, is organized around the "practical elimination" of Indigenous peoples.[10] Of course, Indigenous peoples have opposed, and continue to oppose, Settler colonialism, and many activists used the Canadian-hosted Olympic and Commonwealth games to advance Indigenous rights in Canada. In doing so, they undermined the coherency and authority of Settler colonial narratives about the nation that circulated in the games.

Through a close reading of cultural texts and images created for the games – ads, commodities, opening and closing ceremony recordings, and so on – I demonstrate how the fusion of nationalism and commercialism in Canada is inseparable from the Settler colonial context in which it circulates. I advance a critical understanding of the interrelationship between consumer culture, representation, nationalism, and international sport that is informed by two scholarly fields: media and communication studies and socio-cultural studies of sport. I ask: How do celebratory ideas about Settler colonial history and identity become manifest in, and expressed through, promotional processes and material objects associated with international sporting events hosted in Canada? I reveal that commodities representing the nation are neither superficial nor meaningless goods; rather, they are impassioned objects that hold together unresolved contradictions that lie at the heart of Settler Canadian identity.[11] Reframing their dominant meanings transforms these commodities from uncomplicated representations of national pride into powerful reminders of the history and persistence of Settler colonialism in Canada, as well as the ultimate failure of this country's Settler colonial project.

I begin this introduction by situating the fusion of nationalism and commercialism within a social, cultural, and economic context. I briefly discuss the origins of the Olympic and British Empire/Commonwealth games before focusing on the time period covered in this book. Specifically, between 1976 and 2010, branded nationalism in Canada became more pronounced; politicians in Canada and abroad began championing neoliberal policies; and the Olympic Games grew more commercialized. I then discuss state-led attempts to assimilate Indigenous peoples into Settler society; Indigenous activism centred on self-determination and land rights; and reconciliation initiatives aimed at improving Indigenous-Settler relations. I subsequently discuss three theoretical concepts that inform my analysis of the commercial and cultural dimensions of the Canadian-hosted Olympic/Commonwealth games: commodification, commodity fetishism, and ghostly hauntings. I conclude with a chapter outline.

Nationalism, Commercialism, and the Olympic and Commonwealth Games in Canada

Modern Olympic and Commonwealth games (originally called the British Empire Games) are mega-events: large-scale cultural happenings with dramatic character, mass popular appeal, and international significance.[12] As *sport* mega-events (sometimes called megasports), they feature pre-eminent competition, occur at predictable times, offer opportunities for historical comparison, and transcend traditional meanings of sport.[13] Political and cultural practices surrounding sport mega-events, such as the performance of opening and closing ceremonies and selection of mascots, intersect with non-sporting practices to shape dominant narratives about national identity.[14] While the Olympic Games are more commercially sophisticated than the Commonwealth Games, both events are sponsored by corporations and create opportunities for nationalism and commercialism to converge in meaningful ways.

The French baron Pierre de Coubertin founded the modern Olympic Games in the late nineteenth century. Inspired by the way educators at elite British schools used sport instruction to instill morals in their students, Coubertin introduced his idea for the games at an 1894 congress in Paris, where participants voted to revive the ancient Greek Olympics and establish the International Olympic Committee (IOC).[15] Coubertin developed Olympism as the games' underlying philosophy. According to the Olympic Charter, Olympism aims to place "sport at the service of the harmonious development of humankind, with a view to promoting a peaceful society concerned with the preservation of human dignity."[16] This goal reflects Coubertin's belief that sport-related practices can enhance human development and improve the world.[17] The first modern Olympic Games were held in Athens in 1896 and featured summer sports including gymnastics, tennis, and swimming. Most competitors in Olympic events held in the late nineteenth and early twentieth centuries were White, upper-class, and male since the IOC restricted professional athletes and women, Black, Asian, and Indigenous athletes from participating. The rule that all Olympic athletes be amateurs (i.e., not receive income from competing in sports), persisted until the 1990s.[18]

The founders of the British Empire Games (later known as the Commonwealth Games) took inspiration from J. Astley Cooper, who developed the idea for a "Pan-Britannic and Anglo-Saxon Festival" in the 1890s.[19] He envisioned, but never organized, a multi-sport event featuring cultural and industry-related exhibits "praising the Anglo-Saxon race."[20] A Canadian, Melville Marks "Bobby" Robinson, played a leading role in creating the British Empire Games. Robinson was active in the Canadian sporting scene as manager of the Canadian track and field team and as sports editor of the *Hamilton Spectator*. With support from members of the Amateur Athletic Union of Canada and newly formed British Empire Games Committee, he brought the first-ever British Empire Games to Hamilton, Canada, in 1930.[21] Organizers modelled the event on the Olympics but restricted participation to British athletes who were amateurs.[22] The games returned to Canada in 1954 with Vancouver as host city. They were the first to be called the British Empire *and Commonwealth Games*. The games underwent a further name change in 1978, the year Edmonton hosted them, becoming the Commonwealth Games (i.e., "British Empire" was dropped from the name).

When I began researching this book, I focused exclusively on the three Olympics hosted in Canada. However, I decided to expand my analysis to include the two Commonwealth games hosted in Canada between 1976 and 2010. In doing so, I show that my findings do not apply only to the Olympics but extend to a comparatively smaller and less commercial sport mega-event. Moreover, I identify a common social and political significance of the fusion of nationalism and commercialism in the Canadian-hosted games. Specifically, the commercialization of national identity in both events shapes, and is shaped by, the history and persistence of Settler colonialism. While I limited my archival research to the Canadian-hosted Olympic and Commonwealth games, I also discuss examples of Indigenous cultural representation in the 1967 and 1999 Pan American Games, both hosted in Winnipeg. These examples add another layer of detail to my consideration of the Settler colonial dimensions of Canadian sport mega-events.

Several socio-cultural and economic developments influenced the expression of nationalism in the Olympic and Commonwealth games hosted in Canada between 1976 and 2010. One notable development is the growth of branded nationalism, which is a type of nationalism expressed through commercial practices. The 1976 Montreal Olympic Games and 1978 Edmonton Commonwealth Games occurred a few years before branded nationalism became prominent in this country. However, it was on the rise in 1988 when Calgary hosted the Winter Olympics, and the extent to which consumers embraced corporate brands as representations of distinctly Canadian ways of life increased in the years leading up to the 1994 Victoria Commonwealth Games and, subsequently, 2010 Vancouver Winter Olympics.

To be clear, branded nationalism did not emerge in the 1980s. Rather, it became more pronounced at this time. Companies like the Bank of Montreal, Canadian Pacific Railway, HBC, and Red Rose Tea included patriotic messages in their advertising prior to the 1980s.[23] Moreover, Donica Belisle shows that branded nationalism dates to the 1890s, when Eaton's, Simpson's, and HBC depicted their stores as national icons.[24] Advertisements from this time suggested that English Canadians participated in a commonly shared and nationally significant experience when they read department stores' catalogues and/or shopped at their retail locations.[25]

Catherine Carstairs shows that "the degree to which Canadians have been willing to drape themselves in branded products such as Roots and Molson Canadian gear, embracing them as part of a Canadian way of life," increased dramatically in the 1980s.[26] Several factors contributed to the surge of branded nationalism in this decade. Canadians became concerned that the federal government's free trade policies would lead to American cultural domination in Canada, and companies responded to this concern by encouraging consumers to buy domestic products. Several polarizing events, including a referendum on whether Quebec should separate from Canada and a conflict over Indigenous land rights in Oka, Quebec, which turned violent, weakened national unity. As Canadians began questioning the policies of bilingualism and multiculturalism that had previously united them, companies like the clothing retailer Roots and beer company Molson offered consumers a different image of national identity; this version relied on shared images and experiences rather than the bilingual, multicultural ideal that was prevalent in the 1960s and '70s.[27]

Politicians in Canada and abroad began embracing neoliberalism as an economic model and the related ideology of market fundamentalism around the same time branded nationalism was becoming prominent in Canada. Neoliberals support limited government regulation of society. They reject Keynesian economic policy, which maintains that governments should regulate capitalist economic systems, asserting instead that individual prosperity, freedom, and happiness thrive when governments allow market capitalism to operate largely unfettered.[28] Relatedly, market fundamentalism is a comprehensive worldview and political movement motivated by the belief that market capitalism exists in a natural state outside politics and government and, as such, should not be heavily regulated.[29] Under market fundamentalism, goods and services that were not previously subject to market pressure become treated as commodities that can be priced and sold.[30]

Margaret Thatcher, who became the British prime minister in 1979, and Ronald Reagan, who became the president of the United States the following year, were influential proponents of neoliberalism. Brian Mulroney, Canada's prime minister from 1984 to 1993, was sympathetic to Thatcher's and Reagan's politics. He sought to shift the country away from a social welfare model and towards neoliberalism.[31] During his first term, Mulroney reduced inter-governmental fiscal transfers, partially de-indexed tax credits, and reduced family allowances and old age security benefits. After he was re-elected in November 1988, he introduced more policies aimed at minimizing government spending. The Mulroney government restructured key elements of Canada's social security system, tightened eligibility requirements for family income and old age benefits, and stopped directly financing unemployment insurance.[32]

The Olympic movement was becoming more commercialized around the same time branded nationalism was intensifying in Canada and neoliberalism was on the rise; this confluence of factors created a fertile environment for the expression of branded nationalism in the 1988 Calgary Olympics. Juan Antonio Samaranch became IOC president in 1980 and, under his leadership, the organization became more profit oriented. The IOC began intervening in Olympic host cities' negotiation of broadcast rights, with the organization eventually taking full control of these negotiations. Samaranch also oversaw the creation of the IOC's international sponsorship program, The Olympic Programme (TOP; now called The Olympic Partners Programme), in 1985. Modelled after the profitable sponsorship program designed by organizers of the 1984 Los Angeles Summer Olympics, TOP minimizes the IOC's reliance on income from sales of Olympic broadcast rights by providing it with a lucrative new revenue source in the form of sponsorships.[33]

Victoria hosted the 1994 Commonwealth Games in the shadow of these commercial developments within the Olympic movement. Games organizer George Heller suggested to journalists that the Commonwealth Games Federation should adopt a symbol like the Olympic rings and proposed a five-triangle design as an option.[34] Under Heller's guidance, the Victoria Games raised more income from sponsorships than any previous Commonwealth Games.[35] Heller went on to become president and CEO of HBC from 1999 to 2006, during which time he secured the company's position as official outfitter of the 2010 Vancouver Olympics.[36] HBC contributed to the Vancouver Olympic Games' record-setting sponsorship program, with the games' official report noting that the organizing committee "attained unprecedented domestic sponsorship levels."[37]

Organizers of the Victoria Games and, later, the 2010 Vancouver Olympics, sought corporate sponsorship for these events at a time when several Canadian brands had successfully established themselves as symbols of national identity. Roots incorporates iconic images associated with Canada into its promotional material and clothing design including beavers, maple leaves, scenes from the Canadian Pacific Railway, Algonquin memorabilia, and Indigenous headdresses. By the 1990s, the company was, in Carstairs words, "fully accepted as an authentic Canadian symbol."[38] It outfitted the Canadian Olympians competing in the 1998 Nagano Winter Olympics and the "poor-boy" caps included in Roots' Olympic clothing line became internationally recognized as distinctly Canadian.[39] The coffee chain Tim Hortons occupies a similar position to Roots in the Canadian consumer landscape. It began releasing ads in the 1990s featuring customers telling poignant stories about their lives in Canada. According to Patricia Cormack and James Cosgrave, these ads help Tim Hortons position itself as "a site of national narrative and political enactment."[40] Around the same time, beer brands like Molson and Labatt created promotional campaigns that celebrated national values and culture. A now iconic 2000 Molson ad called "The Rant" features "Joe Canadian" proudly listing features of Canadian identity.[41]

Many companies that link their brand identity to national identity, including Tim Hortons, Molson, and HBC, are now subsidiaries of foreign-owned corporations. As a result, Canadians do not have many opportunities to engage in what Enric Castelló and Sabina Mihelj refer to as *political* consumer nationalism (PCN). This term describes a form of nationalism that consumers express by attempting to influence a nation's economy through their buying habits. For instance, they may intentionally purchase domestically produced goods in order to strengthen a local economy, or try to weaken a foreign economy by boycotting goods imported from that country.[42] Canadians, however, engage in *symbolic* consumer nationalism (SCN) when they buy commodities like HBC red mittens and associate them with national identity and pride. In these instances, individuals express their nationalism by "consuming, using, buying, or wearing products or services that are either produced nationally or otherwise recognized as national."[43] The example of the red mittens, which were made in China, illustrates that SCN includes instances where the design of a product matters more to consumers than where it was produced.[44]

Returning to the concept of branded nationalism, Carstairs does not distinguish between the symbolic meaning of the Roots brand and Roots branded products. When she writes that Roots had become "fully accepted as an authentic Canadian symbol" by the 1990s, she appears to be describing the company and the products it sells.[45] Indeed, their symbolic meanings seem indistinguishable. However, ideas about national identity associated with a company's *brand* are not always identical to those associated with a *branded product*. For instance, when Petro-Canada sponsored the Calgary Olympics and HBC sponsored the Vancouver Olympics, both companies linked their brand identity to national identity in their promotional material. Such ideas influenced the symbolic meanings of Petro-Canada Olympic glassware and HBC red mittens. However, members of local games' organizing committees, journalists, athletes, politicians, and other figures also shaped these commodities' meanings and, as a result, they represent ideas about the nation that diverge from those found in Petro-Canada's and HBC's marketing material.

I introduce the term "commodity nationalism" (e.g., red mitten nationalism) to describe a version of national identity represented through branded objects. This term distinguishes the material ways in which national identity gets shaped and communicated (e.g., the design and consumption of commodities) from the immaterial ways (e.g., advertising). It adds another layer of complexity to our understanding of how Canadian identity becomes commercialized and offers scholars new vocabulary to use when identifying the material dimensions of branded nationalism. I do not intend the term "commodity nationalism" to replace the term "branded nationalism." Rather I use this new term to draw attention to the way Canadians' consumption of branded commodities influences how they define the nation and express their patriotism.

The Settler Colonial Past and Present in Canada

I analyze instances of branded nationalism and commodity nationalism in the Canadian-hosted Olympic and Commonwealth games by considering how the commercialization of Canadian identity operates within a Settler colonial context. In doing so, I contribute to existing critiques of commercial representations of the nation. Carstairs argues that Roots nationalism lacks the positive features of earlier versions of Canadian nationalism such as tolerance, diversity, and community.[46] Similarly, John Wright, Gregory Millard, and Sarah Riegel describe the type of nationalism represented through Roots merchandise as an "in-your-face, though ultimately empty nationalism."[47] While valuable, these arguments do not interrogate the Settler colonial logic that informs ideas about Canadian identity and is circulated through branding practices and commodities.

I am a Settler Canadian who continues to grapple with decolonization as praxis. As Wolfe notes, Settlers do not leave the countries they colonize, and Settler colonialism is not the outcome of a single event or series of events like invasions or battles. Rather, it is a structure, a land-centred project involving a comprehensive range of agencies that aim to eliminate Indigenous societies.[48] The "logic of elimination," according to Wolfe, functions as "an organizing principal of settler-colonial society."[49] This logic manifests in a range of ongoing policies and practices that secure and maintain Settlers' access to territory. In Canada, they include efforts to suppress Indigenous cultures. Anti-Potlatch laws passed in 1885, and persisting until 1951, are a case in point. Practised by Indigenous communities from the Pacific Northwest, potlach traditions vary greatly between groups but "generally involve music, dance, feasting, theatrics, and spiritual ceremony."[50] Participants often claim traditional names, ranks, or hereditary privileges during Potlatches and they are held to mark significant life stages such as births, marriages, and deaths. In addition, participants enhance their status by giving away possessions.[51] Cora Voyageur, David Newhouse, and Dan Beavon contextualize the Potlatch ban in Canada in relation to the capitalist drive to accumulate wealth. They write that the ban likely "resulted from a misunderstanding on the part of Europeans about the potlatch. One can easily imagine the confusion that was felt when a nascent capitalistic world view based on the accumulation of goods was confronted by a world view based on generosity, reciprocity, and distribution."[52]

Indian residential schools were also established in the nineteenth century. Jointly run by the Canadian government and Christian churches, the Settlers who developed and ran them subscribed to the racist idea that Indigenous children were savages who needed civilizing. Indigenous children were forcibly removed from their families and communities and sent to these schools, where they were poorly fed and required to perform arduous tasks like farming, cooking, and cleaning to keep the schools running. Students experienced cruel physical punishment, rarely received encouragement or affection, and some were sexually abused by teachers or religious clergy. The conditions of abuse in residential schools were widespread as "staff abuse of children created conditions for the student abuse of other students."[53] Most residential schools were closed by the 1980s, but a few remained open until the mid-1990s.[54]

The death rate for children enrolled in residential schools was significantly higher than for the general Canadian population. Residential school survivors would later report seeing classmates die, and some even dug graves for the deceased.[55] Infectious diseases, including tuberculosis, were responsible for numerous deaths, but the exact cause of death for many children remains unknown and the total number of fatalities is still coming to light.[56] The National Centre for Truth and Reconciliation (NCTR) and the Truth and Reconciliation Commission (TRC) have documented the identities of 4,117 children who died while attending residential schools.[57] In 2021, several Indigenous nations discovered unmarked graves on the sites of former residential schools. We now know that over 1,000 bodies were buried on grounds that formerly housed the Marieval Indian Residential School in Saskatchewan; Kamloops Indian Residential School in British Columbia; and Kuper Island Residential School in British Columbia.[58] According to NCTR executive director Stephanie Scott, "The recognition of these unmarked graves represents a new chapter in our collective understanding of the devastating impacts of the residential school system."[59] The search for additional graves is ongoing.

The federal government's establishment of residential schools was not an anomaly in Canadian history. Rather, it was the outcome of a systematic effort to assimilate Indigenous peoples into Settler society, one that continued well into the twentieth and twenty-first centuries.[60] In 1969, one year before Montreal won its bid to host the 1976 Summer Games, the federal government released a document called "Statement of the Government of Canada on Indian Policy." Commonly referred to as the White Paper, it sought to eliminate the unique status Indigenous peoples occupied in Canada; proposed abolishing the Department of Indian Affairs, Indian Act, Indian status, and treaty obligations; and argued that Indigenous peoples' rights were protected by federal multicultural policies.[61] According to Christine O'Bonsawin, the White Paper "was tantamount to a Liberal attempt at assimilation. In short, Trudeau's government was recommending the incorporation of indigenous people as an ethnic minority into Canada's national fabric by eliminating their special historical status."[62] Indigenous groups including the Indian Association of Alberta and National Indian Brotherhood produced an official response to the White Paper criticizing the government's conceptualization of Indigenous peoples' rights, and the government ultimately chose not to implement its recommendations.[63]

Opposition to the White Paper marked the beginning of a period of Indigenous activism centred on the issue of self-determination.[64] In 1973, the Supreme Court of Canada ruled on a landmark Indigenous rights case involving the Nisga'a First Nation in British Columbia's Nass Valley. In *Calder et al. v. Attorney-General of British Columbia*, the Nisga'a argued that they retained Aboriginal title because they never signed a treaty with the Crown. Aboriginal title is a legal term that describes Indigenous peoples' inherent right to land. The Supreme Court justices hearing the case agreed that the Nisga'a held Aboriginal title prior to European settlement in the province; however, they were divided on the question of whether the Nisga'a still held it.[65]

Colonial rule in Canada shifted in the 1960s and 1970s in response to the rights-based activism Indigenous peoples mounted in these decades. Whereas Settler colonialism had previously operated through explicitly racist, oppressive, and violent practices, it now became, in Glen Coulthard's words, "reproduced through a seemingly more conciliatory set of discourses and institutional practices that emphasize our [Indigenous peoples'] *recognition* and *accommodation*."[66] Even though section 35(1) of the Canadian Constitution Act, 1982, recognizes Indigenous peoples' right to self-determination, the federal government has largely failed in its promise to uphold this right. The Lubicon Lake Nation's assertion of their rights to oil-rich land in northern Alberta illustrates this point.[67] Companies began extracting oil from Lubicon territory in the 1950s and accelerated their activity in the late 1970s. The Lubicon never signed a treaty with the Crown, and they argued that oil companies lacked the authority to operate on their land. When Calgary hosted the 1988 Winter Olympics, members of the Lubicon Nation used the games to gain public support for their land rights campaign.[68]

Indigenous activists earned a significant victory in 1990 when they successfully held up the ratification of the Meech Lake Accord; the federal government initiated the accord in 1987 to amend the Canadian Constitution. However, the government failed to consult Indigenous leaders about the proposed changes. Members of such organizations as the Assembly of First Nations (AFN) and Inuit Committee on National Issues argued that a proposed clause recognizing Quebec as a distinct society within Canada failed to also recognize Indigenous nations as distinct societies. Their opposition prompted Manitoba politician Elijah Harper, a member of the Oji-Cree First Nation, to withhold his support for the accord, an act that ultimately led to its defeat.[69]

That same year, the city of Oka, Quebec, announced plans to expand a golf course that would impinge on a forested area known as the Pines.

The Kanien'kehá:ka (Mohawk) of Kanehsatake opposed these plans because they consider the area sacred and use it as a burial place. Kanehsatake residents barricaded the entrance to the Pines to prevent construction from proceeding. When Quebec police confronted the protestors, shots were fired, a corporal died, and the police withdrew. Kanien'kehá:ka (Mohawk) from the nearby Kahnawà:ke then blocked three major highways and seized the Mercier Bridge, which connects Montreal suburbs to the city's downtown core, in an act of solidarity with the Kanehsatake protestors. Prime Minister Mulroney responded to the escalating conflict by invoking Canada's National Defence Act and sending more than 4,000 federal troops to Oka. The city agreed to sell the disputed land to the federal government, ending the proposed golf course expansion, and protestors dismantled their barricades.[70]

Victoria hosted the 1994 Commonwealth Games in the aftermath of the Kanien'kehá:ka (Mohawk)-Oka conflict, when the federal government was attempting to strengthen Indigenous-Settler relations. The Canadian government established the Royal Commission on Aboriginal People (RCAP) in 1991 to "investigate the evolution of the relationship among aboriginal peoples (Indian, Inuit, and Métis), the Canadian government, and Canadian society as a whole" and make recommendations aimed at improving this relationship.[71] Indian Affairs and Northern Development minister Jane Stewart addressed RCAP's findings in a 1998 "Statement of Reconciliation," which acknowledged the federal government played a vital role in the development and administration of residential schools. The government committed $350 million for community-based healing projects for former residential school students and established an alternative dispute resolution program to address the abuse teachers and clergy perpetrated against students.[72] The statement, however, conceptualizes Settler colonialism as part of Canada's past, albeit with an ongoing legacy. By failing to acknowledge the colonial present, it divests the government from its obligation to address contemporary practices that contribute to Indigenous peoples' oppression.[73]

The alternative dispute resolution program the government initiated in response to the RCAP report attracted significant public criticism. AFN members argued that it was inadequate and taking too long to resolve individuals' claims.[74] In 2005, the organization launched a $36 billion class-action lawsuit against the federal government on behalf of residential school survivors, deceased students, and their families.

Ottawa settled out of court the following year by accepting the Indian Residential Schools Settlement Agreement, the largest and most complex class-action settlement in Canadian history.[75] Prime Minister Stephen Harper established the Truth and Reconciliation Commission of Canada (TRC) as part of the agreement. In 2008, two years before Vancouver hosted the Winter Olympics, Harper publicly apologized to residential school survivors, their families, and communities for the harm caused by these institutions.[76] He acknowledged that the goal of residential schools was to assimilate Indigenous children into Settler society and that "the legacy of Indian Residential Schools has contributed to social problems that continue to exist in many communities today."[77]

According to the TRC's final report, residential school survivors and their families needed to hear the apology: "They had lived with pain, fear, and anger for most of their lives, resulting from the abrupt separation from their families and their experiences at residential schools, and they wanted desperately to begin their healing. They needed to have validated their sense that what had been done to them was wrong."[78] However, scholars criticize the apology for failing to address the colonial policies and practices that underpinned the residential school system and for discounting an important truth: the schools were part of a Settler colonial system that still operates today.[79]

It is thus essential to recognize that the Settler colonial project in Canada is ongoing; it is equally important to recognize that it is a failure. Residential schools did not successfully assimilate all Indigenous peoples into Settler society. Daily reminders of this truth exist across the country, in the many ways Indigenous peoples practice their cultures, speak their languages, and connect to their histories. Indeed, Settler colonialism is an incomplete process. Audra Simpson articulates this idea beautifully when she writes, "Colonialism survives in a settler form. In this form, it fails at what it is supposed to do: eliminate Indigenous people; take all their land; absorb them into a white, property-owning body politic."[80]

Commodities, Fetish, and Haunting

My analysis of the fusion of nationalism and commercialism is grounded in the proposition that colonialism and capitalism are intertwined, an idea that Coulthard expertly explores in his reading of Karl Marx. In *Capital*, Marx argues that the emergence of a capitalist mode of production separated non-capitalist producers, communities, and societies from their means of production and subsistence.[81] This idea informs Coulthard's critique of capitalism. However, he argues that the driving force shaping the relationship between Indigenous peoples and the Canadian state is dispossession rather than proletarianization.[82] By advancing this argument, Coulthard resists an economic reductionist reading of Marx and instead applies contemporary Indigenous thought and practice to his interpretation of *Capital*. For Coulthard, cultural practices are as important as economic practices in explaining social relations because capitalism works alongside other forms of exploitation to secure the dominance of the Settler colonial state.[83] "Any strategy geared toward authentic decolonization," he writes, "must directly confront more than mere economic relations; it has to account for the multifarious ways in which capitalism, patriarchy, white supremacy, and the totalizing character of state power interact with one another to form the constellation of power relations that sustain colonial patterns of behaviour, structures, and relationships."[84]

Sport-related commercial practices exist within this constellation of power relations. I argue that commodities sold during the Canadian-hosted Olympic and Commonwealth games hold together ideologically charged and contradictory ideas about the nation. It is thus essential to establish a precise definition of a commodity.

Many of the material goods I analyze (e.g., clothing, glassware, coins, postage stamps, stuffed animals, pins, etc.) fit Marx's definition of a commodity: they are material goods intended for exchange in a capitalist system. Yet according to Marx, not all objects are commodities. There is no intrinsic feature of a chair, for instance, that makes it a commodity. Rather, commodities are products intended for exchange, and a defining feature of a commodity is its exchangeability.[85] It must have a use value, defined as the commodity's function and the societal needs it fills, and an exchange value, defined as the quantity and type of goods to which the commodity is considered equivalent. A commodity's exchange value is socially determined. This value is not an inherent part of the object, but rather a judgment people make about the object.[86]

Arjun Appadurai argues that it is not necessary to distinguish between commodities and other things. Rather, a commodity is "one phase in the life of some things."[87] Things, like people, have social lives. They become commodities when they enter a "commodity situation" and their ability to be exchanged for other commodities becomes their socially relevant feature.[88] A "commodity situation" has a temporal component (the commodity phase), social component (the commodity context), and conceptual component (commodity candidacy). Things can move in and out of a commodity situation, and the exchange value of objects in a commodity situation is contextual; it is determined by standards and criteria established within a specific social and historical context.[89]

Appadurai's observations can be applied to the objects included in a Calgary-based Glenbow Museum exhibit, *The Spirit Sings: Artistic Traditions of Canada's First People*, that was affiliated with the Calgary Olympics. The exhibit featured Indigenous artifacts taken from Canada between 1600 and 1800 and subsequently displayed in museums around the world. Some of these objects could have entered the commodity situation earlier in their "lives" if European Settlers, explorers, and missionaries exchanged goods like food and clothing for them (rather than, say, seizing or stealing the objects). Yet the objects moved out of the commodity situation when they became displayed in museums.

While usually exchanged for money, some of the commodities I analyze in this book were exchanged for other commodities. Specifically, visitors to the Canadian-hosted Olympic games adhered to established norms when they exchanged Olympic-themed pins. These norms were outlined in an official guide that notes that individuals should only wear pins they are willing to trade and that it is rude to interrupt a trade in progress.[90] Other objects, the red mittens HBC produced for the Vancouver Olympics, were originally protected from commercial exchange. IOC rules prohibit organizing committees and private companies from selling replicas of torchbearer uniforms in order to prevent imposters from disrupting the relay. The red mittens were originally subject to this regulation, but IOC officials made an exemption when it became clear that consumers were eager to purchase them.[91]

The concept of fetish provides a useful framework for understanding the symbolic and social significance of commodities, like pins and mittens, produced under capitalism. Charles de Brosses coined the word "fetishisme" in 1760 to describe religious practices that he believed relied on primitive ideas about magic.[92] In formulating the concept of commodity fetishism, Marx applies a similar idea to commodities produced under capitalism.[93] He argues that these commodities appear to take on a life of their own, separate from the conditions under which they were made. This situation influences human relationships: "The relationships between the producers," he observes, "within which the social characteristics of their labours are manifested, take on the form of a social relation between the products of labour."[94] In other words, relationships between people become transformed into relationships between things and the labour invested in producing commodities, including the conditions under which the labour occurs, becomes hidden.[95]

In her writing on the concept of fetish, Anne McClintock brings together Marxist and psychoanalytic understandings of the concept, leading to a novel interpretation that relies on a core similarity between Marx's work on commodity fetishism and Freud's work on sexual fetishism and castration anxiety. For McClintock, fetishes hold together conflicting ideas that individuals cannot work through themselves. She writes, "The fetish marks a crisis in social meaning as the embodiment of an impossible irresolution … By displacing power onto the fetish, then manipulating the fetish, the individual gains symbolic control over what might otherwise be terrifying ambiguities. For this reason, the fetish can be called an impassioned object."[96] I apply McClintock's theory to a Canadian context by arguing that commodities representing the nation are fetish objects that hold together unresolved contradictions about the nation's Settler colonial past and present. These objects simultaneously reveal and conceal truths about the history and ongoing persistence of Settler colonialism in this country.[97]

This argument is also informed by Michael Billig's insights on a psychological dimension of consumption. Like McClintock, Billig brings together Marxist and Freudian thought when he writes, "consumerism, or today's fetishism of commodities, is based upon a forgetfulness which, to use Freudian terminology, can be seen as a form of shared repression."[98] Billig argues that consumers push knowledge about the labour invested in commodity production from consciousness. Truths about unsavoury labour practices, like exploitative working conditions in sweatshops, are not unknown to shoppers; rather, such truths do not enter their consciousness and thus do not interrupt their everyday shopping experiences.[99] Similarly, Canadians who use commodities like the HBC red mittens to represent their national pride engage in a type of denial known as disavowal. They are aware of disturbing facts about the history and persistence of Settler colonialism in Canada but fail to recognize the full significance or meaning of these facts.[100]

Crucially, truths about Settler colonialism in Canada have never completely disappeared. Rather, they haunt the nation and, correspondingly, commodities that represent the nation. This argument relies on Avery Gordon's insight that a case of a ghost is "a case of haunting, a story about what happens when we admit the ghost – that special instance of the merging of the visible and the invisible, the dead and the living, the past and the present – into the making of worldly relations and into the making of our accounts of the world."[101] In this conceptualization, the past makes itself felt in the present through ghosts. Moreover, a haunting is a "seething absence" – or "seething presence" – that can be perceived and felt.[102] In this way, information that is not publicly acknowledged, including unspoken truths about the land upon which we live, does not ever fully disappear.

Many commodities I analyze in this book are, to adapt a phrase from Sharon Rosenberg, Amber Dean, and Kara Granzow, "ghosted objects": material goods haunted by ideas about the nation that remain missing from political and commercial narratives about Canadian identity.[103] Rosenberg et al. describe a photograph used in Alberta's 2005 Centenary Celebrations as a "ghost(ed) image."[104] While it ostensibly showed a single Indigenous settlement, the authors discovered that the photograph was actually a composite of several photographs. Their description of the image applies equally to many Olympic and Commonwealth commodities analyzed in this book; they are ghost(ed) objects that represent "a repressed yet haunting presence repeatedly disavowed" by many Settler Canadians.[105]

Confronting the ghosts that haunt commodities can turn them into uncanny representations of the nation. Freud uses the term "uncanny" to describe "everything that was meant to remain secret and hidden and has come into the open."[106] The German word for uncanny is *un-heimlech*, which literally translates as "un-homely": the uncanny renders familiar things like objects, feelings, and ideas unfamiliar.[107] For Gordon, "Uncanny experiences are haunting experiences," and we must confront the uncanny by facing ghosts rather than repudiating them.[108] Canadians can reckon with ghosts by recognizing that some of the commodities they own are unfamiliar and troubling symbols of the nation. This kind of reckoning can lead to a more just society. When we recognize the uncanny, we pay attention to people or things that have been neglected and we are able to make "contact with what is without doubt often painful, difficult, and unsettling."[109]

Canada's colonial history is rife with ghosts. The authors of the final RCAP report write: ghosts "haunt us still. The ghosts take the form of dishonoured treaties, theft of Aboriginal lands, suppression of Aboriginal cultures, abduction of Aboriginal children, impoverishment and disempowerment of Aboriginal peoples."[110] The association between haunting and Settler colonialism became even more salient in 2021 after more than 1,000 bodies were discovered buried in unmarked graves on the grounds of former residential schools. In her piece about the discoveries, Mohawk writer Alicia Elliott argues that "this entire country *is haunted* by the violence enacted to create what we now call 'Canada.'" She further asserts, "We can no longer ignore the human cost of creating this *haunted nation*. In fact, we must remember."[111] The violence of Settler colonialism persists in the present. Like Elliott, Cindy Blackstock, who is a member of the Gitxsan First Nation, uses the language of haunting to make this point. She describes the people buried in the graves, most of whom were children, as spirits with the power to enact change: "I believe those little spirits buried on the grounds of residential schools came to ensure the work gets done to end the injustices facing survivors."[112] The large number of Indigenous children who are separated from their families by the state and placed in foster care is a troubling example of the ongoing injustices to which Blackstock refers.[113]

In this book, I show that commodities representing the nation are haunted by the history and persistence of Settler colonialism in Canada. By "thinking in relation," I use juxtaposition to identify how the symbolic meanings of commodities sold during the Canadian-hosted Olympic and Commonwealth games are informed by truths about the nation that were not acknowledged in the games.[114] Richly layered meanings emerge when seemingly incompatible pieces of information are considered in relation to one another.[115] I use this research tool to advance the following argument: Canadians can only understand the full meaning of games-related commodities when they account for how Settler colonial policies and practices inform their meanings and, more broadly, official narratives about the nation.

Emilie Cameron makes the point that scholars must be wary of using Gordon's theorization of haunting in their work. She argues that analyzing Settlers' encounters with ghosts can privilege and amplify their anxiety about Indigenous peoples' rightful ownership to land. Moreover, "confining the Indigenous to the ghostly also has the potential to re-inscribe the interests of the powerful upon the meanings and memories of place."[116] In her piece describing all of Canada as haunted, Elliott makes a similar argument. She criticizes horror movies about Settlers who live on Indigenous burial grounds and are haunted by the ghosts of the dead. In these films, the Indigenous ghosts remain nameless and nationless while the Settlers are depicted as innocent inheritors of the land they inhabit. Elliott challenges this narrative by focusing attention on the humanity of the children buried in the recently discovered graves on the grounds of former residential schools. They had, she writes, "names and nations and communities. They had families who ached for their return, who asked after them and were deliberately told nothing."[117]

Following this line of thinking, I do not use the language of haunting to describe Indigenous peoples as ghosts belonging to a bygone past or spectral figures haunting Settlers' imaginations. The commodities I analyze are haunted by facts that animate the present, not people who lived in the past. Moreover, I demonstrate that many Indigenous peoples advanced their interests through the Canadian-hosted Olympic and Commonwealth games. Some used these events to gain support for their land rights campaigns and challenge dominant narratives about national identity promoted through the games. Others took advantage of economic and cultural opportunities created by the games, using them to celebrate Indigenous cultures and educate audiences about Indigenous identity. Informed by Janice Forsyth's writing on Indigenous peoples' participation in the Montreal Olympics, I consider how Indigenous participants in the Canadian-hosted Olympic and Commonwealth games creatively navigated Settler-led displays of their cultures, effectively reworking them from the inside.[118] They powerfully demonstrate Simpson's argument that the Settler colonial project in Canada is a failed one.

Chapter Outline

I collected the primary source material for this book from Olympic/Commonwealth related fonds housed in Canadian municipal and provincial archives. I reference reports, marketing material, meeting minutes, press releases, correspondence, and education kits authored by members of the IOC and local organizing committees, politicians, activists, businesspeople, representatives from sport organizing bodies, and members of the public. IOC rules mandate that certain material, including information about corporate sponsorship and Olympic-related finances, remain sealed until fifteen years after the games have ended. Some documents related to the 2010 Vancouver Olympics are therefore inaccessible until 2025. I sourced additional material from publicly available resources, including advertisements, newspaper articles, official Olympic/Commonwealth games reports, and information published on the web.

This book is structured chronologically, beginning with the 1976 Montreal Summer Olympics. In chapter 1, I identify and analyze intersecting narratives about French-Canadian identity that found expression in cultural displays, promotional material, and commodities associated with the Montreal Olympics. These narratives emphasized Quebec's unique cultural and political position in Canada and glorified Settler colonial nation-building practices in the province. They problematically failed to acknowledge Indigenous peoples' presence in the region or depicted their presence as obstacles to Settlers' nation-building goals. Organizers also used symbols of Indigenous cultures to represent the nation at a time when the federal government was attempting to erode Indigenous peoples' rights. Notably, the Kanien'kehá:ka (Mohawk) of Kanehsatake used the Montreal Games to shape perception of their cultures and contributions to Canadian society by inviting Olympic visitors to tour their reserve.

I identify how members of the Montreal Olympic organizing committee depicted the games as a nationally significant event in their fundraising campaigns. They encouraged corporations and consumers to show their support for this Canadian endeavour by sponsoring the games or buying specially produced objects. However, few individuals embraced this idea because Quebec hosted the 1976 Summer Olympics at a time when French and English Canadians were divided along linguistic and cultural lines and many English Canadians viewed the 1976 Summer Olympics as Quebec's, not Canada's, games.

In chapter 2, I investigate how symbols of Indigenous peoples' cultures circulated in the ceremonial and commercial features of the 1978 Edmonton Commonwealth Games. Organizers and sponsors used Indigenous iconography to distinguish English-Canadian identity from British identity, while also honouring the country's cultural and historical ties to the British Empire. Like the Kanien'kehá:ka (Mohawk) of Kanehsatake, some Indigenous groups staged their own cultural displays; others protested when Indigenous athletes were not invited to participate in the lacrosse competitions organizers included as a demonstration sport.

I also introduce a topic that I develop in subsequent chapters. Specifically, conflicts over Alberta's petroleum resources add additional layers of meaning and significance to representations of Indigenous peoples' cultures and the host province's identity in the Edmonton Commonwealth Games. At the time of the games, members of the Lubicon Lake Nation in Alberta were trying to stop companies from drilling for oil on their land. The premier of Alberta, meanwhile, was in a dispute with the federal government over jurisdiction of the region's petroleum reserves. Understood in this context, the celebratory representations of English-Canadian identity featured in the Edmonton Games are haunted by the fact that the nation was established as a Settler colonial state that continues to extract natural resources from Indigenous land.

By the time Calgary hosted the 1988 Winter Olympics, Alberta's dispute with the federal government over its petroleum reserves had largely been resolved, but the Lubicon's land rights campaign was intensifying. In chapter 3, I show that games organizers and sponsors, most notably oil and gas companies, incorporated symbols of Indigenous cultures and Alberta's cowboy history into their depictions of Western Canada. The Lubicon Lake Nation's highly publicized opposition to the Calgary Games drew attention to the human and environmental cost of Settlers' efforts to profit from Canada's natural resources. In doing so, they revealed that the favourable ideas about national identity promoted through the games were unstable and based on a disavowal of this feature of Settler colonialism.

I also analyze the significance of Petro-Canada's sponsorship of the Calgary Olympic torch relay. The company used this event to establish a link between the Petro-Canada brand and national pride. It also sold commemorative Olympic glassware that became popular symbols of Canadian unity and identity, marking purchasers as responsible citizens who financially and symbolically contributed to a national cause. However, members of the Lubicon Lake Nation and their supporters undermined the positive association consumers attached to the brand and the commemorative glassware it sold. Public opposition to oil companies' sponsorship also weakened local politicians' attempts to use the 1988 Winter Games to attract international investment in Alberta's energy industry.

Victoria hosted the 1994 Commonwealth Games after the provincial government had renewed treaty negotiations with local First Nations and events like the Kanien'kehá:ka (Mohawk)-Oka crisis had brought national attention to Indigenous rights in Canada. This context informs my analysis in chapter 4 of Indigenous peoples' extensive participation in the Victoria Commonwealth Games. Indigenous artists and leaders used the games to shape public perception of their cultures. Games organizers and Canadian politicians, meanwhile, used the event to advance the idea that relations between Indigenous peoples and Settler Canadians were being repaired. I also develop a topic introduced in previous chapters, namely, the Settler colonial practice of using symbols of Indigenous peoples' cultures to define the nation. However, the presence of these symbols in commercial and cultural displays associated with the Victoria Games served a new purpose not evident in the Montreal, Edmonton, or Calgary Games: they helped convey the idea that Canada had healed from the trauma of its Settler colonial past. Moreover, organizers of the Victoria Games celebrated Indigenous peoples' artistic traditions and cultures while, at the same time, companies were logging trees on land over which Indigenous groups claimed jurisdiction. Activists used the games to raise awareness of and support for their opposition to these resource extraction practices.

The idea that Indigenous-Settler relations were repaired was conveyed in more complex ways during the 2010 Vancouver Winter Games compared to the Victoria Commonwealth Games. In chapter 5, I describe the FHFN's unprecedented involvement in the 2010 Games. Olympic organizers depicted the FHFN's participation as a central feature of their commitment to the IOC's sustainability and legacy goals, which the organization was actively championing in the 2000s. This practice strengthened the IOC's public image, helped Vancouver Olympic organizers promote celebratory ideas about Canadian social values, and added value to the games' profit-generating features. Moreover, federal and provincial politicians used the games to promote the idea that Indigenous-Settler relations were improving. I investigate how these multiple priorities intersected and expose how the games' cultural and commercial features (i.e., opening ceremony, torch relay, advertisements, licenced goods) collectively represented the nation as a liberal country that has left its Settler colonial past behind.

I also explore how celebratory narratives about Canadian identity and values circulated alongside strong public opposition to the Vancouver Olympics. Activists popularized the slogan "No Olympics on Stolen Native Land" and argued that commercial and social initiatives affiliated with the games would not lead to significant improvements in Indigenous peoples' lives. They would not dismantle the Settler colonial practice of dispossessing Indigenous peoples of their land. Activist opposition to the games exposed the fact that Indigenous-Settler relations were far from being repaired.

Like the Petro-Canada glassware from the Calgary Olympics, the HBC red mittens sold during the Vancouver Games symbolize a version of national identity that is haunted by unacknowledged truths about Settler colonialism in Canada. I devote the final chapter to analyzing the significance of the promotion and consumption of these mittens, as well as HBC's sponsorship of the Vancouver Games more generally. The mittens are the most complex fetish objects I analyze in this book, and they hold together numerous contradictions about the meaning of Canadian identity and citizenship. Many consumers used the mittens to represent their identity as proud Canadians who make meaningful material and symbolic contributions to the nation. However, their actions raise questions that I encourage readers to grapple with, and I conclude the chapter – and this book – by revisiting these questions. They include: What version of national identity, citizenship, and history gets privileged through these consumptive practices? Who and what gets excluded from these commercialized representations of Canada?

1

Commercializing French-Canadian Identity, Indigenous Cultures, and Nationalism in the 1976 Montreal Olympics

In their bid for the right to host the 1976 Summer Olympics, Montreal officials highlighted the appeal of Indigenous cultural displays as well as the European heritage of many Canadian Settlers. Their proposal included a plan for "a vast Canadian cultural festival" featuring performances of Canadian music "expressing the traditions of its Eskimo and Indian aboriginal residents as well as those of its French-Canadian, English-, Scottish- and Irish-Canadian people and Canadians of other origins."[1] They also proposed organizing "Exhibitions of Eskimo, Indian and Canadian art" and a "colourful *Pow Wow* (gathering) of Indians of the Six Nations Federacy in Canada."[2]

By 1970, when Montreal made its bid, Quebec had undergone a period of political and social modernization known as the "Quiet Revolution," a movement aimed at creating new social and political opportunities for francophones and giving them greater control over Quebec's economy.[3] In 1967, some Quebeckers established the separatist Mouvement souveraineté-association, led by René Lévesque, with the aim of making Quebec an independent country. The following year, the group combined with other separatist parties to form the Parti Québécois, also led by Lévesque.[4] The federal government demonstrated a clear preference for Vancouver's ultimately unsuccessful bid for the 1976 Winter Olympics over Montreal's bid for the Summer Games (the IOC scheduled Summer and Winter Olympic Games in the same year until the 1990s). Ottawa promised to pay a third of the cost of the 1976

Winter Games if they were awarded to Vancouver but made no similar promise to Montreal.[5]

Officials from Montreal travelled to Amsterdam in May 1970 to compete against Los Angeles and Moscow for the right to host the 1976 Summer Olympics. Twelve hours before Montreal mayor Jean Drapeau was scheduled to address the IOC, he received word that the organization was now asking the three bid cities to secure financing guarantees. The American and Russian bid teams secured funding promises from their governments, but Drapeau did not do likewise.[6] Rather, he told the IOC that Montreal did not need to secure financial guarantees because he was staking the city's reputation on the Olympics. He promised to preserve the amateur nature of the games and avoid extravagant costs associated with organizing them.[7] Montreal won its Olympic bid on the second round of voting after Los Angeles was eliminated and the IOC members who voted for Los Angeles shifted their support to Montreal.[8]

Trudeau's Liberals were gearing up for the 1972 federal election when Montreal won its Olympic bid. The prime minister, a staunch proponent of federalism, refused to pay for any of the games with federal funds. The organizing committee for the 1976 Summer Games, known by its French acronym COJO (Comité organisateur des Jeux olympiques de 1976), raised money by selling Olympic coins and postage stamps, lottery tickets, admission tickets, programs, and broadcast rights; establishing an official sponsorship, licensing, and supplier program; and providing accommodation for athletes.[9] Together, these initiatives formed the organizing committee's self-financing model, which COJO president and commissioner Roger Rousseau described as "the Golden Rule of the Olympic Games of 1976."[10]

COJO members celebrated their approach to securing privately raised funds for the Montreal Olympics and claimed they were doing valuable work by pushing the Olympic movement in a more commercial direction. The 1976 Games were held at a time when Olympic competitions were broadcast on television networks around the world but before they became, in the words of Robert Barney, Stephen Wenn, and Scott Martyn, an "unrivaled commercial forum."[11] Although COJO officials depicted their profit-generating initiatives as cutting edge, some commentators did not share their enthusiasm. *Vancouver Sun* columnist

Jim Kearney observed in 1974 that former IOC president Avery Brundage would have disliked this approach to funding the games: "It's a good thing Brundage, the last of the unreconstructed amateurs, has retired. The way Montreal is going, even Avery's apoplexy would have wound up being copyrighted. And marketed."[12]

COJO's optimism about its self-financing model was premature. While the organizing committee raised $430 million in private funds, this amounted to approximately one-third of the total revenue needed. The games left Montreal and Quebec with a joint debt of approximately $1 billion.[13] In order to finance them, Montreal spent $8 million and took on $200 million of debt while Quebec spent $25 million and took on $790 million of debt.[14] Although COJO did not achieve its intended goal of relying entirely on private funds, in this chapter I argue that the organizing committee attempted to commercialize something other than Avery's apoplexy: select ideas about national identity and history.

I situate the Montreal Games' commercial dimensions within the broader cultural and social context in which the games were held. First, I identify how COJO's profit-generating initiatives worked in conjunction with games-related cultural displays to convey a politically charged narrative about French-Canadian identity. Moreover, games sponsors and organizers continued the long-standing practice of Settlers using symbols of Indigenous cultures to define Canadian identity, at the same time ignoring the reality that the federal government was trying to assimilate Indigenous peoples into Settler society. Second, COJO officials encouraged Canadian companies and consumers to invest money in the games by sponsoring them or buying specially produced commodities. Although organizers framed these financial contributions as opportunities to contribute to a national cause, few individuals or companies embraced this idea because pre-existing political and cultural tensions between English and French Canadians weakened public support for the Montreal Olympics.

Representing and Commodifying French-Canadian Identity and Indigenous Cultures

I begin this section by identifying the narratives about French-Canadian history and culture that circulated in the Montreal Olympics and situating these narratives within the broader social and political climate of 1970s Canada. I then consider how Indigenous peoples feature in these narratives. My starting point is a handbook produced by COJO. It was required reading for prospective Montreal Olympic hostesses and guides, and they had to pass a test on the material before beginning employment. The handbook notes that their role is "not only to represent COJO but also Montreal, Quebec and all of Canada."[15] In this regard, ideas contained within the handbook provide insight into how Olympic organizers wished to represent the host city, province, and country.

The handbook recounts that English and French forces fought one another for control of present-day Canada, with Britain earning the ultimate victory in 1759. Yet, it continues, "it is nevertheless the French, who left a lasting footprint, to whom we owe the distinctive character of Canada, its double culture that, even today, permeates the everyday life of its citizenry."[16] A section titled "Quebec's Status" states that the province represents "one of the two camps of Canada's cultural and ethnic duality," that it is the only Canadian province with a francophone majority, and that it struggles to participate in central government activities because of the unique linguistic and cultural composition of its francophone population.[17] As a result, the province seeks "as much autonomy as possible within the Confederation," including autonomy over matters of education and finance.[18]

In October 1970, a few months after Montreal won its Olympic bid, the militant separatist group the Front de libération du Québec (FLQ) kidnapped James Cross, a British diplomat living in Montreal. The FLQ published a manifesto opposing what it described as the colonial and capitalist elements of Quebec society and demanding the province's independence from Canada. While the majority of people living in the province opposed the FLQ's use of violence, many sympathized with its position on Quebec sovereignty. When the group kidnapped a public official named Pierre Laporte five days after taking Cross, the federal government responded by invoking the War Measures Act and sending 8,000 troops to Montreal. FLQ members killed Laporte, but police successfully negotiated for Cross's release.[19]

The following year, Quebec politicians disrupted the federal government's plans to amend the Canadian constitution. The Montreal Olympic hostess and guide handbook states that the 1971 Victoria Constitutional Conference considered a charter of federal changes which would have transformed the constitution, and which required unanimous consent from the provinces to be adopted, but that "Quebec couldn't agree to" these changes, a statement that reflects a politically charged perspective about an event that occurred a few years before the 1976 Summer Games.[20] Prime Minister Trudeau scheduled the constitutional reform conference with the first ministers on the condition that Quebec not disrupt the talks. Although Trudeau and Quebec premier Robert Bourassa agreed prior to the conference on the scope of changes to be discussed, many Quebeckers criticized their agreement and the premier bowed to public pressure by asking Trudeau to make additional concessions during the conference. The prime minister refused to capitulate, and the Quebec premier left the conference without an agreement. According to Trudeau's principal secretary, Marc Lalonde, the prime minister felt betrayed by this move and lost trust in Bourassa.[21]

The Olympic hostess and guide handbook lists a series of questions about Quebec's exceptional status in Canada, including "Comparing Quebec to the rest of Canada, one can observe that it has some key differences, can you name one?"; "In what year was French proclaimed the official language in Quebec, and by whom?"; and "Quebec has a thriving art scene. Name a Quebec artist well-known outside Canada as well as their art form."[22] This last question is significant in light of a conflict about the Montreal Olympic arts and culture program that emerged in the lead-up to the games. Artists from outside Quebec felt excluded from the planning process and were angered by COJO's decision to focus primarily on locally produced art. When non-Québécois artists pushed for equal representation in the program, COJO demanded that the federal government finance their contributions.[23] In addition, a group called the Artists Athletes Coalition solicited funding from the Canada Council for a series of Olympic posters to be distributed to schools, sports clubs, and libraries in Canada and abroad. However, council director Tim Porteous would only support the initiative if the group changed the posters' heading from "Montreal" to "Canada."[24] The handbook thus emphasized Québécois artists' accomplishments while artists outside of the province were seeking more recognition in the games.

Mayor Drapeau used the 1976 Summer Games to showcase the strength of French-Canadian society to a national and international audience. About the Olympic stadium he said, "As French Canadians, the only way we're going to survive is to make our mark not only in this country, but on the entire continent. We must never be poor copies of others. We can only survive if we accept the challenge of quality."[25] That is why, he explained, he chose one of the greatest architects of the world, Roger Taillibert, to design the stadium.[26] The Montreal Olympic emblem extends the Olympic rings to form an M and symbolizes the host city's reputation as a world-class city, with the lines extending the M meant to represent Taillibert's Olympic stadium design. According to the games' official report, the emblem evokes "the universal brotherhood of the Olympic ideal, the triumph of the winners, the spirit of fair play in their struggles, and the *elevation of Montréal to the rank of Olympic City*."[27]

The emblem circulated on the bodies of Olympic hostesses and guides through pins affixed to their uniforms. The handbook, the games' official report, and a document COJO distributed to prospective corporate sponsors describe its symbolic meaning.[28] All mention that the M in the emblem design stands for Montreal. None link its design to a feature of national identity. It is understandable that the emblem would represent the host city because cities, not countries, bid for and host the Olympic Games. However, organizers of the 1988 Calgary and 2010 Vancouver Olympics intentionally included symbols of both Canadian and regional identity in their emblem designs. Specially produced Montreal Olympic coins and postage stamps feature the games' emblem alongside the word "Canada" and, in the case of the coins, a picture of Queen Elizabeth II (figure 1.1). When juxtaposed against this text and image, the stylized M in the emblem visually signifies an idea articulated in the hostess and guide handbook: the province represents "one of the two camps of Canada's cultural and ethnic duality" and it is the only Canadian province with a francophone majority.[29]

French-English relations also influenced how COJO organized the games' torch relay. A Greek high priestess, Maria Moscholiou, lit the flame in Olympia, Greece, in a ceremony "enacted in accordance with the customs of antiquity, as related by Plutarch in the life of Numa Pompilius."[30] Torchbearers transported the flame to Athens where officials transferred it to Ottawa through an electronic signal. Some of the original energy from the Greek flame travelled via satellite transmission to Canada, where it was reconverted into electric energy and used to ignite the Olympic torch.[31] Runners subsequently transported the flame from Ottawa to Montreal. Organizers originally considered lighting the torch at the tip of Gaspé Peninsula and having it retrace the steps of early Canadian explorers by travelling along the banks of the Saint-Lawrence,

1.1 Postage stamp featuring the emblem of the 1976 Montreal Olympics.

but federal authorities opposed this approach. According to Daniel Latouche, their reaction to "the idea of a Quebec-only itinerary bordered on hysteria" because it brought up memories of French president Charles de Gaulle's 1967 visit to Quebec, when he delivered a speech in Montreal in support of the Quebec sovereignty movement.[32] COJO members ultimately planned the Olympic flame route to bypass Quebec as much as possible.[33]

Two teenagers, an anglophone named Sandra Henderson and a francophone named Stéphane Préfontaine, jointly carried the torch into the Olympic stadium. Musicians in youth orchestras from thirty countries played the Canadian anthem during the opening ceremony and young people and gymnasts performed on stage. Dancers wearing "folk costumes of the St. Lawrence River Valley" performed a "traditional Québec march step."[34] James Christie described the aspirational tone of the opening ceremony in a *Globe and Mail* article: "The two languages together – *as they might exist in Canada* – were a major part of the afternoon's call for unity."[35] During the closing ceremony, Indigenous dancers wearing colourful outfits entered the stage to the sound of, in COJO's words, "a symphonic suite performed on traditional instruments augmented by Amerindian folk instruments such as tom-toms, rattles, and small bells."[36] I address the significance of this cultural display later in this chapter.

* * *

Narratives about French-English relations in Canada that circulated during the Montreal Olympics were haunted by a truth that bid officials and COJO members only occasionally acknowledged: French and English explorers established a Settler colonial nation on Indigenous land. When Montreal officials bidding for the games presented the IOC with a proposal to organize "a vast Canadian cultural festival" that included a display of Canadian music "expressing the traditions of *its Eskimo and Indian aboriginal residents*," they used inappropriate language to refer to Indigenous peoples. Gregory Younging, author of the book *Elements of Indigenous Style*, includes the words "Eskimo" and "Indian" in his list of inappropriate and offensive terms. Both terms were coined by European explorers and missionaries who settled in North America.[37] The word Inuit began replacing "Eskimo" in the 1960s, a decade before Montreal hosted the Summer Olympics; according to Younging, "The use of *Inuit* was one of the earliest examples of an Indigenous group in Canada changing terminology to assert their identity."[38] Members of the Montreal Olympic bid committee also perpetuated a Settler colonial view of Indigenous people and cultures as property of the state by describing "Eskimo" and "Indian" aboriginal people as belonging to Canada.[39]

Montreal Olympic organizers subsequently constructed narratives about Canadian history that either erased Indigenous peoples from Canadian history or depicted them as part of the nation's past. The hostess and guide handbook depicts Indigenous peoples as existing outside the province's modern history, a depiction that effaces their contemporary presence in the region and ongoing contribution to its development. According to the handbook, some Indigenous people, who "became what the Europeans called 'Indians,' settled in the South; others, the Eskimos, arrived more recently and spread to the North, all the way to Greenland." The text continues, "Nevertheless, the history of Quebec, measured chronologically, and which we well know continues to this day, began in 1534."[40]

The publication also depicts Indigenous peoples as Settlers' enemies who obstructed two colonial powers' competing efforts to assert dominance over the land. "France and England fought not only against the Indians," the handbook notes, "but against one another for supremacy in the New World."[41] A brochure COJO produced about Bromont, Quebec, where the Olympic equestrian competitions were staged, reflects a similar sentiment. It describes the period from 1640 to 1775 in the eastern townships of Quebec as "a hardy and sometimes terrifying one. War was not unknown as French and English troops often made forays into the area to battle Indian hunting parties."[42] Although written from a Settler colonial perspective, these statements make a truth impossible to ignore: Settler colonialism dispossessed Indigenous peoples of their land. The "terrifying" battles described in the brochure were violent confrontations over French and English Settlers' efforts to gain supremacy over Indigenous peoples' land. Indeed, the brochure goes on to note that the period from 1775 to 1840 "was marked by the arrival of the first settlers and the early development of the land."[43]

COJO also affiliated the Montreal Olympic mascot, a beaver named Amik, with selective ideas about Canada's Settler colonial past. Organizers linked the mascot's symbolic meaning with the fur trade in Canada but did not acknowledge that the fur trade brought Settlers into contact with Indigenous peoples whose knowledge, labour, and land they relied upon for success. A picture of Rousseau feeding apple pieces to a beaver accompanied the *Globe and Mail's* announcement that the animal had been selected as the official mascot.[44] The Montreal Olympic official report emphasized the beaver's contribution to early colonial activities in Canada: "Several reasons justified the choice of the beaver as mascot of the 1976 Olympic Games. Recognized for its patience and hard work, this animal has occupied an important place in the economic development of Canada from the time when the fur trade was the major activity in North America."[45] The beaver, Rousseau declared, is "emblematic of Canada" since "no animal has played a greater part in the development of a country than has the beaver in Canada."[46]

Rousseau went on to claim that "any Canadian realizes that it was [the] beaver which opened up this country, which led several large

European companies to open up Canada and led to the settlement of our ancestors here."[47] This statement is haunted by the unacknowledged fact that the first Europeans to settle in Canada were occupying land populated by Indigenous peoples and relied on Indigenous peoples' labour to establish a successful fur trading industry. It is unclear if Rousseau is referring only to French Canadians' ancestors or English and French Canadians' ancestors in this statement. In either case, he excludes Indigenous peoples' presence, and their corresponding involvement in the fur trade, from his account.

The link between the beaver and Canadian fur trade was well established by the time COJO chose the animal as the games' mascot. Beginning in the seventeenth century, Canadian beaver pelts were made into the felt milliners used to make fashionable broad-brimmed hats. Fur traders in Canada depended on Indigenous peoples' labour to obtain and process beaver pelts. Indeed, the entire commercial enterprise relied on commodity exchanges between Settlers and Indigenous peoples, and the fur trade would have been impossible if Indigenous peoples had not shared their knowledge and abilities with European traders.[48] The beaver's association with Canadian history and commerce was cemented in 1867 when Canada became a self-governing dominion, and the beaver became its national symbol. As Margot Francis writes, the animal "was the first article of trade upon which European trade and exploration was based and, as such, it became a crucial medium through which early settlers articulated an imagined relationship with commercial culture."[49]

Mascots were a relatively new addition to the Olympic movement at the time of the Montreal Olympics. Organizers of the 1972 Munich Summer Olympics introduced the first official mascot to the public, a dachshund named Waldi.[50] Yet the practice of using mascots to convey a selective narrative about national identity and history is not unique to Amik. Tara Magdalinski describes Olympic mascots as "cultural narratives that resonate with dominant visions of the nation."[51] She further asserts, "In addition to the promotion of national ideologies, Olympic mascots fulfill overt economic functions and serve as marketing devices for the [Olympic] Games and its sponsors. Given their appealing design as animated creatures that are easily transformed into cuddly toys, mascots are unashamedly constructed to appeal to children and to contribute to the familial marketing of the Games."[52] In the Canadian context, COJO recognized the merchandising potential of a mascot even

1.2 Amik, the mascot of the 1976 Montreal Olympics.

before it chose a beaver to represent the Montreal Games, and the organizing committee was keen to create mascot toys and other products that would appeal to young people. COJO member Richard Gareau wrote in a 1973 memo, "We can benefit enormously from a mascot easily adaptable to different types of merchandise (comics, popular publications, toys, puzzles, jewellery, scarves, ties, hats, etc.)."[53]

Commercializing the mascot by licensing its image to companies helped COJO build its self-financing program; committee member Georges Huel wrote, "we believe the main goal of creating a mascot is to give official licensees the opportunity to produce souvenirs using it."[54] Licensees reproduced the mascot in leather and fur and created beaver puzzles and beaver banks (change holders similar to piggy banks).[55] However, the initial design of Amik may have struck some companies as strange. Journalist James Christie observed wryly, "only recently has it come to anyone's attention that poor Amik was born with neither eyes nor the characteristic teeth. Needless to say, a blind, toothless mascot does not reflect a flattering image of COJO."[56] The mascot eventually received eyes but remained toothless, perhaps in order to make it look cuddly rather than threatening (figure 1.2).

Amik commodities join other Canadian goods, buildings, and logos that carry beaver designs. The animal appears on the Canadian nickel, and a beaver carved from limestone sits atop an entrance to the Canadian

Parliament buildings. In the late nineteenth century, many companies incorporated images of beavers into their logos, including Beaver Brand Chewing Tobacco, Canadian Illustrated News, the Canadian National Railway, Crompton's Corsets, and Sleeman Ale.[57] More recently, the logo for the clothing company Roots features a beaver and, in a 2000 Molson ad called "The Rant," Joe Canadian describes the beaver as "a truly proud and noble animal."[58]

COJO initiated a name-the-mascot contest and chose Amik which, according to the games' official report, is "a word meaning beaver in the Algonquin language, the most widespread among the Amerindians of Canada."[59] This name adds a new dimension to the symbolic significance of the mascot. Although games organizers did not openly acknowledge Indigenous peoples' involvement in the fur trade, the mascot's name is a reminder of this truth. A close reading of the official report also reveals that some COJO members may not have fully understood the meaning of the word "Amik" or the Indigenous language from which it is derived. Specifically, they may have been unaware of the distinction between the Algonquian language *family* and the Algonquin language. Whereas one section of the games' official report describes Amik as an *Algonquin* word, another describes it as part of the *Algonquian* language.[60] Algonquian is not a language, but a language family, "a 'parent' language from which the various Algonquian languages and dialects are descended."[61] Although she does not reference Amik specifically, Christine O'Bonsawin points out that "indigenous people were not included in the organizing and planning of [Montreal] Olympic events and programs, even where indigenous representations were prominently featured."[62] I found no evidence that COJO consulted with Indigenous groups when selecting or translating the mascot's name.

The mascot's name also makes a truth about the residential school system in Canada impossible to completely ignore. Specifically, students were forced to speak English or French and were punished for speaking their mother tongue. The history of language suppression through residential school education in Canada remains an unignorable but unrecognized truth that haunts the mascot. Understood in this way, Amik commodities function as fetish objects that celebrate Settlers' nation-building endeavours; they simultaneously represent and disavow the exploitation, land dispossession, and assimilation practices that underpin these endeavours.

This argument reflects a modern interpretation of the mascot that relies on documents such as the 1996 Royal Commission on Aboriginal Peoples (RCAP) report and multiple Truth and Reconciliation Commission of Canada (TRC) reports published in the 2010s. However, the existence of residential schools and the Canadian government's policy on Indigenous children's language acquisition has been public knowledge since the late nineteenth century. The Canadian Public Works minister Hector Langevin argued in Parliament in 1883, "if you wish to educate these [Indigenous] children you must separate them from their parents during the time that they are being educated. If you leave them in the family they may know how to read and write, but they still remain savages."[63] Moreover, the Department of Indian Affairs' "Programme of Studies for Indian Schools" of 1896 states, "Every effort must be made to induce pupils to speak English, and to teach them to understand it; unless they do, the whole work of the teacher is likely to be wasted."[64] These efforts supported a goal that deputy minister of Indian Affairs Duncan Campbell Scott shared with a federal parliamentary committee in 1920: fully assimilating Indigenous peoples into Settler society. "Our object," he stated, "is to continue until there is not a single Indian in Canada that has not been absorbed into the body politic."[65]

By insisting that residential school students speak only English or French, educators effectively alienated Indigenous children from their families and communities.[66] The authors of the RCAP report articulate this reality eloquently: "the entire residential school project was balanced on the proposition that the gate to assimilation was unlocked only by the progressive destruction of Aboriginal languages. With that growing silence would come the dying whisper of Aboriginal cultures."[67] Residential school survivor Agnes Moses testified in front of the TRC that losing her language damaged her identity and relationship with her family: "The worst thing I ever did was I was ashamed of my mother, that honourable woman, because she couldn't speak English, she never went to school, and we used to go home to her on Saturdays, and they told us that we couldn't talk Gwich'in to her and, she couldn't, like couldn't communicate."[68]

The residential school system thus operated through the "logic of elimination" that Patrick Wolfe argues lies at the heart of Settler colonialism. Indeed, he describes efforts to re-socialize Indigenous children in institutions like missions and boarding schools as an outcome of this logic.[69] More recent events illustrate that the Canadian government continued to develop assimilationist policies well into the twentieth century. COJO unveiled Amik a few years after the government proposed abolishing the Department of Indian Affairs as well as the Indian Act in its 1969 "Statement of the Government of Canada on Indian Policy" (White Paper). The president of the Indian Association of Alberta, Harold Cardinal, described the White Paper as "a thinly disguised programme of extermination through assimilation."[70] A 2015 TRC report suggests that the 1969 White Paper extended historical efforts to assimilate Indigenous peoples into Settler society. Its authors argue that the assimilationist goals that Deputy Minister Duncan Campbell Scott articulated in 1920 were reiterated in the 1969 White Paper, which sought to end Indian status and terminate the Treaties that the federal government had negotiated with First Nations.[71]

COJO's decision to give the Montreal Olympic mascot an Indigenous name exposes a truth about how the Settler colonial state operates, one that Wolfe identifies when he writes, "On the one hand, settler society required the practical elimination of the natives in order to establish itself on their territory. On the symbolic level, however, settler society subsequently sought to recuperate indigeneity in order to express its difference – and, accordingly, its independence – from the mother country."[72] Montreal Olympic organizers "recuperated indigeneity" by naming the mascot Amik and using this name to convey a narrative about the early fur trade in Canada in the shadow of state-sponsored efforts to assimilate Indigenous peoples into Settler society.

***

The design of coins included in the Montreal Olympic commemorative coin collection complemented the ideas about national identity and history promoted through the games' mascot, hostess and guide handbook, and brochures. Although the federal government did not directly fund the Montreal Olympics, it approved the creation of Olympic coin, stamp, and lottery programs by passing Bill C–196 in July 1973.[73] The Canadian Mint issued seven series of Olympic commemorative coins between 1973 and 1976 and added a surcharge ($5 or $10) to each coin's face value.[74]

The Mint also issued a gold coin with a $100 face value.[75] These items were sold at chartered banks, financial institutions, post offices, coin dealers' shops, and major department stores.[76]

Each Olympic coin series had a unique theme: geography (Series One), Olympic symbols (Series Two), early Canadian sports (Series Three), track and field sports (Series Four), water sports (Series Five), team and body-contact sports (Series Six), and Olympic souvenirs (Series Seven). The design of Series Three and Four coins are notable because they include stereotypical images and signifiers of Indigenous peoples. A coin showing an athlete competing in the sport of hurdling depicts the person's face in profile with prominent cheekbones and two feathers tucked into their long, flowing hair. A coin showing lacrosse players, meanwhile, depicts muscular men wearing little clothing on their active bodies and feathers in their hair. In contrast, another coin shows cyclists wearing long sleeve shirts and pants that extend past the knee with short, neatly styled hair parted in the middle. The lacrosse coin is particularly rich in symbolic meaning and its full significance emerges when considered in relation to the history of lacrosse in Canada and the fact that Settlers used the sport to represent and define a unique Canadian identity. The coin design continues Settlers' historical practice of visually distinguishing Indigenous lacrosse players from Settler players. Moreover, the lacrosse coin introduces this representational practice into a commercial environment. Consequently, this commodity helped communicate a selective story about Canadian identity that has historically been conveyed through cultural and sporting practices not associated with the Olympics.

Settlers began depicting lacrosse as a national game inherited from Indigenous peoples in the nineteenth century, at the same time claiming that Indigenous peoples' land belonged to them. Prior to European settlement, many Indigenous nations played ball games similar to modern-day lacrosse. These games feature in some nations' creation stories and various Indigenous languages include words for the game such as "Anishinaabemowin (specifically, Omàmiwininìwak or Algonquin) Pàgàdowe, the Ojibway-specific Baaga'adowewin or Baaga'a-dowe (commonly appears as Baggataway), and/or the Kanien'kéha word Tewaá:rathon."[77] Settlers from Montreal began playing a version of the game, which they later called lacrosse, against members of the Kanien'kehá:ka (Mohawk) First Nation living at Kahnawà:ke and

Ahkwesàhsne in the early nineteenth century.[78] This word derives from the French expression "jouer à la cross," which French speakers used to describe games played with a curved stick.[79]

Matches between Indigenous and non-Indigenous lacrosse players staged in Canada and abroad reinforced the link between lacrosse and a newly emerging Settler Canadian identity. A competition held in Montreal between members of that city's Lacrosse Club and Kahnawà:ke players held on the first Dominion Day in 1867 attracted 5,000 spectators. Canada also organized three lacrosse tours to the British Isles between 1867 and 1883. They featured Kanien'kehá:ka (Mohawk) athletes competing against Settler Canadian athletes, with Indigenous cultural displays such as "war dances" and "powwows," occurring before the start of play.[80] Around the same time, William Beers, an anglophone living in Montreal, began campaigning for lacrosse to be named Canada's national game. He said in 1867, "just as we claim as Canadian the rivers and lakes and land once owned exclusively by Indians, so we now claim their field games as the national field game of our dominion."[81] Beers's statement exposes a Settler colonial desire to establish a home on Indigenous land. Moreover, it reveals that Settlers did not always try to erase evidence of Indigenous peoples' presence and cultures on this land. Rather, they strategically used Indigenous sporting practices (i.e., lacrosse) to shape a bourgeoning Settler colonial identity.

Allan Downey makes the link between the development of lacrosse in Canada and the logic of elimination explicit: "The systematic organization and appropriation of lacrosse, as represented by the new rules, clubs, and bans on Indigenous participation, was a manifestation of that logic [of elimination]."[82] Significantly, Downey asserts that Indigenous athletes who participated in lacrosse tours of Britain in the nineteenth century found creative ways to challenge Settler colonial representational practices. Kahnawà:ke athletes were well versed in the practice of "selling and playing Indian" and intentionally exaggerated performances of their cultures.[83] They also used the tours to earn income, represent their Indigenous identity and nationhood to an international audience, and assert their claim to the sport.[84] This idea is reflected in a speech that Aiontonnis ("Big John Canadian"), a member of the Kahnawà:ke lacrosse team, delivered to Queen Victoria in 1876 before the start of a lacrosse game staged in front of the royal family. The speech reads, in part, "We hope to see you some day in this great land [Canada] which once belonged only to the Indians; but we hope you will come and look upon us playing *our great game* of La Crosse in England against the pale-faced young men of Canada, who now play *our game* like us, and sometimes beat us in fair play."[85]

Settlers relied on visual markers to distinguish between Indigenous and non-Indigenous lacrosse players and to represent their successful colonization of the game; these visual markers also appear in the design of the Montreal Olympic lacrosse coin.[86] Portraits of Settler players in the nineteenth century show team members wearing matching uniforms with carefully crafted poses. In contrast, Indigenous players are casually posed with mismatched outfits, and an 1867 photograph shows Aiontonnis wearing a large, feathered headdress. Kahnawà:ke lacrosse players similarly donned headdresses decorated with beads and feathers when performing pre-game "war dances" on their 1876 tour of England.[87] The Montreal Olympic lacrosse coin design reproduces these visual markers by depicting athletes wearing feathers in their hair and hardly any clothing covering their muscular bodies. This design illustrates that the practice of using stereotypical images to portray Indigenous peoples has not entirely disappeared, nor is it limited to photographs. Rather, it extends to the design of commodities (i.e., coins) produced in the twentieth century.

Feathered bands were also featured in an Indigenous dance sequence included in the Montreal Olympic closing ceremony. However, this performance is not a straightforward example of how clothing and accessories construct differences between Settlers and Indigenous peoples. Rather, it shows that socially constructed value judgments about the difference between Settlers and Indigenous peoples are fictions that can be both created and unravelled through costume. During the closing ceremony, non-Indigenous members of the Fédération des Loisirs-Danse du Québec appeared on stage alongside the Indigenous dancers, and they wore costumes and make-up to blend in with them. The performers moved together in an arrowhead formation, escorted Olympic athletes to the stage, and erected tepees in the colours of the Olympic rings.[88] In addition, the Indigenous participants gave athletes "headbands and feathered headdresses as souvenirs of the Montréal Games."[89] On a symbolic level, these bands recall the Settler colonial practice of using visual markers of Indigenous peoples' culture to define Settler colonial identity. They can also be interpreted as symbolic of the limited role

Indigenous peoples played in the Montreal Olympics: in Jennifer Adese's words, "Indigenous involvement in the planning and executing of the ceremony was permitted to extend little beyond this role of 'playing Indian.'"[90]

O'Bonsawin draws attention to another significant dimension of the games' closing ceremony: "In an attempt to commemorate and showcase indigenous cultures in the Olympic program, and to enhance Canadian national identity at home and abroad, Montreal organizers strategically included indigenous people and imagery in the closing ceremony at a time when Canadian indigenous and government relations were operating under heightened tensions."[91] Specifically, the closing ceremony occurred after Indigenous activists campaigned against the federal government's 1969 White Paper, which argued that Indigenous rights should be subsumed into its multicultural initiatives.[92] The Montreal Olympic closing ceremony scene featuring Indigenous dancers performing alongside Euro-Canadians thus dramatized a problematic feature of Settler colonial society: the practice of using symbols of Indigenous peoples' cultures to define the nation while also attempting to erode Indigenous peoples' rights and assimilate them into Settler society.[93]

The feathered bands that COJO gifted athletes symbolize an uncomfortable truth Wolfe identifies: Settler society both requires the "practical elimination of the natives" and needs to "recuperate indigeneity."[94] This practice has been symbolically and visually represented through clothing, with Settlers dressing up as Indigenous peoples. In one notable example, Hayter Reed, a central architect of the Canadian residential school system, attended the 1896 Governor General's Historical Fancy Dress Ball dressed as the Hodinöhsö:ni' (Iroquoian) chief Donnacona, who greeted Jacques Cartier on his voyage down the St Lawrence River. Reed thus "played Indian" while also working to assimilate Indigenous children into Settler society.[95] Understood in this context, the non-Indigenous dancers who wore clothing and make-up to blend in with the Indigenous performers in the Montreal Olympic ceremony continued a performative practice that cannot be separated from the larger Settler colonial context in which it is situated.

Like Kahnawà:ke lacrosse players who visited the British Isles in the nineteenth century on lacrosse tours, some Kanien'kehá:ka (Mohawk) of Kahnawá:ke who participated in the closing ceremony dance viewed the event as an opportunity to express their cultural identity as "show Indians" in the entertainment industry. They also welcomed the chance to be a part of a globally televised, large-scale celebration; meet some of the world's best athletes; and "promote and strengthen the presence of an emerging pan-Indian identity in Canada."[96] Janice Forsyth notes that the federal government began appropriating large sections of the Kahnawà:ke's reserve to develop the St Lawrence Seaway in 1955, an act that left many residents feeling alienated and in despair. Their participation in the closing ceremony, she writes, "was a symbolic show of a much larger movement of Aboriginal cultural persistence in Canada."[97]

Although COJO incorporated symbols of Indigenous cultures into the design of the Montreal Olympic mascot and coins and arranged for Indigenous dancers to perform in the games' closing ceremony, organizers rejected the Indians of Quebec Association's proposal to mount a cultural exhibit during the games. COJO was not the first sport organizing committee to strategically include Indigenous peoples in some events while excluding them from others. When Winnipeg hosted the 1967 Pan Am Games, organizers selected ten Indigenous youth to carry the torch from Saint Paul, Minnesota, to Winnipeg. The youth, who divided the 90-to-120-mile daily run among themselves, expected to carry the torch directly into the stadium where the opening ceremony was being held. However, that honour went to a non-Indigenous person. The runners watched the ceremony on television, and some returned to the residential schools they attended that same day.[98]

After COJO rejected the Indians of Quebec Association's proposal, the Kanien'kehá:ka (Mohawk) of Kahnawá:ke decided to hold an "Indian Days" celebration during the Montreal Games. They invited Olympic visitors to tour their reserve, located across the St Lawrence River from Montreal, and learn about their culture.[99] Community members sold locally made crafts including necklaces, medallions, bracelets, and watchbands to raise money for a new wing of the local hospital. While they received fewer than the expected 125,000 visitors, the event helped the Kahnawá:ke residents resist the Settler colonial practice of using symbols of Indigenous peoples' cultures to define the nation. Forsyth observes, "While the [Montreal] Olympics organizers drew on their own, white understanding of 'the Indian' to sell a particular version of Canada and the Olympic Games, the Mohawk of Kahnawake constructed their own symbols to show the richness and diversity of Aboriginal lives in Canada."[100]

One community member who went by the satirical name "Chief Poking Fire" sold spoof products to visitors, offering them snake oil made in Pakistan, t-shirts made in India, and rubber arrowheads made in Japan.[101] Some Kahnawá:ke residents worried that visitors would buy the ersatz instead of the hand-made items available for purchase. They were also concerned that visitors, because of their already limited understanding, would be taken in by the stereotypes that Chief Poking Fire perpetuated by performing tribal rites and fire dances, and by arranging for his grandsons to pretend to tomahawk themselves to death.[102] However, Forsyth notes that these cultural displays extended the Kanien'kehá:ka's (Mohawk's) history of using and manipulating stereotypes about Indigenous peoples to influence Settlers' perception of their culture.[103] In this regard, the commodities sold by Chief Poking Fire have important symbolic meanings. They illustrate that defining a cultural object as authentic is a highly complex and contested practice. Moreover, Indigenous peoples, including the Kanien'kehá:ka, (Mohawk) have responded creatively to Settlers' expectations of authenticity.

The Self-Financing Model and French-English Relations

Thus far, I have analyzed the symbolic significance of select Olympic commodities. It is equally important to consider promotional and consumptive practices attached to these commodities. The city of Montreal was responsible for constructing and installing Olympic-related infrastructure and it planned to use the profits from Olympic coin and stamp programs to cover all its construction costs. This strategy was flawed from the beginning. Mayor Drapeau's original cost estimates were unrealistic, and expenses ballooned out of control. Taillibert's complex stadium design proved enormously expensive to build. Moreover, in 1974, labour disputes between the Quebec government and unions representing construction workers on Olympic-related projects stalled work on various Olympic sites. City officials had to pay labourers to work around the clock to compensate for lost time and ensure construction was finished by the start of the games.[104]

The city of Montreal and province of Quebec ultimately spent significant sums of public money on the 1976 Summer Games. Although COJO failed to achieve its goal of financing the games entirely through private funds, the organization adopted fundraising strategies that were, in some ways, ahead of their time. The organizing committee told Canadians they would be supporting a national cause (i.e., the Montreal Olympics) if they bought specially produced coins, postage stamps, and lottery tickets, thus anticipating a commercial practice that became highly popular in the 1980s: using consumer-based fundraising endeavours to fund social causes and public services.[105]

The Montreal Olympic official report reveals that organizers intentionally created opportunities for individuals to invest in the games. "The fundraising programs devised by COJO and the City of Montréal were essentially designed to permit Canadian citizens, as well as the rest of the world, to make voluntary contributions toward the cost of organizing the Games."[106] Committee member J. Neil Asselin articulated a similar idea in 1973 when he described the Montreal Olympic coin program as "a means of encouraging international and individual participation in the financing of the Olympic Games."[107]

COJO also urged vendors to adopt this perspective. At a meeting in February 1975, the COJO Marketing Advisory Committee, Olympic Coin Program, discussed "the need to encourage within the banks an attitude that would regard the sale of Olympic coins not merely as a commercial venture but also as a public service."[108] The postmaster general similarly argued that purchasing Olympic action stamps "allows every citizen to participate, on a purely voluntary basis, in defraying the total cost of the Games."[109] They were the first postage stamps in Canada to raise money for a social cause (the Olympics) through a surcharge.[110] A Canada Post pamphlet noted that this surcharge was intended "to give the public a convenient opportunity to support the Games on a voluntary and personal basis."[111]

Canada Post's view that individuals' spending decisions could be matters of national importance is an example of consumer nationalism. Enric Castelló and Sabina Mihelj use this term to describe "a set of discourses and practices that attach national significance to consumer objects (goods, services)."[112] In this case, Canada Post attached national significance to the Olympic stamps by explaining that consumers could help finance the Montreal Olympics by purchasing these objects. Canada Post also promoted consumer nationalism in the marketing campaign it designed for the Olympic stamps by employing the theme "Help It Happen."[113] It sold special Olympic postage meter dies that marked envelopes with this phrase, and companies who used these postage meters advertised themselves as socially responsible supporters of the Olympics.[114]

COJO complemented Canada Post's promotion of consumer nationalism by depicting corporate investment in the games as a matter of national importance. COJO member Alfred Warkentin included a letter soliciting sponsors for the games in his 1973 marketing plan. It reads, "Association and participation in this monumental enterprise – through the right to make use of the Olympic symbol – is a matter of national pride for Canadian companies."[115] In his marketing plan, Warkentin listed several ways companies would benefit from sponsoring the Montreal Games, including improving their "corporate image and prestige" and gaining the chance to present themselves as "good corporate citizen[s]."[116] Canadian brands, he further argued, would benefit from being associated with the event by capitalizing on "patriotic feeling about the Games being held in Canada and the feeling that all Canadian companies should participate vigorously."[117]

Warkentin also took a more threatening approach: corporate leaders might be convinced to support the games if they became aware of "a 'list' of sponsors which will be seen by Government officials at all three levels of Government." Warkentin continued, "The 'list' presents interesting possibilities. Whether applied to government or not, many companies may simply feel that 'they cannot afford to stay out.'"[118] Furthermore, "Once the Olympics become part of a great national crusade, particularly in Canada, companies which 'stayed out' will be known for that fact – and remembered for it by the public generally."[119] In this statement, Warkentin reverses conventional arguments about the benefits of sponsoring the Olympics. Rather than suggesting consumers will look favourably on brands that support the Games, he warns consumers will criticize brands that do not support them.

* * *

Although Montreal Olympic organizers devised fundraising programs to "permit Canadian citizens, as well as the rest of the world, to make voluntary contributions toward the cost of organizing the Games," few Canadians were motivated to purchase Olympic-related commodities for this reason.[120] The Olympic lottery is an interesting example in this regard. It earned net profits of $235 million, exceeding by sevenfold the organizing committee's initial estimate of profits.[121] Canadians from across the country watched live televised broadcasts of the Olympic lottery draws. A Nielsen TV Index Measurement found that a telecast of the Olympic lottery draw on 28 September 1975 attracted the largest number of CTV viewers and third largest number of Télévision associée (TVA) viewers in that month.[122]

There is no evidence, however, to suggest that the lottery's success was due to its association with the Montreal Games, or that Canadians were inspired by patriotic sentiment to purchase tickets. The Olympic lottery was the first national lottery scheme in Canada, and it helped shift gambling from a criminal activity to a legal practice. The federal government passed an omnibus bill legalizing gambling, along with socially controversial practices like divorce and abortion, in 1969. The bill gave federal and provincial governments the authority to manage and conduct "lottery schemes" and allowed provinces to grant gambling licences to charitable and religious organizations. Canadian lawmakers subsequently amended the *Criminal Code of Canada* in 1985 to give provinces exclusive control over gambling.[123]

In contrast to the financial success of the Olympic lottery, sales of Olympic coins brought in $100 million, amounting to less than half of estimated returns.[124] The Montreal Olympic stamp program, for its part, raised less than the forecasted $10 million.[125] A 1974 consumer survey investigated individuals' reasons for buying coins included in Series One of the Montreal Olympic coin collection. The findings reveal that only a small percentage of consumers were motivated to buy these objects out of a sense of national pride or desire to help finance the Olympics. Almost half of the consumers who bought a prestige set wished to build their coin collection (42 per cent) and less than a quarter purchased a set to support the Montreal Olympics (21 per cent). Only 15 per cent of consumers who bought encapsulated coins wished to support the Olympic Games through their purchase. In comparison, 43 per cent bought encapsulated coins as souvenirs.[126] Avid coin collectors are not generally inclined to purchase coins out of a sense of national duty. Common motivations include the desire to become an active part of the coin collecting community; find a connection to the past; enhance one's social standing and self-image; and/or make sound financial investments.[127]

The Mint might have been able to convince more Canadians to support the games by buying Montreal Olympic coins if it had effectively marketed them to the public. However, the organization had little experience in this area. The minutes of a 1982 meeting between Mint officials and organizers of the 1988 Calgary Olympics read, "The Mint became a Crown Corporation in 1969. When the Montreal Olympic Coin Program was initiated in 1971, there was no formal marketing structure in place; the Mint was a manufacturing organization. A Vice President of Marketing … was installed, but not in time to change the Mint's focus. The Montreal coins were 'marketed on a crash basis through bad distribution.'"[128] The minutes also reveal that the Mint made major mistakes with the Montreal coin program: "The coins were advertised as an investment rather than a commemorative collectable, they were manufactured according to the numbers legally authorized rather than to demand, and the Mint realizes there were far too many multiples made available."[129]

The challenges of convincing Canadians to show support for the nation by buying commodities associated with the Montreal Olympics include, but extend beyond, the Mint's marketing inexperience. Negative public opinion about the games was another important contributing factor. Gareau argued in 1973 that games-related promotion and publicity must "serve the commercial end of COJO 76. In other words, apart from convincing Canada that our Games are a truly Canadian event, all energies must be channelled into the prime objective of translating the value of these Games into dollars."[130] However, many English Canadians did not associate the Montreal Olympics with national pride or unity. According to COJO member Paul Howell, the games were widely considered a regional rather than national project from the very start: "When Montreal made its winning bid … it was clear to Canadians that the Montreal Games would be the Quebec Games."[131]

This idea was also reflected in the observations of a young Canadian who participated in the International Youth Camp affiliated with the Montreal Olympics. Organized by COJO, it offered young people from across Canada and around the world the opportunity to meet one another and attend Olympic events. A Canadian who participated in the camp, Ross Macnab, wrote that he appreciated the chance to meet people from other countries. "It was equally as interesting" he went on, "to discover the great variety of cultures within our own country. An Eskimo, two types of Indians, French Canadians, a Yugoslavian, so many different backgrounds and lifestyles."[132] However, Macnab believed it "was a shame that the Olympic and Camp organizers didn't stress Canada's multicultural heritage. *It appeared that it was not Canada's Olympics, but Quebec's Olympics.*"[133] Macnab's statement reveals that the Canadian pride he experienced when participating in camp activities did not extend to his experience of the Montreal Olympic Games as a whole.

Two letters to the editor published in the *Globe and Mail* illustrate how linguistic and cultural differences between English and French Canadians influenced public perception of the 1976 Summer Games. A letter from a Torontonian named A. Gay Kirkpatrick published on 21 July 1976 reads, "Pierre Trudeau's dream of a bilingual Canada is quite obviously going to be turned into a nightmare by the unilingual Québécois. I attended the opening ceremonies of Canada's Olympics on July 17 … and was simply astounded to hear each initial announcement in French, followed by an English translation. And to add fuel to the fire, the large electronic signboards flashed each country's name during the walk-past, in French only."[134] The newspaper printed another reader's heated response a few days later. Peter Fletcher, who lived in a suburb of Toronto, wrote, "Surely Mr. Kirkpatrick is aware of the fact that French is the official language of the Province of Quebec … with the opinion of many Canadians that *these Games were Quebec's and not Canada's*, it is surprising to see that with the opening ceremonies on Saturday the Olympics are suddenly 'ours.'"[135]

The fact that many individuals associated the Montreal Olympics with the host province rather than the host country helps explain why few Canadian spectators waved the national flag at Olympic competitions. During the first week of the games, Chris Goyens, a COJO spokesperson, complained, Canadians are "getting out-cheered by a long shot … The Americans are wiping us out."[136] Lawrence Martin reported the complaint in the *Globe and Mail* and observed that hardly any Canadian spectators waved flags in the stands. He quoted an unnamed official from COJO's licensing department observing, "There's hundreds of Olympic souvenirs on sale … But it's funny. Nobody came up with an idea for a flag."[137] Thus, even if Canadians had wished to buy commodities to demonstrate their patriotism, they would not have found a Montreal Olympic licensed flag.

By contrast, consumers could easily find commodities featuring the Montreal Olympic emblem, including paper weights, lawn decorations, and necklaces.[138] It even appears on a clothing patch next to the Quebec provincial flag (figure 1.3). I argued earlier in this chapter that COJO did

1.3 Clothing patch featuring the emblem of the 1976 Montreal Olympics and Quebec provincial flag.

not associate the emblem's symbolic meaning with Canadian identity but, rather, with Montreal's status as a world class city. Yet the emblem did not successfully represent this idea, either. Instead, it symbolized Montreal's struggle to host a successful Olympic Games in a country that was divided by political and cultural differences. These struggles were apparent even before the games began, with COJO facing heavy criticism for going over budget and running behind schedule. Rousseau admitted before a committee of the National Assembly of Quebec in July 1975 that the total cost of the Montreal Olympics had increased by at least $100 million in the previous six months, and they would have a predicted deficit of $221 million. A construction timetable also revealed that work on the Olympic stadium was six weeks behind schedule.[139]

The Quebec government took over responsibility for building Montreal Olympic facilities from COJO in November of 1975. By that time, the games were expected to cost $1 billion and have a $600 million deficit.[140] Bruce Kidd concludes that "the Montreal Olympics remain a symbol of extravagant mismanagement and unfulfilled expectations."[141] Even more literally, commodities bearing the Montreal Olympic emblem serve as tangible symbols of these failures. Moreover, the Olympic stadium represented in the emblem through the extended lines of the letter M does not represent the strength of French Canadians in Canada, as Drapeau hoped. Rather, it represents the failure of the games. As Latouche observes, many Montrealers believe the games were "a catastrophe for the city's economy and its reputation, with very little to show except *an over-sized and under-used stadium*."[142]

Conclusion

The Montreal Olympics occurred at a time when French and English Canadians were divided by fundamental cultural, linguistic, and political differences. These divisions influenced narratives about local, regional, and national identity that circulated during the games and shaped the symbolic meanings of Olympic commodities. At the same time, symbols of Indigenous peoples' cultures appeared in the ceremonial and commercial features of the Montreal Olympics, including in the design of the games' mascot and specially produced coins. These representations perpetuated the Settler colonial practice of using symbols of Indigenous peoples' cultures to define Canadian identity. Significantly, Indigenous peoples, including many Kanien'kehá:ka (Mohawk) of Kahnawá:ke, worked within and outside the constraints of the Olympics to undermine Settler colonial representations of their cultures.

These findings demonstrate that the commodification of Settler Canadian and Indigenous peoples' cultures in the Canadian-hosted Olympics was not an outgrowth of the increasingly sophisticated commercial practices the IOC developed in the 1980s. Rather, organizers of the first Olympic Games hosted in Canada designed commodities that contained national symbols and Indigenous iconography. However, in subsequent Olympic Games hosted in Canada in 1988 and 2010, Canadians were more inclined to purchase Olympic-related products to demonstrate their patriotism. Although COJO members attempted to establish a link between nationalism, corporate sponsorship of the Montreal Olympic Games, and consumption of specially produced commodities, they were largely unsuccessful. This failure is instructive, illustrating that several of the political and social factors that make the fusion of nationalism and commercialism through sport possible were missing in the Montreal Olympics.

2

Commercializing English-Canadian Identity, Indigenous Cultures, and Oil in the 1978 Edmonton Commonwealth Games

Members of the Edmonton Commonwealth Games bid delegation travelled to Munich in August 1972 to compete against Leeds, England, for the right to host the 1978 Commonwealth Games. Edmonton's delegation, which arrived in the first week of the Munich Summer Olympics, included Mayor Ivor Dent; president of the Commonwealth Games Association of Canada Jack Davies; dean of Physical Education at the University of Alberta Maury Van Vliet; and Alberta minister of Culture Horst Schmid. The city's bid presentation included a performance by the Alberta All-Girls Drum and Bugle Band and speeches from Davies, Van Vliet, and Schmid. Members of the Commonwealth Games Federation (CGF) voted thirty-four to ten in favour of awarding the 1978 Games to Edmonton over Leeds.[1] They became the first "Commonwealth Games" (i.e., "British Empire" was no longer part of the title) and the first to include a mascot. Organizers selected a brown bear named Keyano, whose Cree name they translated into English as "ours" or "unity," as the mascot.[2]

The federal government provided $12 million in funding for the Edmonton Games, the province of Alberta and city of Edmonton each provided $11.6 million, while the Kinsmen Club of Edmonton donated a further $1 million. Members of the XI Commonwealth Games Canada (1978) Foundation (XICGCF) also raised $3.5 million through the following initiatives: a federal coin and stamp program modelled on the one created for the 1976 Montreal Summer Olympics; a federal lottery; a portion of the returns from a provincial lottery scheme, the

Western Lottery; and corporate sponsorship and licensing initiatives.[3] The XICGCF earned a surplus of approximately $300,000.[4]

Comparisons between the Edmonton Commonwealth Games and Montreal Olympics appeared frequently in the *Globe and Mail*, with journalists praising organizers' efforts to keep the Edmonton Games within budget. Headlines included "Commonwealth Games Won't Be in the Red: Montreal Followed Design, Edmonton Followed the Budget"; "Edmonton Games Likely to Be Spared Montreal-Type Mess"; and "Commonwealth Games: Doing Things Better."[5] Comparisons between the two events, however, were not always favourable. Organizers of the Edmonton Games struggled to convince corporate sponsors to invest in them. A report from the organization's Marketing Division reads, "We found, despite all the publicity that the Montreal Olympics had given to the whole business of licensing, and to the various suppliers and licensees under that programme, that companies were not flocking to our doors offering their services and wares … it became necessary to sell the concept of the importance of our Games to corporations since everyone accepted that they were smaller than the Olympics and of less importance."[6]

Despite the Edmonton Games being less sophisticated than the Montreal Olympics, organizers and sponsors engaged in a practice that was also a notable feature of the 1976 Summer Olympics and, later, Calgary and Vancouver Olympics: using symbols of Indigenous cultures to represent the Settler colonial state. In this chapter, I analyze how Indigenous cultures were represented in the ceremonial and commercial elements of the Edmonton Commonwealth Games. I identify the broader context in which these representations occurred, demonstrating that organizers and sponsors incorporated Indigenous cultural displays in the games while, at the same time, celebrating Canada's Settler colonial origins and ties to the British Empire. Furthermore, games organizers did not invite Indigenous teams to participate in the box lacrosse competitions they staged as a demonstration sport.

A contemporary issue related to Indigenous-Settler relations also influenced the promotional and political practices surrounding the Edmonton Commonwealth Games, namely, the issue of land rights and jurisdiction over oil resources. The games occurred shortly after the Alberta government passed a law preventing local Indigenous groups, who were trying to stop companies from drilling for oil on their land, from exercising their rightful ownership over the land. Moreover, like organizers of Canadian-hosted Olympic Games, Edmonton Games organizers used their event to shape the host region's reputation globally. And Alberta politicians used the games to influence the province's reputation within Canada amidst heightened tensions between the federal and Alberta governments over jurisdiction of oil resources.

Representing and Commodifying English-Canadian Identity and Indigenous Cultures

Organizers of the Edmonton Commonwealth Games celebrated Canada's Settler colonial ties to Britain while also using symbols of Indigenous peoples' cultures to define the nation as distinct from the "mother country." The design of the Queen's baton exemplifies this strategy. The baton relay dates to 1958, when organizers of the Cardiff British Empire Games established the tradition of transporting a baton carrying a message from the head of the Commonwealth, the Queen of England, from London to the host city. Although Prince Phillip typically read the Queen's message contained in the baton at the games' opening ceremonies, the monarch travelled to Edmonton to personally declare the 1978 Games open. The baton travelled by plane from London to Ottawa and subsequently flew to Hamilton, Vancouver, and Calgary. Runners carried the baton on the last leg of its journey, from Calgary to Edmonton.[7]

Games organizers considered three options for the baton's design: a "Canadian Eskimo carving"; "silver, engraved with National Symbols such as Coat of Arms, Maple Leaf, Beaver"; or "constructed of various metals from each Canadian Province with the Provincial Coat of Arms situated on either end and the Canadian Coat of Arms in the Centre."[8] They ultimately settled on the first option and Van Vliet wrote to the commissioner of the Northwest Territories, S.M. Hodgson, asking about the possibility of having the baton "carved out of ivory by Eskimo carvers. In the view of both myself and my Executive, we feel that this would be a very unique and distinctive type of baton and reflect in a cultural sense an art form which exists in no other part of the world."[9]

Hodgson was receptive to this idea and the XICGCF commissioned Inuit artist Nick Sikkuark to carve what a publication about the games describes as "a uniquely Canadian design from Narwhal tusk" (figure 2.1).[10] By characterizing the design as "uniquely Canadian," organizers perpetuated the historical practice of using displays of Indigenous art to define the nation and represent English-Canadian identity as

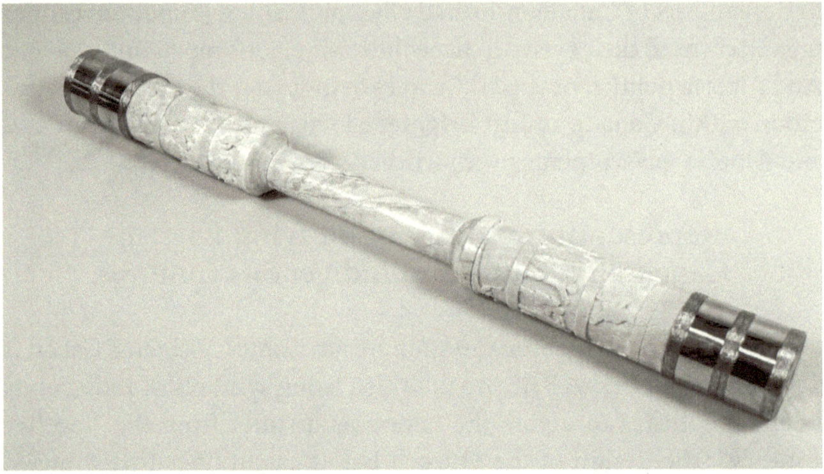

2.1 Queen's baton of the 1978 Edmonton Commonwealth Games.

distinct from British identity. These representations often contained unacknowledged but nevertheless significant reminders of the nation's Settler colonial history. In the case of the Edmonton Games' baton, such a reminder was literally embedded within the object: it contained a message from a representative of the British monarchy, under whose authority Settlers colonized Canada. Recall, for example, that in the seventeenth century King Charles II gave the Hudson's Bay Company (HBC) the authority to trade and negotiate treaties with Indigenous groups and granted the company a commercial monopoly over a large swath of land in present-day Canada. The Edmonton Games' baton thus represents the history of British colonial rule in Canada and is haunted by the fact that Indigenous populations were subjected to this rule. The minutes of a 1976 XICGCF meeting reveal that organizers even considered inviting the Queen to run in the relay: "After some heated debate it was unanimously agreed, whilst the suggestion was unique and would indeed have placed a seal of difference upon the Edmonton Games, Her Majesty not be requested to run the final leg of the relay."[11]

The practice of using Indigenous art to define Settler colonial identity dates to at least the early twentieth century, when English Canadians began depicting Inuit artwork as representations of essential features of the nation.[12] Moreover, an art exhibit staged at the National Gallery in 1927 called *Exhibition of Canadian West Coast Art, Native and Modern*, displayed Indigenous artifacts alongside the works of Settler artists and depicted them as part of Canadian cultural heritage.[13] The exhibit included Emily Carr's paintings of Northwest Coast Indigenous communities. Gerta Moray makes the insightful argument that, in the 1920s and 1930s, "Carr's 'Indian' paintings and her relation to her Native subjects were presented to the public as symbols of the existence of an exotic 'Canadian' prehistory."[14] She further points out that the *Exhibition of Canadian West Coast Art, Native and Modern* was staged at a time when Indian residential schools were operating across the country, the Potlatch was outlawed, and the Indian Act prohibited Indigenous peoples from raising money for political activities.[15]

Gillian Poulter uses almost identical language to Moray when describing the cultural displays that Indigenous lacrosse players participated in during their tours of the British Isles between 1867 and 1883: Indigenous peoples functioned in these displays as "colourful, nostalgic reminders of the *pre-historic* existence of indigenous peoples in Canada, an essential part of its myth of origin."[16] Significantly, organizers of the Edmonton Commonwealth Games originally invited only non-Indigenous athletes to participate in the box lacrosse competitions they included as a demonstration sport in the games.[17] An editorial in the *Edmonton Journal* argued against this decision: "If the Edmonton Commonwealth Games foundation wished to demonstrate a sport unique to this country's culture during the next summer's Games, the demonstration would be far more authentic with descendants of the people who invented it taking part."[18] Ralph Bouvette, chairman of the Indian-Métis 1978 Games Committee, which was struck to co-ordinate Indigenous activities for the games, criticized the exclusion of Indigenous lacrosse athletes as "a deliberate, bloody insult to the native people."[19]

Indigenous athletes were offered a chance to play a cultural role in the competition. However, players rejected this offer, with team representatives asserting, "We don't want to be out there and dance for white people. We don't want to be token Indians."[20] The Indian-Métis 1978 Games Committee presented a proposal to the Canadian Lacrosse Association for two all-Indigenous lacrosse teams to participate in the games.[21] Edmonton Games organizers ultimately agreed to stage a lacrosse competition between two all-Indigenous teams, the St Regis Warriors and Caughnawaga Braves. Yet the federal government did not cover the cost of the competitors' travel to Edmonton and they were not permitted to stay in the athletes' village, watch competitions, or participate in the closing ceremonies.[22] Allen Abel criticized these restrictions in the *Globe and Mail*, writing, "What better way to demonstrate how life often goes for native people than by barring them from the [Athlete's] Village, giving them accreditation that would not permit them to enter any other venue and shipping them out before the closing ceremony?"[23] For Allan Downey, the controversy surrounding Indigenous lacrosse players' participation in the 1978 Edmonton Games "epitomizes a persistent theme in Canadian history – that Indigenous peoples are valued not as athletes or partners within a nation-to-nation relationship, but as performers and spectacles that fit within the assumed absolute sovereignty and control of Canadian sport organizations and, ultimately, the country."[24] As the following analysis illustrates, this theme was also evident in non-sporting activities associated with the 1978 Games.

* * *

Several games-related cultural and commercial practices included Indigenous peoples as, to quote Downey, "performers and spectacles."[25] The Edmonton Games' opening ceremony is one such cultural practice. It began with Queen Elizabeth II and Prince Phillip entering the stage in a car that circled the track. Children then performed a dance which ended in a Canadian flag formation. Journalist James Christie described what occurred next as "a cloying tribute over the loudspeaker to 'the first Canadians, the I-n-n-ndians and the May-tea.' Then came dancers pretending to be French voyageurs and coureurs de bois, who carried canoes and scythes."[26] The order of events in this dramatization draws attention to early Canadian nation-building practices: figures that helped colonize Canada, European voyageurs and coureurs de bois, appear after representations of the so-called "first Canadians," Indigenous peoples.

As host broadcaster for the Edmonton Commonwealth Games, the Canadian Broadcasting Corporation (CBC) aired the opening ceremony on television. However, CBC employees were initially concerned that the ceremony would not make for good television because of a change the CGF had recently made to opening and closing ceremony protocol. In 1976, the CGF decided that athletes should enter the stadium and take their seats before the start of cultural performances. A member of the Edmonton Games' organizing committee speculated that federation members made this change because they "felt that sports festivals, particularly the Olympics, were becoming too much of a commercial spectacular, and that they, the Federation, were determined to do everything possible to see that the Commonwealth Games remained primarily an event for the athletes."[27] From the perspective of the CBC, however, the twelve to fifteen minutes it would take for the athletes to be seated before the cultural display began would bore television viewers.[28] The CGF ultimately allowed organizers of the Edmonton Games to change the standard protocol.[29]

The Edmonton Games' cultural programming, "Festival '78," also included Indigenous cultural performances. An article published in the souvenir magazine produced for the games by the *Edmonton Journal* reads, "The Canadian Folk Arts Festival, the most successful element of the cultural program at the Montreal Olympics, will present folk talent from all 10 provinces and the two territories. Fiddlers and dancers from Quebec, pipes and handbell choirs from the Maritimes, folklore groups from the Prairies, *native Indian and Inuit dancers and singers will perform on outdoor stages in many parts of the city*."[30]

The displays of Indigenous cultures that HBC included in its games-related promotional activities complemented the performances featured in Festival '78. In addition to sponsoring the Edmonton Games, the company's general manager in Alberta, Hal Spelliscy, served as XICGCF vice president of Lotteries, Marketing and Fundraising.[31] HBC published a full-page ad in the 1 August 1978 edition of the *Edmonton Journal* encouraging readers to visit the store's downtown Edmonton location and attend "Commonwealth Games Special Events" featuring Indigenous performers. It reads, "During the Games, we're celebrating with special appearances by Alberta's own native Indian dancers, appearing on the second floor Heritage Stage in our Downtown Store."[32] This ad reflects a colonial perspective of ownership over Indigenous peoples and their cultures through its description of special appearances by "*Alberta's own* native Indian dancers."

Two years before Edmonton hosted the Commonwealth Games, Indigenous dancers performed in the Montreal Olympic closing ceremony and gave athletes feathered bands as souvenirs. Similarly, Indigenous peoples performed on stages located in outdoor spaces in Edmonton, the indoor stadium where the opening ceremony was staged, and within a retail space. Moreover, material representations of

Indigenous cultures circulated alongside some of these performances. The 1 August 1978 HBC ad promises that the area surrounding its Heritage Stage will be "filled with authentic crafts by various native artisans."[33] It also promotes the company's collection of "Eskimo carvings ... Arctic art representing thirteen far northern communities" and provides the following descriptions of Inuit carvings for sale: " beautiful Hudson's Bay fish by Piloposi Napartuk of Povungnituk village" for $48; a "sensitively carved" waterbird from Becher island for $45; and a carving of "the hunter in his quest for survival by Lucassie Angiyow" for $60.[34]

This ad also uses HBC's involvement in the art industry to emphasize the company's long history in Canada, noting, "For over three hundred years, the Hudson's Bay Company has been dealing in traditional Canadian art. And when you've been trading as long as we have, you know how to recognize quality."[35] The ad subtly draws attention to HBC's historical participation in the Canadian fur trade with the statement "when you've been trading as long as we have"; this statement could refer not only to HBC employees' trade in Indigenous art but also their trade in beaver pelts procured by Indigenous hunters and trappers. HBC has never hidden its involvement in this industry. When HBC's profits began declining in the 1930s, executives began downplaying the company's ties to the British Empire and emphasizing its contribution to the Canadian fur trade.[36] Moreover, an HBC ad published in the 2 August 1978 issue of the *Edmonton Journal* promotes its "World Famous" coats, boasting, "Our unique cloth bears the Hudson's Bay Seal of Quality, a standard for the world, and is marked with the lines that used to indicate the number of beaver skins required in trade for a blanket. If you're thinking of Canadian history ... it's hard not to think of the Bay!"[37] This statement can be altered to add an important piece of information: if you're thinking of Canadian history ... it's hard not to think of the Bay *employees' trade with Indigenous peoples.*

This analysis exposes how HBC, a company that helped build the Canadian Settler state, incorporated Indigenous cultural displays and artifacts into its promotional practices. The ad for HBC's collection of Inuit art also tells readers that "The Bay's Canadiana Shop" is "alive with the color of Canada's history and heritage. Proud to be Canadian."[38] Through this statement, HBC aligns its brand identity with its early contributions to Canadian nation-building. However, the "history and heritage" to which the ad refers cannot be separated from the Settler state's displacement of

Indigenous peoples from their lands and suppression of their cultures. As such, the version of nationalism promoted through the ad is tainted by the logic of elimination that lies at the heart of the Settler colonial project in Canada, as well as HBC's contribution to this project.[39]

When hereditary chief of the Dene Tha First Nation, Harry Chonkolay, met Queen Elizabeth II one day prior to the start of the Edmonton Games, he used clothing to draw attention to a topic not openly recognized by games organizers or sponsors: the history and continuation of colonial rule in Canada. Chief Chonkolay appeared before the Queen "unusually attired in a military uniform and head dress."[40] According to the *Edmonton Journal*, "The head dress has become the symbol of 'Indianism' but that's as far as the Chief would carry today's modern native fashions. Instead he wore the military uniform symbolizing his acceptance of rule under the government but power invested under the Indian Act."[41] Chief Chonkolay also drew attention to a truth that haunted the games, namely, that colonial rule is expressed through dishonoured treaties. He told a reporter he regretted not having the opportunity to speak to the Queen about "native rights that have been broken since the signing of peace treaty Number 8."[42]

In addition, members of the Enoch Cree First Nation living on a reserve west of Edmonton collaborated with the Indian-Métis 1978 Games Committee to organize a "Cultural Exposé" held during the same time as the Edmonton Commonwealth Games. Bouvette referenced Indigenous involvement in the 1976 Montreal Olympics, including their participation in the closing ceremony, when discussing the committee's goals: "We were all aware of the extremely pitiful demonstration of native involvement in the Olympic Games in Montreal. We are all convinced that Alberta can do better than that. In Montreal, they literally had white people doing Indian dances."[43] The Enoch Cree worked alongside the Indian-Métis 1978 Games Committee to plan "pow-wow dancing, old-time dancing with fiddles, traditional and contemporary sports, displays, [and] the sale of bannock and other traditional native foods."[44] These cultural practices serve as important reminders that colonization in Canada is an incomplete process; the state has never assimilated all Indigenous peoples into Settler society; and Indigenous peoples continue to assert control over representations of their cultures.

***

The HBC ad published in the 2 August 1978 edition of the *Edmonton Journal* not only promotes the company's wool coats. It also welcomes athletes, officials, and guests to the city, reading, "We are encouraging all our staff … to wear the colours of red, white and blue during the Commonwealth Games. We also invite Edmonton to join us in showing your colours, and as you see people dressed in red, white and blue, to remember to say 'Hello!,' be they tourists or neighbors."[45] The company thus urged HBC employees and locals to show their enthusiasm for the Edmonton Games through their clothing. This ad is an early example of a promotional practice HBC later used in the lead-up to the Vancouver 2010 Winter Olympics when advertising its red mittens (an activity I discuss in the conclusion). In both instances, the company states that individuals can communicate their support for a nationally significant event through their attire. However, a notable difference between these two examples concerns the clothing and apparel designs HBC endorsed. In 1978, the company encouraged locals to wear colours associated with the Union Jack (red, white, and blue), recalling the Commonwealth Games' origins as a sporting event designed to celebrate the British Empire. In the lead up to the 2010 Vancouver Olympics, company representatives promoted an item resembling the national flag; the Vancouver Olympic mittens feature the colours of the Canadian flag (red and white) as well as a symbol on the flag (a maple leaf).

The design of the Edmonton Commonwealth Games' emblem evokes both the Union Jack and Canadian flag: it is a stylized red and blue maple leaf on a white background. The maple leaf's twelve points symbolize Canada's ten provinces and two territories (Nunavut has since become a third territory).[46] The Canadian flag design was relatively new in 1978 and subject to considerable public debate. When federal politicians proposed creating a flag for Canada in 1945, many French Canadians insisted that the design not reproduce other flags – including the British flag – while many English Canadians wanted the Union Jack to remain.[47] Unable to resolve these competing demands, the government did not make any changes to the flag until 1965, when Prime Minister Lester Pearson proposed a design with three maple leaves and no Union Jack. However, many Anglo-Canadians claimed this design was not sufficiently British.[48] The new flag was ultimately designed in red and white with only one maple leaf.

A central issue in the flag debates was, as Eva Mackey puts it, "the difference between the British imperialist view of Canada – which saw Canada as part of the British Empire ... and the nationalist view – which perceived Canada as an independent nation."[49] HBC ads published in the *Edmonton Journal* and the Edmonton Games' emblem design accommodate both perspectives. HBC executives and games organizers used the colours of the Union Jack to appeal to those Canadians who take pride in the country's historical ties to England. At the same time, the company's assertion in its advertising that it was an important player in Canadian nation-building practices and the emblem's maple leaf design promote a version of national identity that is culturally distinct from Britain.

* * *

Organizers of the 1978 Edmonton Games educated young people about the British Commonwealth through a workbook published with funds from the Alberta Department of Education and distributed to elementary schools.[50] The workbook contains lessons about the British Commonwealth as well as the Edmonton Games' mascot that complemented narratives about the nation circulating in the games' cultural and commercial features. Specifically, the workbook emphasizes Commonwealth countries' ties to Britain while also teaching students how Edmonton Games organizers used a feature of an Indigenous culture (a Cree word) to represent English-Canadian identity.

The workbook includes selective, and problematic, information about Britain's empire building missions, with one section noting, "A Commonwealth country was at one time controlled or ruled by Great Britain. Great Britain had sent explorers *into the unknown world to discover new countries and claim them for Britain.*"[51] This statement uncritically discusses Britain's practice of claiming possession of foreign land and extracting profit from the natural resources contained on this land. Moreover, it perpetuates the ideologically charged and misleading idea that there once existed "new" and "unknown" lands available for European settlement. The original inhabitants of these countries would have hardly considered them new or unknown.

The workbook continues by discussing how Commonwealth nations eventually gained independence from Britain: "As many years

2.2 Keyano, mascot of the 1978 Edmonton Commonwealth Games.

passed, these countries decided they wanted to have their own rules or leaders. These countries became independent. Britain was no longer in control of the things that happened in the countries. However, many of these new 'free countries' still wanted to be close to Britain."[52] Students learn that only those countries who recognized the Queen as the head of the Commonwealth were able to join "a new group called the Commonwealth."[53]

Some countries that were formerly members of the British Empire emphasize their independence from Britain by using symbols of Indigenous cultures to represent their unique identity. Patrick Wolfe argues, as I discuss in chapter 1, that a Settler society seeks to "recuperate indigeneity in order to express its difference – and, accordingly, its independence – from the mother country."[54] Montreal Olympic organizers "recuperated indigeneity" by naming the games' mascot Amik, an Algonquin word meaning beaver. Similarly, organizers of the Edmonton Commonwealth Games gave the mascot, a brown bear, the Cree name Keyano (figure 2.2). The games' workbook educates young people about this feature of the mascot, as well as its commercial appeal. The workbook notes that siblings Michael and Dana Perchinsky (aged eleven and nine) made the winning submission to the *Edmonton Journal's* "Name the Commonwealth Bear" contest; the Perchinsky siblings won a 5 foot 3 inch stuffed bear that Pacific Western Airlines transported to their hometown of Fort McMurray, Alberta, for free.[55] The mention of a gigantic stuffed bear exposes young people to the existence of Keyano commodities, including plush toys of Keyano produced by the company Mighty Star International, that they may wish to own.[56]

The workbook also reads, "Michael and Dana's entry, which is a cree word meaning 'ours' or 'unity,' was chosen from among more than 3,700 entries."[57] The fact that games organizers selected a Cree word they translated as "ours" draws attention to a colonial perspective that found expression in the workbook, namely, the view that Indigenous peoples' cultures and lands are resources that the British Empire had once "owned." Yet, the alternative translation of the word "keyano" presented in the workbook has very different connotations from British Empire building practices. Rather, the word "unity" draws an association between the mascot and harmonious relations between people, obscuring the reality that Indigenous-Settler relations were, and continue to be, damaged by attempts to assimilate Indigenous peoples into Settler society. In this regard, Keyano commodities function similarly to Amik commodities. Specifically, they are fetish objects that both represent and disavow the reality of the injustice inherent in the Settler colonial project in Canada.

The workbook includes a series of questions about the mascot's name, including, "What does 'Keyano' mean?" "Why do you think that name was selected as the winning entry?" and "Can you think of another 'winning' name for the mascot?"[58] Authors likely expected students to rely on the workbook's translation of the word "keyano" into English when answering the question "What does 'Keyano' mean?" However, the workbook's straightforward explanation of the word's meaning obscures the complexities and challenges of translating Indigenous languages, including Cree, into English. Vince Ahenakew argues that Cree is "a very difficult language to write and translate; some words have natural English translations, but some have to be manipulated and re-arranged with other words to obtain meaning; and some words change to a question with the tone that is used in pronunciation."[59] He edited an English-Cree dictionary that translates "ours" as "Kiyanaw ohci." However, "ninyanân" is used when answering "ours" to the question "whose?"[60]

Oil Extraction, Indigenous Rights, and Federal-Provincial Relations in Alberta

An acknowledged truth haunts the Edmonton Commonwealth Games' mascot and games-related cultural events. Specifically, games organizers included symbols of Indigenous peoples into the games at a time when the Alberta government was in the process of violating local Indigenous peoples' rights. One year prior to the start of the Edmonton Games, several Indigenous groups living north of Lesser Slave Lake, including members of the Lubicon Lake Nation, attempted to stop companies from extracting oil on land located between the Peace River and Athabasca River. These groups filed a legal caveat asserting they retained ownership over the land. However, before a judge could rule on the case, the Alberta government passed a bill prohibiting individuals from claiming caveats on unpatented Crown land. The bill effectively shut down the Lubicon and their partners' legal claim, placing them outside the protection of the law.[61]

When combined with previous practices like Ottawa's decades-long failure to resolve the Lubicon's land claim, the provincial government's action led to the Lubicon being denied the "right to have rights."[62] As self-governing peoples who lived on the land before Europeans settled in Canada, Indigenous peoples have a unique set of rights that are enshrined in section 35(1) of the Canadian Constitution Act, 1982, which recognizes that Indigenous peoples have the right to self-determination. This section illustrates that not all Canadian citizens have equal rights. Rather, Indigenous peoples belong to nations that have the additional right to exercise political autonomy within Canada.[63]

Hannah Arendt uses the term the "right to have rights" to describe the fact that individuals must belong to a community that recognizes them as rights-bearing individuals in order to exercise any civil or juridical right. She writes, "Not the loss of specific rights, then, but the loss of a community willing and able to guarantee any rights whatsoever, has been the calamity which has befallen ever-increasing numbers of people."[64] The Lubicon were denied the "right to have rights" when their ability to maintain their sovereignty, preserve their culture, and practice their traditional ways of life became jeopardized through oil extraction practices on their land. The Lubicon's alienation from their land meant the loss, in Arendt's words, of "the entire social texture into which they were born and in which they established for themselves a distinct place in the world."[65]

This context informs the symbolic meaning of a commodity sold during the games, "miniature souvenir oil drums containing pure crude oil" produced by a company called Black Gold Souvenirs.[66] These objects can be understood not as feel-good keepsakes of the Edmonton Commonwealth Games but, rather, as containers of a natural resource from which Settlers extract profit at the expense of Indigenous peoples. In this way, they function as tangible representations of a practice (oil extraction on Lubicon land) that is often represented in intangible ways through moral or legal arguments. The miniature oil drums also call attention to the idea that Settler colonialism is not exclusively, or even primarily, an ideological practice. Rather, Settler governments in Settler colonial countries try to control who has the right to live on, and generate wealth from, the land.[67] Commodities I analyze later in this book, such as glassware Petro-Canada produced for the 1988 Calgary Winter Olympics, symbolize this idea in even more complex ways than the souvenir oil drum. However, the miniature oil drum is notable because it is an example of a commodity central to Alberta's identity – as the centre of Canada's oil and gas industry, as discussed below – and was sold a few years before Calgary hosted the Olympics.

Like many commodities analyzed in this book, the souvenir oil drums have multiple and intersecting symbolic meanings. In addition to containing a natural resource that lay at the heart of the Lubicon's conflict with the province, the souvenirs represent Alberta's identity as an oil-rich province. Indeed, an article in the *Edmonton Journal* from July 1964 describes how three brothers intended to convert "Edmonton's pride into fluid assets" by selling canned crude oil as souvenirs.[68] One of the brothers, Ed Kostyshyn, proclaimed, "This city needs a distinctive souvenir," and added, "we're the oil capital ... don't you think we should have a real Alberta souvenir?"[69]

Numerous companies working in the oil and gas sector, including Petro-Canada, Imperial Oil, Shell Canada, and Trans-Canada Pipelines, sponsored the 1978 Edmonton Commonwealth Games.[70] Hal Pawson, who contributed to Edmonton's successful bid to host the games, asserts that locals hoped the event would strengthen the city's global and domestic reputation. Significantly, bid officials depicted the province's oil and gas riches as a central feature of the city's identity. In Pawson's account, bid delegates wished "to 'put Edmonton on the map,' as we smugly put it, not really believing in our hearts that was necessary. After all, hadn't Edmonton been on the map a goodly number of years, at the very least since 1947 and the discovery of oil 18 miles southwest of the Alberta capital, near Leduc? (I now suspect our real reason was to prove to the rest of Canada – and at least that large part of the world known as the Commonwealth – that if Edmonton put its mind to it, this community of 'doers' could handle just about anything, including a project as large as the Commonwealth Games.)"[71]

Bid officials did not pioneer the practice of using sport-related events to advertise oil companies' activities in Alberta and depict the cities that supported these activities favourably. When Vancouver hosted the 1954 British Empire and Commonwealth Games, organizers published a Souvenir Book/Program of Events that included promotional messages about corporations and Canadian cities. Imperial Oil's sponsored page included an image of a pioneer well, describing it as "the pioneer well in what has proved to be Canada's most important oil discovery – in the rich farming country near the town of Leduc, Alberta."[72] Readers also learned that Edmonton was the "centre of Canada's vast multi-million dollar oil, gas and petrochemical developments" and Calgary is "one of Canada's enterprising and growing cities. It ranks high for its interests in flour milling and meat packing. Oil, too, adds to the prosperity of its people."[73] The publication thus conveys a consistent narrative about the wealth of Western Canada's petroleum resources and works to strengthen a corporation's brand (Imperial Oil) as well as two cities' reputations (Edmonton and Calgary).

The fact that the Edmonton Commonwealth Games' souvenir oil drum contained crude oil is also significant considering that, at the time of the games, Premier Peter Lougheed and Prime Minister Pierre Elliott Trudeau were engaged in a protracted conflict surrounding jurisdiction of the province's oil and gas reserves. The conflict began when Lougheed became premier in 1971. After coming to office, he argued that the province should have the authority to make its own decisions about the rich natural resources found in Alberta. Having such decision-making power would help improve Western Canada's standing in the country. As he put it in a speech, "We have to try to protect the Alberta public interest – not from the public interest of Canada as a whole – but from central and eastern Canadian domination of the West."[74]

Trudeau, however, was unwilling to cede control of Alberta's oil and gas industry. In September 1973, the prime minister responded to rising global oil prices by freezing the price of domestic petroleum products, reducing the depletion allowance companies could claim by 8 per cent, and, most troubling to Lougheed, setting an export tax of 40¢ per barrel of oil.[75] Lougheed responded by announcing that he would lift a cap he had set on the price companies paid the province to extract oil from the land.[76] Relations between Edmonton and Ottawa were so tense in the late 1970s that Trudeau joked he "heard what for me is a rare and wonderful sound, the sound of Albertans applauding," when Queen Elizabeth II officially opened the 1978 Commonwealth Games.[77] Lougheed used the games as an opportunity to reiterate his commitment to fighting for Western Canada's interests. At a banquet honouring the Queen held one day before the opening of the Edmonton Games, he commented, "As Albertans, we seek to have the western region, and Alberta in particular, be even more a part of the mainstream of all aspects of Canadian life."[78]

This perspective influenced one local's interpretation of the Edmonton Commonwealth Games' postage stamps, all of which included the games' red, blue, and white emblem.[79] Alberta resident Altaf Jina complained about these stamps in a letter published in the *Globe and Mail*. Although one stamp shows the Alberta legislature (others show figures competing in various sporting events, and one features an inside view of a track and field stadium), Jina noted, "Out here in Alberta there is much distrust toward Ottawa and sometimes I think the federal Government is going too far in demonstrating its contempt of Albertans. Take, for example, the newly issued Commonwealth Games stamps. Edmonton, the host city, is not even mentioned. The Post Office has done Edmonton a great injustice and has injured the pride of festive Edmontonians."[80] Jina's complaint draws attention to the important symbolic work that commodities produced for the Commonwealth Games perform. For Jina, the stamps' designs are not simply images related to the Edmonton Games. Rather, they reflect the federal government's mistreatment of Western Canadians. This perspective illustrates a key insight of this chapter and, indeed, the entire book: the symbolic meanings of commodities are influenced by the social, political, and economic contexts in which they are produced and consumed.

Conclusion

Organizers and sponsors of the Edmonton Commonwealth Games used symbols of Indigenous peoples' cultures to represent the nation. In doing so, they continued the historical practice of strategically using Indigenous iconography to depict English-Canadian culture as unique and separate from British culture. At the same time, reminders of Canada's ties to Britain were prominent features of the games. Ceremonies like the Queen's baton relay showcased the monarch's authority as Canada's head of state, while the colours of the Union Jack appeared on the games' emblem. Cultural and commercial practices associated with the games, including HBC's sponsorship practices, brought together symbols of Indigenous peoples' cultures and Canada's colonial ties to the British Empire.

This analysis illustrates that, as in the Montreal Olympic Games, representations of Indigenous peoples' cultures in the Edmonton Commonwealth Games existed alongside reminders of Settler colonial nation-building in Canada. This evidence was not hidden in the Edmonton Games. Rather it was an integral component of many features of a sporting event that was originally designed to celebrate the bonds of the British Empire. Indigenous lacrosse players' exclusion from full participation in the games, as well as commercial and cultural practices that promoted Alberta's oil riches, made a truth impossible to ignore: colonial nation-building practices in Canada helped establish a nation that continues to be governed by Settler colonial policies and practices.

3

Commercializing Western Canadian Identity, Indigenous Cultures, and National Unity in the 1988 Calgary Olympics

Members of the Calgary Olympic Development Association (CODA) travelled to Baden-Baden, Germany, in September 1981 to bid for the right to host the 1988 Winter Olympics. CODA chairman Frank King writes that he and his team were "dressed in what we referred to as 'dignified western' attire: blue sports jackets with a western cut, grey slacks, white shirts, and navy striped ties."[1] The chief of the Kainai (Blood) First Nation, Lambert Fox, his wife, Yvette, and two members of the Royal Canadian Mounted Police (Mounties), accompanied bid officials.[2] Cortina D'Ampezzo, Italy, was eliminated in the first round of voting and International Olympic Committee (IOC) members selected Calgary over Falun, Sweden, in the second round with a vote of forty-eight to thirty-one.[3]

Calgary prepared to host the 1988 Winter Games at a time when the Olympic movement was becoming more commercialized. The 1984 Los Angeles Summer Olympics marked a turning point for the movement. Organizers did not rely on public funds to pay for the games but instead developed private fundraising projects that generated a surplus of over USD$220 million.[4] IOC members used the 1984 Summer Games' successful sponsorship program as a model for The Olympic Programme (TOP; now called The Olympic Partners Programme), which they developed the following year.[5]

The Calgary Olympic Organizing Committee (Olympiques Calgary Olympics '88), OCO'88 for short, generated $559 million in revenue and over $32 million in profits. It earned its largest single amount, over

$326 million, from the sale of Olympic broadcast rights. Organizers rescheduled the 1988 Winter Games to coincide with the yearly calculation of network ratings known as broadcaster sweeps; these calculations help determine a network's advertising rates.[6] The organizing committee jointly ran the American TV rights negotiations with IOC officials and a sports marketing firm called Trans World International, marking the first time committee members and local organizers cooperated as equal partners.[7] ABC ultimately agreed to buy the rights for USD$309 million, the most any network had ever paid to secure the rights. ABC was not able to recoup its costs and lost USD$40 million broadcasting the 1988 Winter Games.[8]

OCO'88 also received $90 million from domestic sponsors, suppliers, licensees, and contributors, as well as an anonymous donation; these profits far exceeded organizers' original goal of $50 million. Other sources of income included $49 million in funding from the federal government; $3 million from the province; $200 million from sales of Olympic coins and postage stamps; and $100 million in provincial lottery aid.[9] Canadian companies that sponsored the Calgary Games included General Motors of Canada, Labatt, and the Royal Bank of Canada (RBC).[10] Moreover, a group of forty "corporations in the Calgary petroleum community" collectively sponsored the Calgary Olympics for $4.8 million.[11] Known as Team Petroleum'88, the group aimed to unite "the petroleum community behind the Games" and "provide a meaningful program of recognition of the Canadian Petroleum Industry."[12]

Team Petroleum'88's investment in the games contravened a central tenet of TOP, the global sponsorship program developed by the IOC in 1985, which grants companies "category-exclusive marketing rights" to the Summer and Winter Games (e.g., because Coca-Cola is a TOP sponsor, no other beverage company can be a global Olympic sponsor for the duration of Coca-Cola's contract with the IOC).[13] However, OCO'88's domestic sponsorship program was separate from TOP and members of the organizing committee, many of whom had deep ties to the petroleum industry, were unwilling to give only one petroleum company the right to sponsor the games.[14] Companies working in the petroleum industry also supported individual events associated with the games, with Petro-Canada sponsoring the torch relay and Shell Canada sponsoring a Glenbow Museum exhibit called *The Spirit Sings: Artistic Traditions of Canada's First People.*

Members of the Lubicon Lake Nation used the Calgary Olympics to publicize their campaign to stop companies from drilling for oil on their land, focusing much of their anti-Olympic activism on the oil industry's investment in the games. At the same time, OCO'88 worked with the federal government to establish a Natives and the Olympics Committee "to ensure a coordinated federal-provincial effort to facilitate Native participation, culturally and economically, in the Olympics."[15] Led by Indigenous activist and Treaty 7 representative Sykes F. Powderface, the committee organized cultural exhibitions as well as a powwow, fashion show, and national youth conference.[16]

In this chapter, I identify how representations of Indigenous peoples' cultures in the Calgary Olympics intersected with celebrations of Alberta's oil and gas wealth and its cowboy heritage. Using details of the Lubicon's public opposition to the games, I argue that unacknowledged facts about the provincial and federal governments' mistreatment of Indigenous peoples haunt these narratives. I also investigate a significant commercial feature of the Calgary Games that was not present in earlier Olympic and Commonwealth games hosted in Canada: the promotion and consumption of a commodity symbolizing national identity. Specifically, many Canadians embraced specially produced Petro-Canada Olympic commemorative glassware as symbols of their patriotism. In doing so, they disavowed an uncomfortable truth: the wealth Settlers derive from natural resources in Canada sometimes comes at the expense of Indigenous peoples' rights.

Representing and Commodifying Western Canadian Identity and Indigenous Cultures

CODA members celebrated Alberta's oil riches and the province's cowboy heritage when bidding for the right to host the 1988 Winter Olympics, and these later became prominent features of the narratives about national and regional identity that circulated during the Calgary Olympics. These narratives also inform the meaning and significance of Indigenous cultural displays featured in several events associated with the games. When King and CODA president Bob Niven travelled to Moscow for the 1980 Summer Olympic Games, they gave IOC members containers filled with samples of Alberta's tar sands as gifts. Like the souvenir oil drums sold during the Edmonton Commonwealth Games, these containers are tangible symbols of the province's petroleum wealth. King writes in his memoir that IOC director Monique Berlioux was not expecting to receive such a gift: "I will never forget the look of total surprise on Madame Berlioux's face when these fresh-faced oilmen from Calgary presented her with a sample of Alberta tar sands as we departed. This was literally a tacky gift."[17] King also gifted white cowboy hats to IOC members when he visited Lake Placid for the 1980 Winter Olympics, items that would eventually become a signature of Calgary's Olympic bid team.[18]

Calgary bid officials also relied on the long-standing practice of representing Indigenous peoples' cultures as defining features of Canadian identity. In 1981, King presented a Luxembourgian IOC member with "an Indian tomahawk made in the style of tomahawks of old."[19] That same year, IOC president Juan Antonio Samaranch visited Canada. CODA members and Calgary mayor Ralph Klein arranged for Samaranch to meet a Siksika (Blackfoot) First Nation chief named Leo Pretty Young Man, who made the IOC president an honorary chief.[20] CODA members also collaborated with Indigenous groups from the southern Alberta area covered by Treaty 7, which includes Calgary, to make their Olympic bid appealing to IOC officials. King and Klein wrote a joint letter to minister of Indian Affairs and Northern Development William McKnight in 1987, observing, "You will no doubt be aware that throughout the period from 1979 to 1981, the Treaty #7 Bands were instrumental in assisting the Calgary Olympic Development Association (CODA) in winning the right to host the 1988 Olympic Winter Games. Indeed, it is fair to say that without their assistance and co-operation, Calgary might not have been successful in that great undertaking."[21]

King's description of a dance that Chief Lambert Fox and Yvonne Fox performed during Calgary's bid demonstration reveals that Indigenous cultural performances strengthened the city's Olympic bid. Because cities bidding for the games mounted cultural displays concurrently in one large room, they competed for IOC members' attention. The Foxes danced "to the beat of native tomtoms" while two Mounties handed out photographs of their colleagues in uniform.[22] CODA used the Foxes' dance to draw attention away from the other displays, including Italian opera singers' performances in support of Cortina D'Ampezzo's bid. King writes, "As soon as the Italian choir started to sing, we would turn up our recorded Indian drum music to full volume. Lambert and Yvonne Fox danced magnificently, singing their distinctive Native chants."[23]

Calgary's Olympic bid demonstration is an example of what Eva Mackey describes as "nationalist narratives of tolerance," stories about the nation featuring Indigenous peoples and minorities as "the colourful recipients of benevolence, the necessary 'others' who reflect back white Canada's self-image of tolerance."[24] Mackey argues that one such narrative, "the Benevolent Mountie myth," is exemplified by a postcard showing a young Mountie and an Indigenous leader named Chief Sitting Eagle shaking hands.[25] In the same way, Calgary's Olympic bid display gave the impression that the Mounties handing out photographs and the Indigenous performers peacefully co-exist.[26] Crucially, Mackey asserts that narratives of tolerance, such as the benevolent Mountie myth, do not erase Indigenous peoples' presence in Canada. Rather, they misrepresent the "brutal history of conquest and cultural genocide that Canada is founded upon."[27] Calgary Olympic bid officials did not openly acknowledge this history; however, it is inseparable from the cowboy theme that featured centrally in the city's Olympic bid and, later, the 1988 Winter Games.

The "brutal history" to which Mackey refers includes Settlers' introduction of cattle into modern-day Treaty 7 land in the nineteenth century. When these animals began occupying grazing areas that had once belonged to bison, they displaced the bison and increased the spread of bovine tuberculosis. Indigenous peoples lost their primary source of food when the bison population declined, and many began facing starvation by the early 1870s. To compound matters, tuberculosis spread to Indigenous populations, whose immune systems were already compromised because of malnutrition. The federal government established a Home Farm program in 1870 that did little to address the magnitude of the famine. Moreover, officials used rations to coerce Indigenous peoples into signing Treaty 7 at the same time as Indigenous peoples were resorting to desperate measures, such as eating grass, to satiate their hunger. Government officials denied food assistance to Indigenous groups living off reserve and forbade the sale, barter, or exchange of food grown on reserve to anyone outside the reserve. This policy forced Indigenous groups who had not yet signed treaties to do so in order to avoid starvation.[28]

The devastating consequences of Settlers' introduction of cattle into modern-day Alberta haunted two intersecting narratives about the nation that OCO'88 promoted in the Calgary Games. One narrative celebrated Indigenous peoples' cultures and emphasized their contributions to contemporary Canadian society. Another narrative paid tribute to Western Canada's "cowboy" heritage. In the pages that follow, I identify how Indigenous peoples participated in the Calgary Games through the Natives and the Olympic Committee; discuss how games organizers promoted the theme of Western hospitality; and situate these narratives within the context of practices in Western Canada that operated according to the "logic of elimination" that lies at the heart of the Settler colonial project in Canada.[29]

As the head of the Natives and the Olympic Committee, Powderface celebrated the committee's pioneering work in a 1987 letter to journalists: "For the first time in the modern Olympic Games, the Organizing Committee has recognized the Aboriginal people and encouraged them to develop a program and be part of the Games."[30] He wrote that committee members planned to showcase Indigenous practices from the past with a powwow; celebrate contemporary Indigenous cultures with cultural exhibits; and focus on the future through a youth conference.[31] The committee organized a cultural exhibit during the games that featured Indigenous handicrafts, stories, and traditions; according to Powderface, the exhibit demonstrated that Indigenous peoples "are contributing to a growing country through industry, business and resource development. This element will enhance OCO'88's objectives to present to the world what Calgary is today. The future is the Natives greatest strength – their people, children, education and determination."[32]

Powderface's letter reveals that, like the Kanien'kehá:ka (Mohawk) of Kahnawá:ke who participated in the 1976 Montreal Olympic closing ceremony, some Indigenous peoples used the Calgary Games to positively represent their cultures to Olympic audiences. Yet, as in the Montreal Games, these representations co-existed with depictions of Settler Canadian identity that did not openly recognize the country's colonial history. Specifically, organizers of the Calgary Games built on the positive image of Western Canadian culture that CODA cultivated during the bid phase. Their representation of Western hospitality, however, is haunted by unacknowledged truths about that region's history, such as the fact that many Indigenous peoples living in Alberta in the nineteenth century struggled to feed themselves and their families.

OCO'88 entertained a proposal from the Calgary Stampede Board to include an "Indian attack and wagon-burning" scene in the opening ceremony but ultimately decided against it.[33] Instead, members of the

"Kainai (Blood), Apátohsipikáni (Northern Peigans), Tsuu T'ina (Sarcee), and Nakoda (Stoney)" First Nations entered the stadium on horseback while a commentator asked the audience to "please welcome *our* Native Albertans."[34] Cowboys subsequently appeared riding chuckwagons and Mounties performed a "musical ride," a choreographed performance on horseback set to music. In a continuation of the cowboy theme, Canadian athletes marching in the Parade of Nations wore red coats with leather fringes and white cowboy hats.[35] Later in the ceremony, Daniel Tlen performed "O Canada" in the Southern Tutchone language.[36] The Calgary Olympic opening ceremony extended representational practices that bid officials first developed in Baden-Baden: defining Western Canadian identity through the figures of the Mountie, cowboy, and "Indian."[37] Jennifer Adese astutely identifies this dynamic in her analysis of the ceremony, noting that "These three figures have been the backbone of the city's identity, replicated annually in the form of the Calgary Stampede."[38]

The Olympic cauldron was surrounded by an enormous teepee. The authors of OCO'88's official games' report did not hide the fact that organizers used this structure to represent Western Canadian identity: "In keeping with the Western theme, the cauldron was framed by a symbolic teepee 65 metres, or 10 storeys, high."[39] One OCO'88 member wrote about representations of Western identity in the games as follows: "Generally speaking the underlining tone of our theme as the 'leading melody' would be a North American western nature, hospitable, friendly, adventurous, trusting, honest, down to earth, not relying on convention or contract to get the job done. A hearty pride without conceit, enthusiastic openness, unbiased viewpoints that readily accept new thoughts and ideas. Laid back attitude that offers visitors comfort."[40]

OCO'88 intended that the games' emblem, which features five interlocking Cs that intersect to form a snowflake and maple leaf, symbolize both the host city and nation. According to the 1988 Calgary Olympic report, "The small Cs were designed to represent Calgary and the large Cs to represent Canada. The five interlocking C's [*sic*] represented the theme 'Coming Together in Calgary,' the stylized Maple Leaf represented Canada and the snowflake design represented the Olympic Winter Games" (figure 3.1).[41] Although not mentioned in this formal description, the emblem design also includes a symbol of Western Canadian identity, namely, a cowboy boot. Gary Kingston observed in the *Vancouver Sun* that the Calgary Olympic emblem "was part snowflake, part maple leaf

3.1 Emblem of the 1988 Calgary Olympics.

and, if you look close enough, you can make out the shape of a cowboy boot in the tips of the snowflake."[42] Indeed, the edges of the bifurcated snowflake tips are not identical in length. Rather, one tip slopes down to resemble the boot's vamp (front part of the upper shoe) while the other, shorter tip slopes down to resemble its heel. The Calgary Olympic emblem appeared on a range of commodities and circulated alongside another symbol of Western Canadian identity, white cowboy hats. In fact, white cowboy hats decorated with the Calgary Olympic emblem and pins designed with miniature versions of these hats were available for sale during the Calgary Olympics.[43]

The games' mascots, two polar bears named Hidy and Howdy, also represent Western Canadian identity. Organizers designed Hidy wearing a blue dress and Howdy wearing a blue vest, and both mascots wear white cowboy hats with red bands that match red scarves tied around their necks (figure 3.2). OCO'88 asked leaders from four major Canadian department stores to recommend a mascot. The general manager for the Alberta region of HBC, Hal Spelliscy, led the group; he had previous experience with an international sporting event in Canada, having served as a member of the 1978 Edmonton Commonwealth Games' organizing committee. The group recommended a brown bear mascot after deciding that the mascot should be widely appealing, especially to children; non-political; unique; identifiable with winter; and easy to reproduce in print and commodity form.[44] OCO'88 ultimately designed Hidy and Howdy as polar bears because a brown bear had already been selected as the mascot for the 1980 Moscow Summer Olympic Games.[45]

OCO'88 members explicitly linked the design of the mascots to the host region's identity by describing their "colorful costumes" as representative of "the Western hospitality of Calgary."[46] A local high school student submitted the winning entry to OCO'88's name the mascots contest; the games' official report notes that "Hidy" and "Howdy" are "a creative blend of proper names and typical western greetings."[47] The mascots' smiling, happy expressions work in concert with their outfits and names to represent the games' "North American western nature" theme.[48]

OCO'88 produced and distributed Olympic Education Resource Kits to elementary school students (grades 1–6), junior high schoolers (grades 7–9), and senior high schoolers (grades 10–12) in Alberta. These kits introduce students to the mascots and encourage them to consider the meaning of their cowboy outfits. The junior high education kit includes a picture of the mascots along with the question: "What symbols did the artist include in her drawing of Hidy and Howdy?"[49] The implied answer is clear: the artist included a symbol of Western Canadian identity in her drawing by showing the mascots wearing cowboy hats.

An OCO'88 elementary school education resource also includes information about Alberta's "pioneer history" that fails to recognize that Indigenous peoples lived in the region prior to European settlement. The kit notes, "Calgary is named after the Scottish seashore home of Colonel Macleod of the North West Mounted Police (N.W.M.P.). It began as a frontier fort of the N.W.M.P. on a point between two blue rivers."[50] Students learn that "Calgary's present prosperity is built on the oil industry, but its roots go back to the days of cowboys and ranchers."[51] Of course, Indigenous peoples lived in modern-day Alberta long before the Mounted Police arrived. Siksika (Blackfoot) elder Wilton Goodstriker recounts, "The year 1874 saw the arrival of the Mounted Police into Blackfoot territory … the police asked if they could winter

3.2 Hidy and Howdy, mascots of the 1988 Calgary Olympics.

there (present-day Fort Macleod). They were granted permission for one winter, and it's been a long winter."[52]

Commodities designed with the Calgary Olympic emblem, cowboy hats, and games' mascot design serve as commodified symbols of Western Canadian identity and in this role, they hold together a contradiction inherent in OCO'88's depiction of "North American western nature" and "the Western hospitality of Calgary."[53] On one hand, Settlers from Western Canada pride themselves on being welcoming. On the other hand, they welcomed, and continue to welcome, individuals to land they colonized, and European Settlers were decidedly unfriendly to Indigenous peoples who lived, and continue to live, on the land. This fact is evident in the federal government's cruel treatment of Indigenous populations facing starvation in the Plains region. Coercing these groups into signing treaties with the Crown through immoral tactics, like forcing Indigenous peoples to go hungry, is a highly disturbing example of the Western Canadian trait of "not relying on convention or contract to get the job done."[54]

* * *

The significance of the Calgary Olympic mascots includes, but also extends beyond, the fact that they hold together contradictions in the meaning of Western Canadian hospitality. The mascots worked alongside Calgary Olympic education kits to expose young people to Olympic-related commercial practices. These kits also promoted highly problematic ideas about Indigenous peoples' cultures. In this section, I identify how Olympic organizers exposed young people to selective narratives about Olympic-related commercial practices and Indigenous cultures.

Olympic organizers designed Hidy and Howdy to appeal to young people. The Calgary Olympic official report reads, "The use of two mascots, a male and a female, allowed them to interact with each other and with members of the public. That they were soft, furry animals made them appealing. Children, in particular, were thrilled by public appearances of Hidy and Howdy."[55] High school students dressed as the mascots made 2,800 public appearances in the fourteen months leading up to the games and attended corporate functions hosted by Olympic sponsors including Coca-Cola, Petro-Canada, and RBC.[56] By producing multiple identical mascot costumes, organizers planned for the mascots to attend different functions at the same time.[57]

OCO'88 doubled the profit potential of its mascot program by selecting two animals that could each be sold as commodities. A 1983 OCO'88 memo discusses the value of Olympic mascots in commercial terms, noting, "A mascot is selected by an Olympic Organizing Committee for two key purposes – promotion and marketing. Most often a mascot has been selected that is especially appealing to children. A mascot helps to promote the 'fun' side of the Games; it serves as an effective means of creating positive awareness. The mascot is an integral part of any advertising or promotional activity."[58] This profit-based approach to selecting mascots became even more pronounced in the years following the Calgary Olympics. As Tara Magdalinski notes, "Since the 1988 Calgary Winter Games, there has been a proliferation in the number of mascots associated with the Olympics, perhaps initially to ensure gender equity but subsequently to increase their merchandising potential."[59]

Mascot commodities, such as pins and stuffed animals, were often marked with the Olympic rings and Calgary Games' snowflake emblem, and an activity in the junior high kit taught students that these symbols represent brands whose commercial value must be protected through copyright. A section on Olympic symbols begins by describing the five ring Olympic symbol and its meaning. It then includes an activity in which students design a personal symbol and consider the following scenario: "A student walks into the classroom wearing your symbol. Describe your feelings and what you would say to that person. How would you decide who gets to keep it?" The next question is "Why would the Olympic Movement copyright its symbols?"[60] Significantly, this activity coincided with the IOC's recent implementation of TOP, which increases the value of the copyrighted Olympic symbols companies pay to use in their promotional material.

An OCO'88 education resource also contained a highly problematic depiction of Indigenous peoples' cultures as less sophisticated than Settler culture. A section of the junior high education resource titled "Games People Play: A Comparison of Competition in Pre-Industrial and Industrial Cultures" discusses the Northern Games and Arctic Games, which students learn feature sports like badminton, cross country skiing, and hockey. Yet "the most unusual events are traditional Arctic sports, developed over the years by Inuit to test stamina, strength and endurance (for example, the high kick in which athletes leap into the air from one foot or both feet)."[61] Students are subsequently encouraged to play "Inuit games" in their classroom or school playground and consider how such activities "differ from popular games in Canada."[62] By contrasting so-called Canadian games with Inuit games, the text and accompanying activity construct a hierarchical binary between Settlers' and Indigenous peoples' cultures that privileges the former and denigrates the latter.

***

Members of the Lubicon Lake Nation led an anti-Olympic campaign that exposed an important truth not recognized in the ideas about the nation conveyed through the Calgary Olympic emblem, Hidy and Howdy, and education resources produced for the games. Specifically, at the time of the Calgary Olympics, the Alberta and Canadian governments were violating the rights of a local Indigenous group. In 1899 and 1900, representatives from the federal government travelled to northern Alberta to negotiate Treaty 8 with Indigenous peoples living in this area. Although they tried to make contact with all Indigenous groups living on land covered by the treaty, they did not penetrate the wilderness far enough to reach the Lubicon, who are members of the Cree First Nation.[63] The federal government took steps to establish a Lubicon reserve in 1939, but the outbreak of the Second World War and subsequent changes in eligibility requirements for treaty status prevented a reserve from ever being created.[64] Companies began extracting oil located on and around Lubicon territory in the 1950s. By 1984, over 400 oil and gas wells existed within fifteen miles of Little Buffalo, the main Lubicon town, and over 100 oil companies and subcontractors were operating in the area.[65]

Oil extraction practices on Lubicon land impeded the Lubicon's ability to hunt and trap, consequently cutting them off from their main source of food and income. Company bulldozers pushed snow and debris into piles that blocked animal trails and buried the snares set out by hunters. Some members of the Lubicon Lake Nation accused oil workers of intentionally destroying their trap lines. The average Lubicon family earned more than $5,000 from trapping in the winter of 1979–80. Four years later, those earnings had sunk to $400 and more than 90 per cent of the Lubicon workforce was on social assistance compared to 10 per cent in 1978.[66]

In 1982, one year after Calgary won its bid to host the Winter Games, the Lubicon filed an injunction against ten oil companies drilling on their land. They asked the Alberta Court of Queen's Bench to order a stop to all oil extraction practices in the area surrounding their community until their land dispute with the federal government was settled. Justice Gregory Forsyth presided over the case, and he prioritized oil companies' interests over the Lubicon's cultural and physical survival. The judge rejected the Lubicon's argument that their way of life was being destroyed by oil companies' activities. He also argued that the Lubicon would be unable to compensate these companies for their financial losses if the Lubicon's land claim, which was still pending at the time, proved unsuccessful.[67] The federal government subsequently appointed former justice minister and Supreme Court of BC justice E. Davie Fulton as a special envoy to the Lubicon Lake Nation to investigate their situation. In 1986, Fulton recommended that Ottawa establish a Lubicon reserve and compensate the Lubicon for lost livelihood caused by oil extraction on their land. Politicians in Ottawa, however, did not act on his recommendations.[68]

Dawn Martin-Hill conducted interviews with members of the Lubicon community that reveal the extent to which their cultural identity and material livelihood are tied to the land. Chief Bernard Ominayak explained, "We survived off this land for many years, and everything that we do surrounds land. For example, through our prayers and the ceremonies that we have, everything is tied back to the land."[69] He also observed, "our ways are disappearing fast … once we lose that connection with the earth and the animals, this land around us, whatever we have survived off of for these many years, it's weakening us."[70] The first suicide in memory in Little Buffalo occurred in 1985 when a father of six took his own life. The man's estranged wife said that he had been depressed: "He believed in the old way of life. Trapping was very important to him because that was the only way of life he knew. There was some cutlines [seismograph lines] running through his trapline – quite a few."[71]

Six months before Calgary hosted the Olympics, the Lubicon community experienced an outbreak of tuberculosis, the same disease that had spread throughout the Treaty 7 region of Alberta following the decline of buffalo populations in the nineteenth century. Twenty-seven Lubicon contracted active tuberculosis while many others were found to be infected and at risk of developing symptoms. A lung disease spread by coughing, tuberculosis disproportionately affects groups whose resistance to the disease has been compromised by poor living conditions, inadequate diet, and stress. The tuberculosis outbreak thus reflected the declining socio-economic conditions in the Lubicon community caused by oil company activity in the region.[72]

In 1986, Ominayak called for an international boycott of the Calgary Olympics, arguing that they were "being organized by basically the same interests that are committing genocide against the Lubicon Lake Indian people."[73] Many CODA and OCO'88 officials had ties to the oil industry. King worked as senior vice-president of manufacturing for the oil company Turbo Resources while also serving as CODA chairman.[74] In his memoir, King describes a meeting he attended with local business leaders interested in developing amateur sport in Calgary. He chatted with Bob Niven, who would later become his CODA colleague, "about life in the Calgary oilpatch" while waiting for the meeting to start. By its end, the attendees had decided to mount a bid to host the 1988 Winter Olympics.[75]

Ominayak travelled to Europe prior to the start of the Calgary Games to raise support for the Lubicon's cause. He focused attention on the Glenbow Museum exhibit *The Spirit Sings*, sponsored by Shell

Canada. A press release notes that the exhibit includes "an estimated 500 of the rarest and most revealing artifacts of early Canadian Indian and Inuit culture. What is surprising is that almost all of these works of art and artifacts will be borrowed from more than forty institutions and private collectors in twenty-two countries. Few are in Canadian collections. They left Canada from the 17th to 19th centuries as souvenirs or gifts from native peoples to explorers, traders, missionaries, and colonial officials."[76] Ominayak led an international campaign aimed at convincing museums to show solidarity with the Lubicon's cause by refusing to lend artifacts to the Glenbow Museum for *The Spirit Sings* exhibit. Many curators agreed to this request, but the exact number of participating institutions is disputed; Glenbow Museum officials claimed twelve museums were boycotting the exhibit while a close adviser to Ominayak, Fred Lennarson, claimed twenty-three museums were boycotting it.[77]

A curator of *The Spirit Sings* exhibit, Julia Harrison, defended the Glenbow Museum's decision to accept sponsorship money from Shell Canada on the grounds that public institutions were becoming increasingly reliant on corporate funding to operate: "In this era of declining government support, cultural institutions (including universities) have no option but to seek outside support for projects they undertake."[78] Shell Canada, meanwhile, depicted its sponsorship of *The Spirit Sings* as evidence that the company makes valuable contributions to the nation. A press release about the exhibit quotes Shell Canada president Jack M. MacLeod: "The exhibition of these treasures is an important event for Canadians and for visitors to Canada. It will give us all a chance to expand our understanding of Canadian native heritage, and will add an exciting dimension to the Olympic Arts Festival … Shell's participation in this project is consistent with our commitment to Canada."[79]

The Lubicon's high-profile opposition to the exhibit undermined the positive association the company hoped to establish between its brand and the nation. Lennarson pointed out the irony inherent in the fact that "a display of North American Indian artifacts to attract people to the Winter Olympics is being organized by interests who are still actively seeking to destroy Indian people: namely, the Alberta Government and its oil-company allies."[80] The Lubicon and their supporters' public protests exposed the fact that Shell's espoused commitment to Canada involved drilling for oil on Lubicon land.

K.B. Wamsley and Mike Heine argue that OCO'88 developed a Native Participation Program to divert attention away from the Lubicon's anti-Olympic campaign. They write, "The program was structured to channel Native involvement into less controversial areas, and it was explicitly designed to counter the international publicity generated by the boycott of *The Spirit Sings*."[81] In this interpretation, the work of the Natives and the Olympic Committee did less to highlight the vibrancy of Indigenous cultures and more to distract from the Lubicon's demands for justice.

Greg Smith of the Piikani (Peigan) First Nation similarly argued that OCO'88 intentionally incorporated a symbol of Indigenous peoples' cultures into the Calgary Olympic medal design to draw attention away from Indigenous groups' opposition to the games.[82] OCO'88 held a contest to determine the medal design. Friedrich Peter submitted the winning entry, which includes a stylized Indigenous headdress. According to one news article, the medals feature "the profiles of a Greek athlete and a Canadian Indian. Symbols of winter sports – such as snow skis and a bobsled – are intertwined with the feathers of the Indian's headdress" (figure 3.3).[83] Members of the Indian Association of Alberta argued that the medal design misrepresented the cultural importance of the headdress.[84] A Calgary HBC store continued this problematic practice by selling what it described as the "ultimate [Calgary] Games memento – a Blackfoot Indian headdress."[85] Frank Oberhoffner, a store employee, said, "We wanted a wow and we've got it. No one else in town will have anything else like this."[86] A tourist bought the headdress for $3,000 within an hour of it going on sale.[87]

The Mohawk Council echoed criticisms of the Calgary Olympic medal design when they spoke out against the Glenbow Museum's decision to include sacred objects, among them a chief's headdress and False Face mask, in *The Spirit Sings* exhibit. The council petitioned the Alberta Court of Queen's Bench to order these objects be removed from the exhibit, along with several pouches and knives. Mohawk grand chief Joe Norton told a *Globe and Mail* reporter, "These articles should not be displayed. We are fed up … We will no longer be ridiculed or insulted by the demonstration of things that were bought or stolen from our people at some time in their history."[88] The court ultimately ruled against the council's request. However, the Chicago Field Museum of Natural History decided not to send "several Cree headdresses" to the museum "when it learned of the Lubicon situation."[89]

3.3 Medals of the 1988 Calgary Olympics.

Curators of the Glenbow Museum also came under fire for their approach to securing the objects featured in *The Spirit Sings*, most of which belonged to museums located outside Canada. Some argued that the museum should have attempted to repatriate these objects rather than borrow them on a short-term basis. As Christine O'Bonsawin writes, "Critics believed that decisions made by the Glenbow Museum curatorial officials constituted a second and more disgraceful wave of thievery of indigenous artifacts, as these objects were being returned to their country of origin on a temporary basis only."[90]

The exhibit was originally titled *Forget not My World*, a strong if unintentional reminder of the contradiction that lies at the heart of representational practices in the 1988 Calgary Olympics. Specifically, cultural events affiliated with the games, such as the Glenbow Museum exhibit, showcased symbols of Indigenous cultures at a time when oil drilling activity on Lubicon territory was threatening that group's survival. Members of the Glenbow Museum Scientific Committee received letters from the public objecting to the title *Forget not My World*.[91] The minutes of a 1986 meeting between Glenbow Museum director Duncan Cameron and the committee read, "The committee wished to urge Mr. Cameron in the strongest possible terms, to consider attempting to change the title," with one committee member noting that the title "suggested an attempt to retrieve something out of oblivion."[92] Cameron would only consider changing the title to *The Spirit Sings* if Shell Canada and OCO'88 gave their permission. Cameron "agreed that if the committee could, as the outcome of the weekend meeting, formulate a [new] title which he [Campbell] could feel would be marketable, then he would offer it for the approval of Shell and OCO."[93]

Some members of the public perpetuated the Settler colonial practice of claiming ownership over Indigenous peoples' cultures and lands when describing *The Spirit Sings* exhibit. A press release quotes King stating, "As the original habitants *of our great country*, *our native peoples* have a rich and colourful tradition. It is especially significant that an exhibition exploring their culture will be featured during the XV Olympic Winter Games."[94] Similarly, Arnold Edinborough published a review of the exhibit in the *Financial Post* that reads, "The most striking impression of the whole exhibition is the sense it gives a modern Canadian of the depth of history, the richness of the native artistic tradition and the scope of *this great land of ours* … Here we have a rich history and identity, *which is ours* and with which we should ally ourselves."[95] In this review, Edinborough depicts the Indigenous artifacts displayed in *The Spirit Sings* exhibit as relics from the Canadian past. In doing so, he continues a long-standing practice of depicting symbols of Indigenous cultures as, to quote Gerta Moray (whose research on Emily Carr's artwork I discuss in chapter 2), "symbols of the existence of an exotic 'Canadian' prehistory."[96]

Petro-Canada and Glassware Nationalism

In a move similar to that of Shell Canada, whose president claimed that the company's sponsorship of *The Spirit Sings* was "consistent with our commitment to Canada," Petro-Canada used its sponsorship of the Calgary Olympic torch relay to show its support for a national cause. In this section, I show that Petro-Canada fostered branded nationalism by developing Olympic-related promotional campaigns that associated its brand, and commemorative torch relay glassware, with national pride, a promotional message activists undermined by protesting Petro-Canada's sponsorship of the torch relay.

The Calgary Olympic official report notes that the Olympic torch relay "came within a two-hour drive of 90 per cent of the Canadian population" and reached 800 villages, towns, and cities.[97] Canadians sent close to seven million entries to the nationwide lottery used to select torch bearers (many people submitted multiple entries).[98] King observed, "the response of Canadians to the ritual had been overwhelming. Thousands of people had stood in bitter cold for hours just to get a chance to see the flame, to hold it, to take a little bit of it away with them."[99]

According to market research conducted by Petro-Canada, 79 per cent of Canadians surveyed were aware that the company was sponsoring the Calgary Olympic torch relay.[100] Petro-Canada was still a Crown corporation in 1988 and the Olympic Torch Relay Media Guide quotes company president Ed Lakusta highlighting the company's Canadianness: "We're a Canadian company, and Canadians expect us to do things which enrich our national life. The enthusiasm the Relay has generated in communities across the country is simply amazing. We're proud to be associated with an event that is creating memories that will last a lifetime for so many Canadians."[101]

While there is no evidence to suggest that the national pride Canadians associated with the torch relay was insincere, Petro-Canada told individuals what to expect and how to act through the television ads it released in the lead-up to the games. These ads suggested that Canadians should not miss the chance to take part in the torch relay as spectators because it was going to be a nationally significant and emotionally resonant event. Individuals subsequently used slogans from these ads and relay-related commodities to express the national pride they associated with the Calgary Games. Petro-Canada nationalism thus emerged within a specific environment created by games organizers, Petro-Canada's promotional activities, and citizens' involvement in the relay as torch bearers and spectators.

One Petro-Canada ad implies that Canadians will miss out on an important event if they do not witness the torch relay in person. As groups of people walk toward the torch relay route, a voiceover tells viewers, "There's something special happening in Canada, in big cities and small towns all across this country of ours. People are getting ready to share in the experience of a lifetime. As the Olympic torch is passed from hand to hand on its glorious 18,000-kilometre journey to Calgary for the Olympic Winter Games, don't miss the opportunity to be part of this. Because this is ours, and it's ours to share."[102] A man wearing a stylish coat over a business suit reluctantly leaves his house to join a crowd waiting for the Olympic torch bearer to arrive. However, his expression changes and he becomes teary-eyed when a smiling blonde woman holding the torch comes into view. The man exchanges a meaningful look with a person dressed in a plaid flannel shirt and the pair are clearly moved by the emotional intensity of the event. This scene suggests that the torch relay can unite all Canadians, regardless of age or class. It ends with the following jingle: "Share the spirit, (share the flame), share the glory, (share the flame), share this moment in our never-ending story, come together heart to heart, everybody has a part, share the flame (Canada), share the flame, share the flame."[103]

Another ad shows a young boy excitedly anticipating the arrival of the torch relay. A voiceover says, "When the Olympic torch is proudly carried through your community, it's an experience you won't want to miss."[104] Shawna Richer later wrote in the *Globe and Mail* that "the torch relay of the 1988 Calgary Olympics set a new standard for a Winter Games, from its 18,000-kilometre distance to the patriotic passion of Canadians who clamoured to carry the flame."[105] She further observes that "Spontaneous roadside cheers, tears and outbursts of the national anthem, even on the darkest, most frigid nights, were routine occurrences along the torch relay route."[106] Alan Hobson makes a similar observation in *Share the Flame: The Official Retrospective Book of the Olympic Torch Relay*. He writes, Canadians "ran out of their houses and shouted to the passing [torch relay] cavalcade, 'We love you, Canada.' They stood in their high school gyms and their public squares and they sang their national anthem with newly glowing hearts."[107]

Canadians sometimes expressed their national pride and enthusiasm for the Calgary Olympics by using phrases from the Petro-Canada ads. The official torch relay retrospective book includes a picture of two school-aged girls with home-made signs that read "Share the Flame Canada."[108] Another woman, Donalda Garner, sold seven goats from her farm in Regina to raise the money she needed to travel with her parents to Quebec, where she had been selected to run as a torch bearer; after arriving, they stayed at the home of another torch bearer, Pierre Fafard. Hobson writes that the Garners and Fafards forged "bonds that will endure long after the flame has reached its destination. For Garner it epitomized the true meaning of 'share the flame.'"[109]

Activists sympathetic to the Lubicon's cause protested Petro-Canada's sponsorship of the Calgary Olympic torch relay and their opposition weakened the positive association the company attempted to establish between its sponsorship of the event and national pride. Protestors appeared along the relay route in every province except Prince Edward Island, and many held signs that referenced, but altered, Petro-Canada's promotional messages.[110] A journalist reported in the *Globe and Mail*, "Mocking Petro-Canada's Olympic torch slogan of 'Share the flame,' protesters carried signs saying 'Share the shame' when the torch arrived on Parliament Hill in Ottawa."[111] Activists in Fredericton, meanwhile, lined the relay route holding signs that read "Don't *share the nightmare* of the genocide of Indians."[112]

The Canadian Alliance in Solidarity with Native Peoples published a flyer asserting that sharing the flame "doesn't mean watching while a forest fire incinerates the animals, birds, fish and plant life of the land."[113] The flyer also riffs on a line from the "share the flame" jingle ("everybody has a part") while also referencing *The Spirit Sings* exhibition: "What part can Natives have when their artifacts and culture from the past are being exploited by the very forces who are annihilating that way of life – today?"[114] Matthew Coon-Come, grand chief of the Quebec Cree, articulated a similar sentiment at a protest: "I say we should share the flame, we should *share the blame*, we should *share the shame*."[115] A couple from Red Deer, Alberta, published a letter in the *Globe and Mail* criticizing the federal and provincial governments' treatment of the Lubicon in similar language: "*it is our shame* that we care more for the grand Olympic show glorifying the human spirit than we do for real suffering human beings."[116]

These messages exposed an important truth: Petro-Canada nationalism relies on a disavowal of the human and environmental cost of oil extraction practices. Sometimes, law enforcement officials and politicians prohibited anti-Olympic activists from promoting their cause in public spaces. In doing so, they sidelined the protestors' messages and made it easier for Settler Canadians to engage in the type of disavowal required to embrace Petro-Canada nationalism. In Toronto, police demanded that more than one hundred protestors leave Nathan Phillips Square, where they had gathered in anticipation of the Olympic torch's arrival. When the protestors, who were sympathetic to the Lubicon's cause, moved to a nearby intersection, police claimed they were blocking pedestrian crosswalks and demanded they move once again.[117] Lubicon activists were also treated with hostility when they gathered in the Olympic Plaza, located in downtown Calgary, to meet the torch relay. According to a *Washington Post* article, "teenage spectators pelted the Lubicon Lake band protesters with shards of ice as police officers stood idly by. One policeman angrily told a *Calgary Herald* reporter that he hoped the newspaper would accurately describe the crowd's reaction to 'those effing Indians.'"[118]

The Olympic Plaza served as an exclusionary space where Indigenous protestors were harassed while oil industry workers were celebrated. The host city and OCO'88 jointly spent $5.6 million to build the area, which was "to serve as the focal point for a wide range of activities designed to enhance the Olympic experience for the general public."[119] A few weeks before the start of the games, OCO'88 held a ceremony in the plaza to thank 3,500 oil industry workers who signed up to volunteer for the games. One journalist covering the event praised Calgary citizens for "finally showing off their Olympic spirit" and reported that "the threat of the Lubicon Indian band disrupting the Games to publicize their land claims is generally scoffed at."[120] Local officials later prohibited activists from distributing leaflets on Stephen Avenue Mall, a location where members of the public met each night of the games to celebrate the day's events. The Calgary Civil Liberties Association opposed this prohibition and, according to the *Globe and Mail*, "suggested aloud to anyone wanting to listen that freedom of expression was thought not to be compatible in Calgary with the Olympic spirit."[121]

King dismissed anti-Olympic protestors for dampening the show of positivity and unity that many Canadians displayed during the games. He writes in his memoir, "the negative placards of Lubicon supporters along the torch relay route seemed out of place and ineffective. The public and the media moved unsympathetically around the protesters, and the message lost momentum. Under the glow from the ubiquitous Olympic-torch candles, people hugged and shook hands in friendship. There was no room for defiance or confrontation here, and the protesters' message was overwhelmed."[122] Cartoons and editorials published in the *Calgary Herald* similarly dismissed these protests. Wamsley and Heine, for instance, describe a cartoon from the 15 March 1987 edition of the newspaper depicting "a group of Natives who man a barricade in an attempt to hinder the progress of the torch relay. The Native protestors literally get burned by the stupidity of their 'bright idea,' viz., their attempt to deter the progress of something as forceful as the Olympic symbolism of good-will being carried across Canada."[123]

Wamsley and Heine argue that individuals who criticized Lubicon activists for politicizing the Olympics failed to recognize that OCO'88 organizers also politicized the games. At issue, they write, was "the discursive delimitation of the 'proper' politics in the context of the 1988 Olympics."[124] Specifically, the decision to include symbols of Indigenous cultures through *The Spirit Sings* exhibit and accept sponsorship money from oil companies are also deeply political actions.[125] This incisive argument can be taken one step further: by failing to recognize the political dimensions of the Calgary Olympics, supporters obscured the Settler colonial context in which the event was being held. Consequently, they made it easier for Settlers to disavow the fact that Petro-Canada nationalism is tainted by practices such as the extraction of oil on Lubicon land.

* * *

Petro-Canada sold commemorative Calgary Olympic torch relay glassware, which turned out to be popular consumer goods. These commodities are material representations of the ideas about national pride and unity that many Canadians associated with the Calgary Olympics. They are decorated with the Calgary Olympic emblem, Olympic rings, and a stylized Olympic torch with a maple leaf emerging from its flame. The maple leaf in the torch relay logo gestures to the Petro-Canada logo which also includes a maple leaf. However, the company's name does not appear on the glasses. They were sold at Petro-Canada gas stations across the country, and consumers ultimately bought 50 million glasses, amounting to more than double the Canadian population at the time.[126] Phil Churton was a district manager for the company in 1988 and described public demand for the objects as overwhelming: "People were clamouring. We couldn't keep up."[127] Gas station operators frequently called his office asking for more glasses because they had run out of stock.[128]

King celebrated the success of the torch relay by observing, "You can't invent ways to bring people together like this relay. *You can't buy the pride it has unleashed*. It gives all Canadians a chance to participate in some way."[129] While it may not have been possible to purchase the pride Canadians displayed during the Calgary Olympic torch relay, it was possible for a commodity to symbolize that pride. Indeed, Petro-Canada created an ad suggesting that the torch relay glasses served this purpose. The ad shows clips of torchbearers transporting the Calgary Olympic torch alternating with images of athletes studying and training. A voiceover tells viewers, "For 88 days, the Olympic torch relay brought us together in a celebration of the Canadian spirit. It also brought Canada an enduring legacy: the Petro Canada Olympic Torch Relay Legacy Fund. Every time you bought an Olympic torch relay glass, you contributed to this awards program. It will allow our promising athletes and coaches to continue their education and training. The Olympic Torch Relay Legacy Fund: *The pride we shared leaves a promise for the future*."[130] The final scene shows the stylized Olympic torch icon that appears on the glasses alongside the phrase "Olympic Torch Relay Legacy Fund: Sustaining the Olympic Spirit."[131]

The ad suggests that Canadians shared in a collective expression of patriotism and national unity when they participated in the Calgary Olympic torch relay and bought commemorative glassware. In doing so, it promotes glassware nationalism, a version of national pride that Canadians experienced during the Calgary Olympics and expressed by buying the glasses. The glasses, however, are fetish objects that embody an "impossible irresolution" in the meaning of citizenship and belonging in Canada.[132] They represent both the national pride and unity the relay inspired in individuals, and at the same time, the Alberta and Canadian governments' unjust treatment of the Lubicon and their exclusion from the expression of national unity shown during the relay. Interpreting the objects' symbolic meaning in this way transforms them into uncanny symbols of a Settler colonial country that derives profits from the natural resources found on Indigenous peoples' land.

The ad also emphasizes the fact that Canadians contributed money to a fund for elite athletes, the Torch Relay Legacy Fund, when they bought the drinking glasses. It implies that Canadians invested in a nationally significant cause, support for high-performance Canadian athletes and coaches, through their purchases. Although it does not name the Petro-Canada glassware directly, OCO'88's senior high education kit exposed students to a similar idea to the one promoted through the ad. The kit reads, "As an integral part of the Torch Relay, a legacy for amateur sport organizations will be provided through the sale of limited-edition products licensed by OCO'88's Marketing Department."[133]

Canadians bought the Petro-Canada glassware at a time when neoliberalism was on the rise, and individuals were increasingly expected to engage in economically valuable activities and reduce the strain they placed on publicly funded services.[134] This insight adds another dimension to the symbolic meaning of glassware, illustrating that it represents Canadians' identities as citizens who make financially valuable contributions to the nation. In this example, Canadians used their consumer dollars to support a social cause (funding for elite Canadian athletes). Moreover, the commodities are a feature of the broader neoliberal drive to commercialize previously uncommercialized elements of society. In this case, individuals' patriotism became commercialized through the Petro-Canada glassware.[135]

Like Petro-Canada, OCO'88 members depicted the act of consuming Olympic-related products as patriotic acts that helped fund a nationally significant cause. At the 1985 launch of the Calgary Olympic coin program, King said, "We are proud and delighted to endorse the Olympic Coin program and we are confident that not only will Canadians embrace this vehicle for supporting the Games, but it will be an international best seller as well."[136] Canadian associate minister of National Defence Harvie Andre also attended the launch, and he reinforced King's message that Canadians could express their support for the games by buying the coins. Canadian athletes, Andre said, "desperately need our support. Canadians can show their support by embracing this commemorative coin series."[137] He went on to note, "Our future Olympians will appreciate the financial vote of confidence and will be encouraged to victory knowing that Canadians are already cheering behind them. As proud Canadians, let's show the world leadership. Let's support our Canadian athletes in their pursuit of excellence."[138]

By suggesting that Canadians could cast a "financial vote of confidence" for Canadian athletes through the consumption of Olympic coins, Andre created an association between civic engagement and consumption. He also encouraged Canadians to engage in symbolic consumer nationalism (SCN), which is "the reproduction of nationalism through consumer-based practices."[139] In this example, the act of exchanging money for a commodity appears on par with activities like casting a vote in a political election. Canadian minister for Fitness and Amateur Sport Otto Jelinek similarly suggested that individuals could "speak" with their wallets by buying Olympic coins. He made the following statement at the launch of the Calgary Olympic coin program: "Every time a Canadian buys an Olympic coin, they are *making a positive statement of support* for Canada's Olympic athletes and ideals."[140] Jelinek named Canadian athletes who were in the audience when he added, "With three percent of the face value of each coin going to the Canadian Olympic Association, that purchase is also *making a positive financial statement of support* that will help ensure that future Ken Reads, Gaetan Bouchers, Alex Baumanns and Laurie Grahams will have the opportunity to show that they, too, can compete with the best athletes in the world."[141]

Representing and Commodifying Alberta's Oil Industry

Petro-Canada's sponsorship of the Calgary Olympic torch relay complemented Team Petroleum '88's collective efforts to promote the oil and gas industry through its investment in the games. In this section, I consider the significance of Team Petroleum'88's promotional practices by showing that the group worked alongside OCO'88 to situate Alberta competitively within the global petroleum market. This strategy is evident in the instructions that OCO'88 gave individuals scheduled to speak at a 1987 banquet honouring Team Petroleum'88: "Recognition should be made of Team Petroleum '88's hosting of the world's oil and gas industry at the Games and its promotion, with the City of Calgary and Alberta, of Calgary and Alberta to attract industry and development."[142]

A news release announcing that Western Natural Gas would be supplying gas to light the Olympic cauldron also draws attention to the petroleum industry in Alberta. It quotes John Fisher, the company's senior vice president and general manager: "The flame on the Calgary Tower and flames at the venue sites will do Calgary proud before the eyes of the world. As well as being a showcase for Calgary and the Olympics, the flame will remind everyone of the central role of the energy industry in Alberta's development."[143] The Team Petroleum'88 emblem shows oil drilling equipment on either side of the Olympic rings and Calgary Olympic emblem, and pins featuring the Team Petroleum'88 emblem were available for sale during the games (figure 3.4). Team Petroleum'88 members were encouraged to use the emblem in corporate, public, and employee relations programs as well as general communications. However, they were not permitted to use it to market or advertise a specific product, and these guidelines helped focus attention on the entire oil and gas industry rather than individual companies that contributed to Team Petroleum'88's sponsorship initiative.[144]

3.4 Team Petroleum'88 logo.

This focus on business investment in Alberta complemented OCO'88's depiction of Calgary as a city that honours its frontier history but is not stuck in the past. A booklet about Olympic sponsorship opportunities describes the 1988 Winter Olympic host city: "Set in the foothills below the majestic Rockies, Calgary continues as the centre for traditional grain and livestock production. Now, it has added a vast petrochemical industry to that 'rodeo' heritage, which has propelled Calgary to become the most dynamic business centre in the country."[145] Moreover, a training manual for games volunteers depicts the city as a progressive and economically vibrant place with a rich cowboy history: "Calgary is a Western city, unique in Canada. It was founded by rugged pioneers who valued the warmth and friendliness of humans meeting in the wide and vast expanses of the west. Our city grew, fuelled by industries that thrived on risk and vitality. Today we are a modern city, culturally rich, technologically fruitful, and future oriented. But in our best tradition we still retain the qualities that distinguished the pioneers."[146] This idea was also represented visually through a Kodak-sponsored hot air balloon festival staged during the games. It featured balloons in several shapes including propane bottles, gasoline pumps, and cowboy hats.[147]

The training manual also notes, "In spite of its reputation, Calgary is not a cowboy town."[148] For David Whitson, this statement illustrates that politicians wished to represent the host city as modern and advanced: "Burdened, in some ways, by the city's history as a 'cowboy town,' civic and provincial leaders (like [Alberta premier Peter] Lougheed) saw the Olympics as a perfect stage on which to demonstrate that Calgary was a vibrant and forward-looking metropolis, as opposed to stuck in its agricultural past."[149] OCO'88 certainly depicted Calgary as modern and business-friendly but Whitson's argument that the city was burdened by its history as a frontier town is not entirely convincing. In this chapter, I have shown that symbols of the region's cowboy history featured prominently in the games' cultural and commercial features (e.g., opening ceremony, emblem design, mascot design) and Calgary Olympic organizers did not downplay Calgary's identity as a "cowboy town." Rather, they promoted the idea that the city's recent oil and gas wealth complements its ranching industry.

OCO'88's Youth Committee included an ad for Calgary in a section of its senior high school education kit called "Selling Calgary." The ad reinforces this message about the city's identity by showing symbols of the city's cowboy heritage along with symbols of its oil riches. The ad features a man extending his hand to the viewer, as if to shake hands, in two different settings. One side of the poster shows him dressed in a cowboy hat, standing in a rural setting surrounded by mountains, skiers, grazing cows, and horses pulling a cart. The other side shows the same man dressed in a suit standing in a metropolitan area next to a woman in a stylish fur coat, with skyscrapers in the background. The education kit instructs students to identify the audience for the ad and draw a parallel between the way Calgary sells itself and the way OCO'88 sells the Olympic Games.[150] This activity illustrates that OCO'88 taught students about city branding even before scholars and professionals formally described and quantified the phenomenon. Scholarship on this topic emerged in the early 2000s in the fields of marketing and business studies.[151] Simon Anholt's 2007 book, *Competitive Identity: The New Brand Management for Nations, Cities and Regions*, is a formative text on this topic. According to Melissa Aronczyk, Anholt is widely credited as a key figure in the development of nation branding.[152]

Aronczyk uses the term "living the brand" in a 2008 article and, subsequently, 2012 book to describe "a concerted and comprehensive strategy by national citizens of all strata of society to assimilate and communicate" a nation branding message.[153] OCO'88 trained its volunteers to "live" Western Canada's brand decades before Aronczyk began publishing research on this phenomenon. The organizing committee relied heavily on volunteer labour, with a total of 11,680 volunteers making up 97 per cent of OCO'88's workforce. OCO'88 placed high demands on Calgary Olympic volunteers by requiring them to attend training sessions for at least one year and work a minimum of 120 hours during the games.[154] The volunteer training manual instructs volunteers on how to "live the brand" by informing them that "Calgary is famous for its hospitality and true western warmth" and encouraging them to "smile and be friendly" while on duty.[155] OCO'88 required these unpaid workers to be "well groomed and aware of overall appearance" and "have a genuine interest in people from diverse cultures."[156]

When discussing their involvement in the 1988 Winter Games years after the event, volunteers described how they "lived" the Calgary brand. One person made the following statement in a 2006 focus group that organizers of the 2010 Vancouver Olympics commissioned in the lead-up to those games: "I was proud to be a volunteer for a wonderful organization [OCO'88] and represent my city."[157] Another focus group participant made a similar point: "I didn't volunteer officially but I still feel that I was national ambassador to the world. I went out of my way to make people feel welcome – I felt it was my duty and because it was so much fun!"[158]

Not all the representations of Alberta's oil and gas riches in the Calgary Olympics would meet Anholt or Aronczyk's definition of region branding practices, as most games-related practices did not reach the scale or sophistication of contemporary marketing campaigns intended to shape a region's global reputation. However, Olympic sponsors and government officials collectively used the 1988 Calgary Winter Games to remind global investors that Alberta was open for business and that the province had established strong relationships with energy companies. Conveying this message was particularly important because conflicts between Edmonton and Ottawa in the 1970s and early 1980s negatively affected oil and gas operations in the province. Relations between Canadian prime minister Pierre Trudeau and Alberta premier Peter Lougheed became more acrimonious in the years following the 1978 Edmonton Commonwealth Games. The most intense conflict between the leaders occurred in October 1980 when the Trudeau Liberals unveiled the National Energy Policy (NEP). The policy introduced new taxes on the petrochemical industry, including a Petroleum and Gas Revenue Tax.[159] Some Albertans were so angry about the NEP that they put bumper stickers on their cars that read "Let the Eastern Bastards Freeze in the Dark!"[160]

This conflict made energy companies wary of operating in the province. Lougheed retaliated against the NEP by reducing crude oil production by 15 per cent or about 180,000 barrels a day. The Canadian Petroleum Association claimed that the Liberal's policy caused drilling activity in Canada to decline by 22 per cent and led to the loss of 15,000 jobs. The Toronto Stock Exchange's (TSE) oil and gas index dropped more than eight hundred points after Trudeau announced his new energy policy, and stock owners sold so many shares of Canadian petroleum companies that the TSE temporarily suspended trading on several petroleum stocks.[161] Relations between Edmonton and Ottawa improved in 1984 when Prime Minister Brian Mulroney came to power. He decreased federal involvement in the petroleum industry and dismantled the NEP in a series of accords reached with oil-producing provinces, effectively decreasing federal involvement in the industry.[162] Even before Petro-Canada was privatized in 1991, Mulroney directed it to operate like any other private-sector oil company, rather than as an instrument of public policy, which was Trudeau's approach.[163]

OCO'88 and Team Petroleum'88 successfully used the Calgary Olympics to draw attention to the idea that Alberta's oil and gas industry was once again thriving. However, the Lubicon's opposition to oil companies' sponsorship of the Calgary Olympics undermined organizers and sponsors' efforts to depict the host region in a favourable light. The headline of a 27 February 1988 *Washington Post* article about the Lubicon's anti-Olympic protest makes this clear: "Indian Band Protests in Calgary; Battle for Rights Threatens to Mar City's World Image."[164] A headline published in the *Sydney Morning Herald* conveys a similar message and directly addresses games' organizers' celebration of Calgary's cowboy heritage. It reads, "Indians Hope to Dent the Good-Guy Image of Calgary's Cowboys."[165]

The actions of European museums who showed support for the Lubicon by refusing to donate items to *The Spirit Sings* exhibit were also damaging to Calgary's reputation. Felix Valk, director of the Museum voor Volkenkunde in Rotterdam, for instance, observed that the exhibit risked being seen "as a kind of cover-up, a nice façade hiding the real world of today's native peoples."[166] Calgary's mayor travelled to Europe a few months before the 1988 Winter Games began, launching what

Wamsley and Heine describe as a "goodwill-tour" to repair the city's reputation.[167] Understood in this context, commodities symbolizing the strength of Alberta's petroleum industry, such as pins marked with the Team Petroleum'88 logo, hold together contradictory ideas. On one hand, they represent the idea that the host region is home to a profitable oil and gas industry. On the other hand, they represent the human cost of petroleum extraction in Alberta.

Conclusion

Calgary Olympic organizers and sponsors used symbols of Indigenous peoples' cultures to represent the host region and nation while also emphasizing Western Canadian "cowboy" history. Companies working in the oil and gas industry, meanwhile, sponsored games-related cultural practices and conveyed the idea that Alberta is a resource-rich and business-friendly province. These representations were haunted by the violence of European Settlement in Western Canada in the nineteenth century and by games organizers and sponsors' misappropriation and misuse of Indigenous cultural artifacts.

The anti-Olympic protests mounted by the Lubicon and their supporters undermined the value of the petroleum industry's involvement in the games by exposing the fact that extractive practices in Alberta were threatening local Indigenous communities' cultural and physical survival. Their protests are particularly significant in relation to three features of the fusion of nationalism and commercialism present in the Calgary Games. First, companies such as Petro-Canada used the games to establish a link between their brands' identity and celebratory ideas about national identity. Second, Canadian consumers embraced an Olympic-related commodity, commemorative torch relay glassware, as a symbol of their national pride and identity as Canadians. Third, corporate sponsors worked alongside Olympic organizers and local politicians to shape the host region's public image. Notably, these features were present to a much greater extent in the 1988 Winter Games compared to previous Canadian-hosted Olympic and Commonwealth games. The reality that oil companies' activities were threatening the Lubicon's survival tainted all three practices. Anti-Olympic protestors made it impossible to completely disavow this fact and, in doing so, exposed the deep ties between nationalism, commercialism, and Settler colonialism.

4

Commercializing Indigenous Cultures and Lumber in the 1994 Victoria Commonwealth Games

When Victoria officials competed against Cardiff, Wales, and New Delhi, India, for the right to host the 1994 Commonwealth Games, they presented members of the Commonwealth Games Federation (CGF) with a petition supporting their bid signed by 33,000 people. Officials also developed what they described as a "bullet-proof" financing plan that included income from corporate sponsors.[1] The majority of CGF members, a total of twenty-nine, voted to award the games to Victoria; nineteen members voted for New Delhi and nine voted for Cardiff.[2] The Victoria Commonwealth Games Society (VCGS) financed the games through a mix of public and private funds. It received $62 million from the federal government; $44 million from the provincial government; and raised $54 million through private fundraising measures, including establishing corporate sponsorship; supplier, supporter, and licensee programs; and selling broadcast rights.[3] The VCGS earned a surplus of $4.6 million.[4]

VCGS president George Heller solicited corporate sponsorship for the games by arguing that the Victoria Games' logo, a stylized ribbon in the shape of a "V," was "becoming one of the most valuable marketing symbols in Canada. It is only available to our marketing partners and will enhance the recognition of your products and services."[5] Heller thus suggested that games' sponsors could strengthen their brands by using the logo in their promotional campaigns. In doing so, he made a similar argument to the one used by the International Olympic Committee (IOC) to promote its global sponsorship program. Yet he also recognized that symbols associated with the Commonwealth Games were not as valuable as the Olympic rings, observing that "the Commonwealth Games is a good product that can be built upon."[6]

Heller was trying to keep pace with the IOC's profit-generating activities while also recognizing that the Commonwealth Games were not as lucrative as the Olympics. Yet, in the Canadian context, the VCGS was more advanced than Olympic organizers in one area, namely, Indigenous inclusion in the games. The VCGS adopted a more progressive and sophisticated approach to collaborating with Indigenous peoples compared to the ones adopted by organizers of the 1976 Montreal and 1988 Calgary Olympics. While organizers of the 2010 Vancouver Olympics later maintained, accurately, that they achieved "unprecedented Aboriginal participation,"[7] VCGS members pioneered some of the practices that Vancouver Olympics organizers later adopted to ensure that Indigenous peoples played a meaningful role in the games' planning process.

Representations of Indigenous peoples' cultures were more complex and ambivalent in the Victoria Games compared to earlier Canadian Olympic and Commonwealth games. VCGS members perpetuated the long-standing practice of using Indigenous iconography to define the Settler colonial state; however, Indigenous peoples exerted significant control over representations of their cultures. Moreover, some participants openly discussed Canada's Settler colonial past, and a games-related education resource addressed this topic.

In this chapter, I identify how politicians used the Victoria Commonwealth Games to promote the idea that relations between Indigenous peoples and Settlers in British Columbia were improving. I show that these narratives circulated at a time when activists were trying to stop logging companies from clear-cutting forests located on unceded Indigenous territory in the province. These activists exposed the reality that certain Indigenous groups' priorities were incompatible with some of the economic practices occurring in BC at the time of the games. Moreover, ideas circulating in the games about repaired Indigenous-Settler relations were undermined by reminders that Settler colonialism is a land-based structure that persists in Canada.

Representing and Commodifying Indigenous Cultures

Officials began planning the Victoria Commonwealth Games soon after two events in Canada brought national attention to Indigenous peoples' right to self-determination: the defeat of the Meech Lake Accord and the 1990 Kanien'kehá:ka (Mohawk)-Oka conflict. In addition, the BC government began renewing treaty negotiations with local First Nations in 1992, two years before Victoria hosted the Commonwealth Games. Indigenous peoples participated in the games within this political context. They actively shaped the meanings of their contributions and drew attention to Indigenous groups' historical and ongoing resistance to Settler colonialism in Canada. Yet some individuals questioned whether the Victoria Games would – or could – benefit Indigenous peoples in the long term.

The VCGS established a Native Participation Committee (NPC) to promote and co-ordinate Indigenous peoples' involvement in the Victoria Games. Operating with a $4.7 million budget provided by the federal government, it organized events, including a youth conference and canoe regatta.[8] According to the NPC, the conference offered participants the opportunity to "meet youth from other tribes sharing our culture through song, dance and language" and "hear the power and strength of our elders as they pass their inherited knowledge on."[9] Moreover, committee members wrote that the regatta marks "the rebirth of the canoe races first held on the Gorge in the 1850s and will lead up to the 1994 Commonwealth Games."[10] It coincided with the final leg of the Queen's baton cross-country trip, and the canoes accompanied the Queen's baton as it travelled into Victoria's Inner Harbour.[11] Willie Seymour, a Coast Salish man who served as the regatta's master of ceremonies, said that the event helped repair past wounds: "These canoes have journeyed the highways of our forefathers. It has been a journey of healing, unity, respect, recognition and a revisiting of our sacred areas."[12]

The executive director of the United Native Nations in Vancouver, Dan Smith, celebrated the fact that local Indigenous peoples became involved in the games early in the planning process and participated in a meaningful rather than tokenistic way in the event. Smith told a *Vancouver Sun* reporter, "In the last few years, the people of Canada have encouraged their governments to resolve the plight of the aboriginal people. I see more positive things taking place. Our participation in the Commonwealth Games is evident because the government's attitude and the people's attitude toward aboriginal people has changed."[13] BC premier Mike Harcourt acknowledged that Indigenous peoples lived in Canada prior to European Settlement when he wrote in the *XV Commonwealth Official Souvenir Magazine*, "Aboriginal people, *in whose traditional territory the Games are being held*, have been actively involved [in the Victoria Commonwealth Games]."[14]

Indigenous athletes participated in lacrosse competitions that the VCGS included in the games as a demonstration sport, and the games' *Official Souvenir Magazine* notes that lacrosse "was developed by the Algonquin peoples of the St. Lawrence River area in eastern Canada."[15] A postage stamp included in the Victoria Commonwealth Games' stamp collection shows athletes playing lacrosse, and a *Canada News-Wire* article about the item recognizes that Indigenous peoples played the sport before Europeans settled in modern-day Canada: "One of the stamps being issued by Canada Post this month will feature Lacrosse, one of Canada's two national sports. Lacrosse was played by the First Nations long before the Europeans arrived … The stamp features athletes participating in a men's field lacrosse game, with colourful roses in the foreground."[16] In contrast to the Montreal Olympic coin discussed in chapter 1, the design of the Victoria Games' coin does not include stereotypical signifiers of Indigeneity.

Members of the Iroquois Nationals lacrosse team competed in the Victoria Games alongside members of the Canadian men's national program; players from the Canadian women's lacrosse team took part in a separate competition that did not include an Indigenous team.[17] This development is notable when compared to the lacrosse competition included in the 1978 Edmonton Commonwealth Games. Organizers of those games neglected to invite Indigenous athletes to participate in the competition, adding a game between two Indigenous lacrosse teams only after facing public pressure to do so (I discuss this controversy in chapter 2).

Indigenous peoples also participated in numerous cultural events associated with the Victoria Commonwealth Games. A total of 450 Coast Salish, Kwakwa̱ka̱'wakw (Kwakiutl), and Nuu-chah-nulth (Nootka) peoples performed in the games' opening ceremony, and Coast Salish artist Richard Krentz worked with carvers from Indigenous communities throughout the Northwest Coast to carve the world's largest totem pole as a legacy of the games. Krentz and his collaborators carved the 55-metre pole from a 250-year-old red cedar tree grown in the Nimpkish Valley. According to an article in the *Vancouver Sun*, "Songhees Chief Norman George bestowed the name Spirit of Lekwammen, a Coast Salish word meaning 'Land of the Winds,' on the totem pole."[18] A design from the pole appears on the Victoria Games' commemorative medals.[19] In addition, the artist Roy Henry Vickers, who is of Ts'msyen (Tsimshian), Haida, and Heiltsuk descent, carved a totem pole called "The Legend of the Salmon People" to stand outside the Saanich Commonwealth Place, a swimming and aquatics venue built for the 1994 Games.[20]

Daniel Francis argues that the totem pole is "just one aspect of Native culture that has been adopted by non-Native Canadians as a symbol of their own."[21] For instance, in the 1920s, Canadian Pacific Railway (CPR) executives partnered with local and federal governments and museum experts to preserve Gitxsan (Gitksan) totem poles that appear along railroad lines in BC. CPR officials marketed these poles as tourist attractions, and totem poles have since come to serve as unofficial symbols of the province.[22] However, Krentz and Vickers explained the meaning of the totem poles they carved for the Victoria Games in quite different terms, with no suggestion that these poles symbolized the province. Krentz and his collaborators intended that the "Spirit of Lekwammen" totem pole "send a message of hope – that it is possible for people of different nations, languages, cultures and beliefs to work together in harmony to achieve a common goal."[23] Vickers associated his "The Legend of the Salmon People" pole with the idea that Indigenous peoples have resisted, and continue to resist, the logic of elimination that lies at the heart of Settler colonialism. He addressed this idea at a ceremony for the raising of the pole, which "went up with the blessings of five coastal native Indian bands."[24] Vickers said, "This has much to do with where we are as an aboriginal people today. We are an aboriginal people who have dealt with discrimination and cultural genocide over four generations, and we have our cynics. We have people who have a lot of anger and are very bitter … But that's all negative. If you walk in a positive way, if you walk on the road of recovery, if you walk in your power, then you are respectful not only of the earth you walk on and yourself as a person, you are respectful of every other person who is a precious human being. And when we come to one another in that spirit, nothing but good happens."[25]

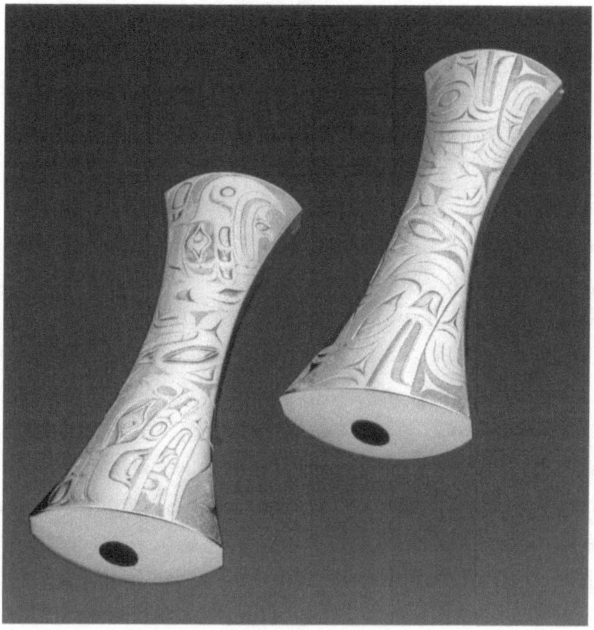

4.1 Queen's baton of the 1994 Victoria Commonwealth Games.

The design of the Queen's baton also represents Indigenous cultures in Canada. BC Hydro sponsored the relay and worked in collaboration with the NPC to commission three Indigenous artists to design the baton: Coast Salish artist Charles Elliott; Kwakwa̱ka̱'wakw (Kwakiutl) artist Richard Hunt; and Nuu-chah-nulth (Nootka) artist Art Thompson. The baton "features symbols of the artists' families and cultures: a wolf and frog from the Salish, a wolf from the Nuu-Chah-Nulth, and a raven with a frog in its mouth, along with a young thunderbird, from the Kwagiulth [Kwakwa̱ka̱'wakw]" (figure 4.1).[26] This design also appears on material goods circulating through the games: it marks the left side of the 1994 Commonwealth Games postage stamps and appears on the games' medals.[27]

Thompson's cousin, who goes by the name Ki-Ke-in, spoke at the Victoria Games' medal launch. He drew attention to the fact that Indigenous peoples have successfully resisted the federal government's past attempts to assimilate them into Settler society: "In 1884 in BC, the colonial government outlawed everything you see here today – the regalia and even the names from the native soil."[28] Ki-Ke-in noted that Thompson attended a Port Alberni residential school but eventually "freed himself of the anger that all aboriginal people in BC know ... I'm so proud of this man it's hard to put into words. Finally, in this province and in this country, aboriginal people are being given a place that is more than a token."[29] Understood in relation to Ki-Ke-in's comments, the Queen's baton represents the idea that Indigenous peoples are healing from past traumas and the Canadian state is mending its broken relationship with Indigenous peoples.

While these developments are important, Indigenous participation in the Victoria Games did have some limitations. NPC co-ordinator Danny Henry stated publicly that the VCGS did not always treat NPC members as equal partners. A 1993 *Canadian Press* article summarized his concerns: "While high-priced Games consultants stay in fine hotels and are wined and dined ... there's insufficient money for similar treatment for visiting native elders performing essentially the same function with [Henry's] committee."[30] In addition, games organizers removed Henry from the agenda of a corporate sponsors' conference at the last minute, claiming there was not enough time to fit him in.[31] Chief Dan Sam of the Tsartlip First Nation argued that Indigenous peoples' participation in the games would not lead to long-term social change. He observed, "The Games are a good thing, but the way I see it is, we get recognized for 10 days and when it is over, we are left with nothing. For us, it's back to Square 1."[32]

The Victoria Commonwealth Games' opening ceremony was based on a Settler's interpretation of Indigenous Potlatch traditions. It was produced by Jacques Lemay, who also produced the Calgary Olympic opening ceremony. The Canadian Broadcasting Corporation (CBC) published a *Broadcasters Handbook* for the games which includes the following statement from Lemay: "Ultimately, the Opening Ceremony closely follows the ageless West Coast tradition of the POTLATCH. We are indeed inviting the world into our 'Big House' and we will share our songs, traditions and dances with the world. We will host them and feast with them."[33] Lemay's description of the Potlatch tradition as "ageless" reflects a Eurocentric interpretation of Indigenous cultures, one that positions them as existing outside Western chronological conceptualizations of time and progress.

***

BC premier Mike Harcourt used the Queen's baton relay to set a productive tone for the treaty negotiations the provincial government had initiated with local First Nations in 1992. In contrast to other parts of the country, few treaties were signed between First Nations in BC and the Crown. Vancouver Island governor James Douglas signed fourteen purchase treaties with participating First Nations in the early 1850s. However, when Joseph Trutch took over from Douglas as governor in 1867, he refused to recognize Indigenous peoples' right to the land. Trutch argued that all of BC belonged to the Crown and no further treaties were negotiated. In 1973, the Supreme Court of Canada heard the *Calder et al. v. Attorney-General of British Columbia* case. In their ruling, the seven Supreme Court justices agreed that the Nisga'a First Nation held Aboriginal title prior to European settlement in BC, although they were divided on the question of whether the Nisga'a continue to hold Aboriginal title. The province established the BC Claims Task Force in 1990 and created the BC Treaty Commission in 1992.[34]

When the Queen's baton arrived in Victoria's Inner Harbour surrounded by canoes paddled by Indigenous peoples, the premier drew a link between the event and the Treaty Commission's goals. The *Vancouver Sun* quotes him saying, "It's a magnificent start not just to the Commonwealth Games but also to the start this fall of treaty negotiations to complete a process which should have been completed in 1858."[35] An uncomfortable truth underpins Harcourt's efforts to use the games to promote the province's commitment to treaty negotiations. At the same time as he was promoting this message, his government was permitting companies to extract natural resources on Indigenous peoples' land without their permission. Put another way, the province recognized Indigenous peoples' rights through the treaty process but did not stop corporations from violating these rights.

One year prior to the start of the Victoria Games, members of the Tla-o-qui-aht (Clayoquot) First Nation threatened to boycott the games if the province did not address their concerns over the logging of old-growth forests in Clayoquot Sound. Members of the Tla-o-qui-aht (Clayoquot), along with the Ahousaht (Ahousat) and Hesquiaht First Nations, opposed the BC government's 1992 decision to allow the logging company MacMillan Bloedel to operate in the Sound. Approximately 20 per cent of the region had already been clear-cut and the government granted MacMillan Bloedel permission to log an additional two-thirds of the forest. Although the Tla-o-qui-aht (Clayoquot) claim land rights to an area within the Sound, the province did not consult with them before granting the company logging rights.[36]

A group going by the name "independent state of Qwa-Ba-Diwa" criticized Vickers for carving his "The Legend of the Salmon People" totem pole out of a red cedar that was grown in Vancouver Island's Walbran Valley and procured by the logging company Fletcher Challenge. A member of the group wrote an open letter to Vickers asserting, "The tree will be removed from our territory … by the predator, Fletcher Challenge. This company operates without respect and without our consent. We trust you will not do the same."[37] In addition, the forestry company TimberWest Forest Ltd of Vancouver sponsored Vickers' totem pole for $50,000.[38] This sponsorship activity illustrates that a problematic corporate practice associated with the Calgary Olympics (Shell Canada's sponsorship of *The Spirit Sings* exhibit) was also present in the Victoria Commonwealth Games. Specifically, companies working in controversial extractive industries (i.e., oil and lumber) funded games-related events intended to showcase and celebrate Indigenous cultures.

Activists protesting MacMillan Bloedel's activities in Clayoquot Sound gathered near the Victoria Commonwealth Games' rowing venue a few weeks prior to the start of the games.[39] They raised signs with slogans like "Protect the Common Wealth" but were forced to leave the area when government authorities successfully sought a court order from the BC Supreme Court to evict them.[40] The VCGS thus incorporated symbols of Indigenous peoples' cultures into the games through the design of the Queen's baton and games' medals while also excluding protestors from an area where athletes and spectators had gathered. Understood in this context, the objects, and related commodities like postage stamps featuring the Queen's baton design, are fetish objects that hold together unresolved contradictions in the meaning of contemporary Indigenous-Settler relations in BC. On one hand, they represent the idea that relations are on the mend. On the other hand, they represent the limited progress that has been made in this area and call attention to the province's ongoing violation of Indigenous peoples' right to land.

In a likely bid to gain public support for its logging activity in Clayoquot Sound, MacMillan Bloedel placed a full-page ad in the official souvenir magazine of the Victoria Games offering free tours of "a working forest." Visitors would "see up-to-date harvesting techniques, a modern sawmill and reforestation areas on Vancouver Island. Plus, along the way you'll view spectacular scenery, ocean fjords and wildlife."[41] Another ad, this one paid for by the province of BC, shows a bear standing in a sea of grass with thick forests in the background. It promotes the province's commitment to environmental sustainability and social progress, reading, "Where dreams run wild. Where forests grow tall and rivers run free. Where the air is clear and clean, and we never hear the words – endangered species. In British Columbia, Canada, we're making this dream a reality. By doubling our parks and protected wilderness areas. And changing the way we manage our forests. This is our commitment. Creating a new world standard. To leave this planet a better place for our children."[42] By focusing on the theme of environmental protection, this ad attempts to distract readers from the fact that the government's decision to allow companies to clear-cut trees in Clayoquot Sound is neither environmentally nor ethically sound.

These political and commercial practices illustrate that although Indigenous peoples used the Victoria Games to advance their interests, their potential to achieve this goal was constrained by Settler colonialism in Canada. One of the artists who helped design the games' Queen's baton, Charles Elliott, questioned the value of Indigenous peoples' inclusion in the games. A *Canadian Press* article notes, "At a time when B.C. native bands are fighting provincial and federal governments over disputed rights to land and resources, it occurred to Elliott that Games organizers might be courting Indian involvement to thwart protests or critical international media attention."[43] Elliott ultimately decided not to boycott the games but instead communicate a message about Indigenous resistance through the stylized frog design he created for the Queen's baton. Frogs represent transformation and change in some Indigenous cultures, and Elliott argued that his design "stands for the change that's going on in this society, that aboriginal people in this province are beginning to assert themselves and seeking some social justice."[44]

Elliott's design contains what a *Canadian Press* article describes as "a hidden clarion call" for Indigenous peoples.[45] This information adds an additional layer of meaning to the Victoria Games' Queen's baton and medals. While they ostensibly represent the view that Indigenous-Settler relations are improving, they also contain a covert message about the ongoing need for Indigenous peoples to resist Settler colonialism and advocate for their rights. By intentionally designing the Queen's baton in this way, Elliott worked within the institutional and wider social and political limitations of the Victoria Commonwealth Games to inspire change.

While Elliott decided to participate in the games, former leader of the Union of BC Indian Chiefs Philip Paul encouraged local First Nations groups to boycott them. He argued, "The Commonwealth is a conglomeration of people who have colonized Indian and Third World countries generally. There is no way Indian people should back them or become tokens."[46] Paul's statement draws attention to the Commonwealth Games' links to British imperialism. They were, after all, originally called the "British Empire Games," and a tension existed between Indigenous participation in the Victoria Games and the events' ties to the British Empire. This tension was reflected symbolically in the colour scheme of a special logo designed for the games by Coast Salish artist Susan A. Point, "Echoing the Spirit – Transformation of the Coast Salish Spindle Whorl." Point designed the logo, intended to represent Indigenous peoples' involvement in the games, predominantly in the colours of the Union Jack: red, white, and blue.[47]

A "special Echoing the Spirit set of First Nations pins" was available for sale, and these commodities held together unresolved tensions underpinning Indigenous peoples' involvement in the games.[48] While Indigenous artists created games-related products that celebrated their cultures and symbolized their resistance to the logic of elimination at the heart of Settler colonialism, these works were created and showcased through a sporting event that is associated with British imperialism, a political and ideological practice that drove the colonization of English Canada.

The "Echoing the Spirit" pin set, furthermore, represents a truth reflected in a statement included in the *Broadcasters Handbook*: it welcomes readers to "Camosak, the name the native inhabitants had for Victoria when the British arrived to stay in the 1840s. For those who live here, it is a special place, on a special island."[49] This statement tacitly recognizes a central feature of Settler colonialism: outsiders establish a country on land inhabited by Indigenous peoples (i.e., the British *arrived to stay* by setting up a government that operated according to the logic of elimination central to the Settler colonial project). The pin set represents both the colonial project and resistance to it. Indeed, activists opposed to the logging of old-growth forests in Clayoquot Sound exemplify how Indigenous peoples continue to resist Settlers' claim of ownership over their land.

Like the "Echoing the Spirit" logo, the Victoria Games' V-shaped logo was designed in red, white, and blue. In addition, Union Jack-themed decorations appeared in the host city in the lead-up to the 1994 Games.[50] The VCGS sent letters to businesses, school districts, shopping malls, and other institutions encouraging them to build enthusiasm for the games by planting red, white, and blue flowers throughout the city and decorating buildings with these colours.[51] Pierre Berton of the *Toronto Star* wrote that during the Commonwealth Games, Victoria was "ablaze with Imperial colours" because locals planted "vast sheets of red salvia, blue lobelia, and white impatiens."[52]

Like the organizers of the 1978 Edmonton Commonwealth Games, the VCGS promoted English Canada's ties to Britain while simultaneously including Indigenous iconography in cultural displays. Significantly, the Union Jack's popularity as a symbol of Canadians' allegiance to Britain was beginning to wane in the final decade of the twentieth century. This trend was revealed in the findings of focus group interviews Hall & Hall Associates conducted with residents of greater Victoria. The company showed participants sixteen design options for the Victoria Commonwealth Games' logo, and they found that respondents' feedback was consistent across age and gender with one exception: "younger respondents, those under 35, who have known only Canada's red and white maple leaf flag during their lifetime, think of red, white and blue as 'American.' Older respondents (those 35 plus) see these three colours as appropriate reminders of our Commonwealth links."[53] One focus group participant who fell into the twenty-five to thirty-four-year-old age range commented, "Get away from the red, white and blue colour scheme because it is so American."[54] By contrast, a participant who was over the age of thirty-five commented, "The colours red, white and blue will suggest the Commonwealth."[55] These responses illustrates that younger Canadians may not have been familiar with, or emotionally connected to, the flag debates that preceded the selection of Canada's current red and white flag (I discuss these debates in chapter 2).

Mascots and Education Resources

The Victoria Games' mascot and education kits exposed young people to ideas about the nation, and Indigenous-Settler relations in Canada, that were as complex and ambivalent as the ideas circulating in other games-related cultural practices. For instance, the name organizers gave to the Victoria Games' mascot, a smiling orca whale named Klee Wyck, draws attention to an Indigenous-Settler exchange that would have been familiar to many Canadians (figure 4.2). The mascot's name was inspired by the Canadian painter Emily Carr's account of her visits to Indigenous communities in BC. The VCGS held a contest to name the mascot and four people separately submitted the winning entry; they all described Klee Wyck as a nickname for Carr, meaning "the laughing one." One submission reads, "What better name for our Commonwealth mascot, the noble Orca, than KLEE WYCK. An Indian name meaning 'the Laughing One,' it was the one given to Emily Carr, our very own famous Victoria artist."[56]

Carr explains how she acquired the nickname in her 1941 memoir *Klee Wyck*, which describes her travels to Indigenous communities located on the west coast of Vancouver Island. While in Ucluelet, the artist met a Nuu-chah-nulth (Nootka) woman named Mrs Wynook who called her "Klee Wyck." A missionary heard their exchange and asked Mrs Wynook what the name meant. Carr writes, "Mrs. Wynook put her thumbs into the corners of her mouth and stretched them upwards. She pointed at me; there was a long, guttural jabber in Chinook between her and the Missionary. Finally, the Missionary said, 'Klee Wyck is the Indians' name for you. It means 'Laughing One.'"[57]

VCGS director Linda Schlechte Petch celebrated the mascot's link to Nuu-chah-nulth (Nootka) culture through its name. She is quoted in a 1991 press release explaining that "the panel chose this name above others because it met all the criteria for the Games' mascot and allows this noble animal to retain its integrity and at the same time links it to *our native heritage*."[58] In this statement, Petch problematically claims ownership over Indigenous peoples' history, continuing a long tradition of Settlers making such claims. Arnold Edinborough, for instance, articulated a similar sentiment in his review of *The Spirit Sings* exhibit associated with the 1988 Calgary Olympics. "The richness of the native artistic traditions and the scope of this great land of ours" constitute "a rich history and identity, which is ours and with which we should ally ourselves."[59]

A 1991 Mascot Steering Committee report reveals that the VCGS believed it had mistranslated the mascot's name: "Research done by the Steering Committee indicates that Klee Wyck does not, in fact, quite translate from Chinook into English as 'The Laughing One.' This, apparently, was Emily Carr's interpretation of what her Indian friends were

4.2 Klee Wyck, mascot of the 1994 Victoria Commonwealth Games.

calling her, communicated to her by them through sign language. The actual translation is closer to 'the smiling one,' and its correct anglicized written translation is one word, not two."[60] Despite this observation, the committee recommended "that the story of how Klee Wyck was named become an integral part of the mascot's mythology."[61] It further recommended that "the name Klee Wyck be used in most instances without translation or further definition" but that "when translation is offered, it be shown as 'The Laughing One.'"[62]

Several texts about Carr, including Maria Tippett's biography of the artist and Grant Crabtree's 1946 documentary called *Klee Wyck*, translate the name as "the laughing one."[63] However, a group of astronomers interpreted the word differently. The scientists discovered a new asteroid in January 1991 and named it in honour of the Victoria Commonwealth Games' mascot.[64] A citation in *Dictionary of Minor Planet Names* describes Klee Wyck as the name "given by Vancouver Island's coastal people to the famous Victoria artist Emily Carr on one of her many painting expeditions into the coastal wilderness in the early 1900s. The name in the Nuu-Chah-Nulth people's language translates to 'the smiling one.'"[65]

The VCGS sold mascot commodities including stuffed animals, magnets, swimming caps, backpacks, and sweatshirts.[66] Organizers designed the mascot wearing a medal marked with the games' logo in order to make the whale a "trade markable proprietary character."[67] These commodities hold in tension different translations of the name Klee Wyck. Rather than resolving these differences, objects like plush toys of the mascot symbolize how Carr's cross-cultural exchange with Mrs Wynook was mediated by a colonial official (i.e., a missionary). Significantly, Carr and other Settlers failed to completely control the meaning of the exchange and confusion about how to properly translate the nickname into English persists.

The significance of the mascot's name can also be understood in relation to Carr's written account of her visits to Northwest Coast Indigenous communities. Clarke, Irwin and Company bought the rights to *Klee Wyck* in 1951 and included the book in its Canadian Classics series of educational publications. The publishing house edited the version of the book it sold to schools by removing more than 2,300 words as well as "almost every derogatory adjective or descriptor concerning missionaries at Ucluelet and other places, observations concerning their negative reactions to First Nations beliefs, a passage describing a musty church interior and references to residential schools."[68] This edited version of the book thus represents a selective account of Canadian identity and history that omits important truths about practices aimed at assimilating Indigenous peoples into Settler society. The Victoria Games' mascot similarly represents a selective account of the host region and nation, one that makes it possible for consumers to ignore the history and persistence of Settler colonialism in Canada.

* * *

In contrast to the edited version of *Klee Wyck* available to Canadian schoolchildren, in which references to Settler colonial practices were expunged, the "Youth and Education Learning Resource Kit" that the VCGS distributed to schools across BC explicitly addresses this topic. One booklet included in this kit, called "AA en mas" ("Come and

Compete"), is particularly notable in this regard. It does not reproduce the colonial logic reflected in many education practices affiliated with the Canadian-hosted Olympic and Commonwealth games, such as the lesson comparing "Competition in Pre-Industrial and Industrial Cultures" in a Calgary Games' education kit. Rather, authors of the "AA en mas" booklet recognize that Indigenous peoples "practised (and still do practise, in many cases) many sports and games, songs, and dances as part of their culture."[69] They characterize these activities as resources Indigenous peoples use to resist Settlers' treatment of Indigenous cultures as inferior to European cultures: "Today, traditional and contemporary First Nations games and sports help to revive the old pride in being a Native Indian person."[70]

The "AA en mas" resource informs readers that Indigenous peoples lived in Canada long before Settlers arrived and colonized the land. Its message to students reads, "In this resource book, you will find out about the first culture that there ever was in North America – First Nation."[71] Furthermore, "First Nations people were playing racquet and ball games long before *Canada was colonized.* At least 48 different tribes throughout Canada and the United States played lacrosse."[72] The book goes even further by recognizing the devastating impact of colonization in Canada: "For about two hundred years, after contact with the Europeans that came to Canada, many First Nations traditions were attacked, blocked, or outlawed. There was a lot of trouble as rapid changes were forced on a very old culture. People were no longer proud to be Native Indians or First Nations people."[73] Whereas lessons included in education resources linked to the Montreal, Edmonton, and Calgary games gestured to Settler colonialism in Canada without directly confronting this topic, the "AA en mas" booklet included a frank acknowledgment.

The workbook also serves as an example of how non-Indigenous educators can develop culturally appropriate resources by collaborating with Indigenous community members. Authors worked with Indigenous cultural advisers to produce the "AA en mas" resource, and a section in the book encourages teachers to "enlist the assistance of representatives from your local First Nations community … In addition, you may wish to ask for input from First Nations students you have in your class or school."[74] Authors also worked with Coast Salish, Nuu-chah-nulth (Nootka), and Kwakwa̱ka̱'wakw (Kwakiutl) collaborators to translate sport-related words from their languages into English. Students learned the meanings of these words and how to pronounce them. For example, the "xa" in we-xa ("lift" in Kwak̓wala) "is like 'ha' but you drop the uvula down into the throat to block some air – like the end of a snore."[75] In comparison to the Victoria Games' mascot, whose name reflects Settlers' interpretation of the words Klee Wyck, this education resource includes words from Indigenous languages translated into English by Indigenous peoples who speak these languages.

The education resource includes instructions on how to plan a "Commonwealth-First Nations Games Day." "One possible format is based on the Potlatch format of the Northwest Coast First Nations" and teachers can arrange, if possible, for a First Nations elder to say a prayer.[76] Further, they should "Explain what a potlatch is, how it connects to this Games Day and some history of Commonwealth and First Nations sports."[77] Future research could investigate how teachers followed, and/or creatively interpreted, instructions in the resource. Did some teachers use the Commonwealth-First Nations Games Day to explore the idea introduced in the education resource that "after contact with the Europeans that came to Canada, many First Nations traditions were attacked, blocked, or outlawed"?[78] Did they encourage students to consider the significance of the fact that the Victoria Games' opening ceremony was modelled on a Settlers' interpretation of the Potlatch?

Conclusion

Indigenous peoples made meaningful contributions to the Victoria Games through their involvement in the NPC and games-related cultural events. These contributions helped expose audiences to the richness and vibrancy of Indigenous cultures located in BC. They also helped politicians promote the idea that relations between Settlers and Indigenous peoples in the province were being repaired. Reminders of Canada's Settler colonial past that appeared in the games did not undermine the coherency of this political message. These reminders thus served a different purpose in the Victoria Games compared to the previous games analyzed in this book. Whereas many cultural and commercial elements of the Montreal, Edmonton, and Calgary games were haunted by unacknowledged but clear evidence of the violence of Canada's Settler colonial past, this past was frequently acknowledged in the Victoria Games. Moreover, politicians in BC used the games to promote the idea that the province's commitment to renewing treaty negotiations with local Indigenous groups offered an opportunity to move beyond this violent past. Yet, activists used the Victoria Games to draw attention to facts that contradicted and complicated this message by showing that the Settler colonial practice of extracting profit from Indigenous land continues in Canada.

Commodities representing Indigenous peoples' cultures appeared in the games in the form of postage stamps representing the Queen's baton, specially designed "Echoing the Spirit" pins, and mascot toys. Other commercial practices, such as the publication of an ad for MacMillan Bloedel in the games' souvenir book, helped promote controversial resource extraction practices in the host province. However, the Victoria Commonwealth Games were less commercially sophisticated than the Calgary Olympics. Moreover, compared to the 1988 Winter Games, promotional and profit-oriented initiatives associated with the 1994 Commonwealth Games did not intersect as intensely with the ideas about national identity promoted by organizers and sponsors. This comparison illustrates that the fusion of nationalism and commercialism in the Victoria Games was less sophisticated than in the Calgary Games. The 1994 games also lacked a notable feature of the 1988 Winter Olympics: although the VCGS created a licensing program and sold specially produced commodities, consumers did not embrace any of these commodities as symbols of their national pride and/or identity.

5

Commercializing Reconciliation and Indigenous Cultures in the 2010 Vancouver Olympics

When Vancouver officials bid for the right to host the 2010 Winter Olympics, they promised that Indigenous peoples would play a meaningful role in the games. The Sḵwx̱wú7mesh (Squamish) National Council publicly supported the city's bid and the Vancouver Bid Corporation (VBC) told the International Olympic Committee (IOC) that "planning is underway for extensive involvement of Aboriginal people in the 2010 Games."[1] The organization also argued that the strong relationship between Indigenous and non-Indigenous Canadians reflects Olympic values: "Canada brings together the cultures of the world, as well as an ancient and rich First Nations culture, in one harmonious society: a living embodiment of the Olympic ideal."[2] The VBC even mentioned Canadian policy on Indigenous rights in its Bid Book, noting that Canada "became the first country in the world to constitutionally entrench the rights of Aboriginal peoples" through Section 35 of the Charter of Rights and Freedoms.[3]

The IOC awarded the 2010 Winter Olympics to Vancouver over PyeongChang, Korea. The games were held on the territory of the Lil̓wat (Lil'wat), xʷməθkʷəy̓əm (Musqueam), Sḵwx̱wú7mesh (Squamish), and Tsleil-Waututh First Nations, which came to be known during the Vancouver Olympics as the Four Host First Nations (FHFN). The IOC and Vancouver Olympic organizers officially partnered with these First Nations, marking the first time in Olympic history such a partnership was struck. Compared to earlier Canadian-hosted Olympic Games, the extent of Indigenous peoples' participation in the 2010 Winter Games was unprecedented. An honorary firekeeper blessed the Vancouver Olympic flame every time it passed through one of the 119 Indigenous communities located along the torch relay route.[4] During the games' opening ceremony, representatives from the FHFN officially welcomed athletes and visitors to their territory. The chiefs of these First Nations joined Canadian governor general Michaëlle Jean and IOC president Jacques Rogge as members of the Olympic Official Party, the first leaders of an Indigenous nation to be so included.[5]

The FHFN partnered with the Vancouver Organizing Committee for the 2010 Olympic and Paralympic Winter Games (VANOC) to develop an Aboriginal Licensing and Merchandising Program which sold "authentic Aboriginal products."[6] Proceeds from this program contributed to VANOC's $1.9 billion operating budget. Organizers also established a separate $599.8 million venue construction program funded by the Canadian and BC governments. VANOC announced in December 2010 that both its operating budget and venue construction program broke even, earning neither a surplus nor a deficit.[7]

The organizing committee raised $756.8 million from its domestic corporate sponsorship program, which was distinct from the IOC's international sponsorship program, and included three tiers: national partner, official supporter, and official supplier. In addition, sales of Olympic licensed merchandise totalled $57 million in royalties, with more than 45 licensees selling commodities available in 1,600 retail stores across the country. VANOC also earned over $230 million through ticket sales.[8]

Indigenous peoples' involvement in the Vancouver Olympic Games advanced several groups' agendas. The FHFN ensured that Indigenous peoples exerted control over how their cultures were represented in the games. Indigenous groups also shared in the wealth created by the sporting event. Meanwhile, the VBC and VANOC met the IOC's sustainability and legacy goals by championing Indigenous-related social causes. Canadian politicians, for their part, used the 2010 Games to publicize the success of government-led initiatives aimed at improving Indigenous-Settler relations. By considering how these different groups pursued their goals, I explore the promises and limitations of Indigenous peoples' participation in the Vancouver Olympics. I show that various groups advanced social causes, including reconciliation between Indigenous peoples and Settlers in Canada, within a heavily commercialized

Olympic environment. Moreover, numerous stakeholders attempted to profit materially from the FHFN's participation in the games.

Olympic organizers depicted Canada as a progressive country that honours Indigenous peoples' cultures. However, activists involved in the "No Olympics on Stolen Native Land" campaign promoted an alternative perspective. They argued that social and political initiatives aimed at improving Indigenous peoples' quality of life and/or reconciliation between Indigenous peoples and Settler Canadians will not be successful if governments and corporations continue to undermine Indigenous peoples' right to land and self-determination. Activists thus undermined the optimistic ideas about social change that Olympic organizers and sponsors promoted through their sustainability and legacy initiatives.

The Four Host First Nations and Vancouver's Olympic Bid

Members of the FHFN helped Vancouver bid officials win the right to host the 2010 Winter Olympic Games. VBC chairman Jack Poole stated, "If it hadn't been for the full support of the Four Host First Nations in our bid, we likely wouldn't be talking about Vancouver 2010 today."[9] Members of the bid corporation established an "Aboriginal Participation Strategy and Secretariat" and created a position on its board of directors "appointed by local First Nations."[10] The Líl̓wat (Lil'wat) and Sḵwx̱wú7mesh (Squamish) First Nations, whose land is located in modern-day Whistler, became involved in Vancouver's Olympic bid process earlier than the xʷməθkʷəy̓əm (Musqueam) and Tsleil-Waututh First Nations, whose land is located in modern-day Vancouver, probably because the city's Olympic bid included plans to build new venues in Whistler but not in Vancouver.[11]

In November 2002, the Líl̓wat (Lil'wat) and Sḵwx̱wú7mesh (Squamish) First Nations signed a Shared Legacies Agreement with the province of BC and VBC. It identifies three central objectives: "to respect the [Líl̓wat (Lil'wat) and Sḵwx̱wú7mesh (Squamish)] Nations' historic and current presence in the region; protect the Nations' Aboriginal rights and title; and to take advantage of economic opportunities, including the proposed hosting of the Games."[12] The following year, the xʷməθkʷəy̓əm (Musqueam) and Tsleil-Waututh First Nations signed a Memorandum of Understanding with the VBC (but not the province of BC). Their agreement was finalized in July 2003, one day before Vancouver won its Olympic bid; it establishes a foundation for the groups' cooperative working relationship and commitment to share in the games' benefits and legacy.[13]

The VBC depicted its partnership with the FHFN as an important component of its sustainable development plan at a time when the IOC had begun to embrace this concept as a guiding principle of the Olympic Movement.[14] Bid officials listed Indigenous peoples' involvement in the games as one of four "key sustainability elements" in their plans, along with environmental preservation, inner-city commitments, and Paralympic inclusion.[15] The IOC adopted *Olympic Movement's Agenda 21: Sport for Sustainable Development* in 1999. The document asserts, "The starting point of sustainable development is the idea that the long-term preservation of our environment, our habitat as well as its biodiversity and natural resources and the environment will only be possible if combined simultaneously with economic, social and political development particularly geared to the benefit of the poorest members of society."[16]

Although *Olympic Movement's Agenda 21* is primarily concerned with environmental preservation, it also commits to strengthening the involvement of women, youth, and Indigenous peoples in sport. For instance, it reads, "Indigenous populations have strong historical ties to their environment and have played an important part in its preservation."[17] Indigenous peoples' contribution to Vancouver's Olympic bid thus helped the city show the IOC it was committed to a goal outlined in *Olympic Movement's Agenda 21* – support for Indigenous peoples' cultures and participation in sport – and gave Vancouver a strategic advantage over other bid cities. It also distinguished Vancouver's bid from Montreal's and Calgary's earlier Olympic bids, which did not explicitly champion social causes aimed at improving Indigenous peoples' well-being.

Championing Indigenous inclusion in the games was part of the VBC's broader efforts to adopt a social cause through the games, a strategy that was becoming an increasingly important feature of the bid process. A member of Vancouver's bid committee observed in 2000, "The format for Olympic Bids is changing dramatically, as the IOC moves to an evaluation approach that is more focused on the substance of the Bid, rather than the relationships developed through the bidding process. At the same time, the IOC has taken a far more active role in promoting societal issues in conjunction with sport, including the environment, anti-doping, inclusiveness, etc. While the need to have a technically flawless bid is apparent, it is also evident that bids must appeal to the priorities of the decision makers even more than before."[18]

IOC members have always affiliated the Olympic movement with positive social values. The Olympic Charter, for instance, describes Olympism as "a philosophy of life" that "seeks to create a way of life based on the joy of effort, the educational value of good example, social responsibility and respect for universal fundamental ethical principles."[19] However, the organization's growing emphasis on social issues in the bid process was likely a response to a bribery scandal that damaged the IOC's public image. News emerged in 1998 that Salt Lake City officials had paid IOC members to support their city's Olympic bid. A Canadian IOC member, Dick Pound, led an investigation into the matter and recommended that the organization expel six members and adopt a code of ethics.[20] The IOC subsequently released a multi-platform ad campaign in 2000 called "Celebrate Humanity" that promoted Olympic ideals. It was designed by the IOC's Marketing Department with the aim of strengthening the Olympic brand.

Understood in this context, the VBC's partnership with the FHFN likely appealed to IOC members because it was consistent with their efforts to strengthen the association between the Olympic brand and positive social values. In this case, Vancouver bid officials championed inclusivity through their partnership with the FHFN. Moreover, the VBC developed a sustainability policy that prioritized Indigenous peoples' involvement in the games while also advancing profit-oriented goals. According to VANOC, "The three main themes of the Corporation's sustainability policy were environmental stewardship, economic opportunity and social responsibility. These were highlighted in the Candidature File and other agreements signed by the Bid Corporation."[21] In this conceptualization of sustainability, initiatives aimed at "maximizing economic opportunity" appear compatible with the goal of "conserving resources" and "hosting inclusive and accessible Games."[22] These ideas also align with the "Celebrate Humanity" campaign, which promotes ideals such as hope for a better world while also strengthening the economic value of the Olympic brand.[23]

* * *

The VBC's partnership with the FHFN was important on a domestic level as well. Vancouver bid for the 2010 Winter Olympics after Victoria hosted the 1994 Commonwealth Games and Winnipeg hosted the 1999 Pan Am Games. Indigenous peoples collaborated with organizers of these events, participated extensively in them, and exerted significant control over representations of their cultures. VBC members likely felt pressure to keep pace with these developments. Moreover, organizers of the 1999 Pan Am Games addressed an injustice experienced by Indigenous torch bearers in the 1967 Winnipeg Pan Am Games. In 1967, organizers asked a group of Indigenous runners to transport the games' torch from Saint Paul, Minnesota, to the host city, but did not allow them to take part in the games' opening ceremony. When the event returned to Winnipeg in 1999, organizers apologized to the surviving runners for this slight and invited them to participate in the games' opening ceremony, where they passed the torch to a star of the 1999 Manitoba Aboriginal Summer Games, Ida Whitford. Charlie Nelson, a torch bearer in 1967, stated that contributing to the opening ceremony of the 1999 Pan Am Games was inspirational: "We passed the flame to the next generation. We will help them to be strong and continue to have dreams."[24]

Members of the VBC were also cognizant that renewed treaty negotiations between the BC government and local First Nations established in the 1990s had not led to the creation of many new agreements. Because Olympic competitions would be staged on land not governed by treaty, members of the FHFN could have put the VBC's bid in jeopardy by challenging the province's authority to host the Olympic Games in Vancouver and the surrounding area. In addition, Indigenous land rights became a more pressing political issue in the province after the Supreme Court of Canada ruled on an Aboriginal title case concerning two First Nations located in northern BC, the Gitxsan (Gitksan) and Wet'suwet'en First Nations. In *Delgamuukw v. British Columbia*, the court clarified the definition of Aboriginal title and the ways it could, and could not, be extinguished. The justices ruled that First Nations who possess Aboriginal title maintain authority over their ancestral land and must be consulted about all resource extraction practices occurring on their land.[25] Chief Ernest Campbell of the xʷməθkʷəy̓əm (Musqueam) First Nation reminded VBC officials that the proposed games would be held on Indigenous land in a 2002 letter to the organization. When requesting a seat on the corporation's board of directors, Chief Campbell noted that "nearly two-thirds of the events planned for the Vancouver/Whistler 2010 Winter Olympics are scheduled to take place within Musqueam traditional territory."[26]

Some individuals questioned the extent to which hosting the 2010 Vancouver Olympics would benefit local Indigenous groups. Taiaiake Alfred criticized the economic development deal the Lílwat (Lil'wat) and Sḵwx̱wú7mesh (Squamish) First Nations struck with the province. He described it as a "blatant pay-off for their support of the Olympic bid" and "a sell-out designed to benefit elite politicians on both sides of the colonial divide."[27]

The social benefits of hosting the games in Vancouver also became subject to public debate after Mayor Larry Campbell held a non-binding plebiscite in February 2003 on the following question: "Do you support or do you oppose the City of Vancouver's participation in hosting the 2010 Olympic Winter Games and Paralympic Winter Games?"[28] Opponents of the city's Olympic bid argued that if the games came to Canada, they would economically benefit a small group of Canadians and disadvantage many more. Hosting an Olympic Games would not boost BC's economy in the long term and public money spent on the games would be better spent on social services like health care and education.[29] Moreover, the "No Games 2010 Coalition" suggested that organizers were not being transparent about their activities: "Secret deals are being negotiated with select First Nations bands, and municipal and corporate entities."[30] Supporters of Vancouver's Olympic bid tried to counter these criticisms by arguing that the economic growth generated by a Canadian-hosted games would benefit Canadian society as a whole. A VBC document titled "Answering the NO side" asserts, "The Games are an investment in our future" and have the potential to create "a larger economic pie, permanently."[31] The document also responds to the accusation that the VBC was arranging secret deals with interested parties: "A Shared Legacies Agreement with First Nations was negotiated between the Bid, the Province and local First Nations. This agreement was also made public and has been extensively reported on by the *Vancouver Sun* and other media. We believe that it is an excellent example of the Olympics helping to improve the economic and social sustainability of the affected First Nations."[32] This argument is consistent with how members of the VBC framed their approach to sustainability in the Candidature File. To use the language of the three "sustainability themes" contained in the file, Vancouver bid officials suggested that the Shared Legacy Agreement would maximize "economic opportunity" for Indigenous peoples while also promoting "social responsibility" by celebrating and strengthening their cultures.[33]

VBC members also tried to raise public support for their Olympic bid by partnering with a Canadian bank, CIBC, to establish an official youth bid ambassador program. A total of twenty young people aged fourteen to seventeen served as ambassadors who were responsible for building awareness and enthusiasm for Vancouver's Olympic bid.[34] Youth from the xʷməθkʷəy̓əm (Musqueam) and Sḵwx̱wú7mesh (Squamish) First Nations participated in the program. Fourteen-year-old Rebecca Campbell celebrated the opportunity to represent the xʷməθkʷəy̓əm (Musqueam) community, saying, "I think it is very exciting that Vancouver is making a bid for the Olympics due to the fact that Vancouver sits on the traditional territory of the Musqueam First Nation. What a great way to represent my people and city by being a CIBC 20 for 10 Youth Bid Ambassador!"[35]

Representing and Commodifying Reconciliation and Indigenous Cultures

The results of the 2003 plebiscite revealed that 64 per cent of voters supported Vancouver's bid to host the 2010 Winter Olympics, and the city won its bid later that year. The FHFN made history by becoming the first Indigenous group to officially partner with an Olympic organizing committee. The Truth and Reconciliation Commission of Canada's (TRC) final report praises this partnership: "In the spirit of reconciliation, which aligns easily with the spirit of the games themselves, the Four Host First Nations and the Vancouver Olympic Committee formed a partnership that ensured that Indigenous peoples were full participants in the decision-making process – a first in Olympic history."[36]

The FHFN worked with VANOC to ensure that Indigenous peoples benefited socially and economically from their participation in the Vancouver Olympics. In the pages that follow, I discuss examples of Indigenous peoples' involvement in games-related cultural and commercial practices and identify improvements in the way their cultures were represented compared to earlier Canadian-hosted games. However, many Indigenous peoples and Settler Canadians could not benefit from the games because of the context in which they were held. Specifically, the 2010 Winter Olympics were a highly commercialized event hosted in a Settler colonial country, on land that Indigenous peoples never ceded to the Crown, at a time when the federal and provincial governments had established deeply flawed reconciliation initiatives.

The Vancouver Olympic medals, designed by Corrine Hunt, feature images of orcas "in the style of a traditional West Coast First Nations bentwood box."[37] Each medal is decorated with a unique, hand-cropped segment of the design. Hunt is of Kwakwa̱ka̱'wakw (Kwakiutl) and Tlingit heritage. Her proposal to VANOC reads, "From the beginning of her career engraving rings, bracelets, pendants, and broaches, Corrine has searched for unique ways to bring the stories of her First Nations culture to contemporary life."[38] Another section of the proposal quotes Hunt directly: "Designing the medals for the 2010 Olympics presents a remarkable opportunity for me to once again retell familiar stories for our current times."[39] Hunt's medal design is a marked improvement over the design of the 1988 Calgary Olympic medals. In chapter 3, I show that members of the Indian Association of Alberta criticized the stylized headdress design featured on the Calgary Olympic medals because it disrespected the cultural importance of this item. By contrast, Hunt's design represents her contemporary interpretation of an Indigenous cultural object (i.e., a bentwood box).

The emblem of the Vancouver Olympic Games also features a contemporary interpretation of an Indigenous cultural object. The emblem is a stylized Inukshuk (plural: Inuksuit) with five coloured stones stacked on top of each other to resemble a person extending their arms (figure 5.1).[40] Inuksuit are stone objects that the Inuit, who live in northern Canada, use as directional markers. Unlike the Vancouver Olympic medals, however, the emblem was not designed by an Indigenous artist. A Settler named Elena Rivera MacGregor came up with the idea for a stylized Inukshuk, which won VANOC's emblem design contest.[41]

Although Rivera MacGregor's design reflects a Settlers' interpretation of the Inukshuk, it was endorsed by several Indigenous leaders. BC premier Gordon Campbell wrote a letter to Nunavut premier Paul Okalik asking him to support VANOC's decision to include an Inukshuk "as the key element of the [Vancouver] Olympic Emblem."[42] Campbell identifies one reason why VANOC made the choice: "The Inukshuk is

5.1 Emblem of the 2010 Vancouver Olympics.

a unique part of the Inuit cultural identity and a distinctive symbol of Canadian culture."[43] Premier Okalik endorsed the emblem and joined VANOC members in Vancouver at the public unveiling of the emblem in 2005.[44] Inuit Tapiriit Kanatami president Mary Simon praised the design for raising awareness of Inuit culture. Simon, who is currently serving as the first Indigenous governor general of Canada, said, "It is with pride that Inuit stand with the FHFN in sharing the story of our culture, showing the world the people behind the Inukshuk."[45] The Vancouver Olympic emblem appears on a wide range of commodities including pins, hockey pucks, t-shirts, baseball caps, umbrellas, and jackets.[46] People could also literally embody the design. The Royal Canadian Mint, which distributed special Olympic-themed coins featuring the emblem, designed the floor of its Olympic Pavilion to include a large indented Inukshuk inside a loonie. Children could lie inside the indent while their parents took pictures of them.[47]

The Vancouver Olympic emblem appeared on the Olympic torch, which passed through 1,036 communities and places of interest including 118 Indigenous communities; twelve Indigenous youth served as flame attendants and travelled with the torch to make certain the flame was never extinguished.[48] For Michael Putulik, an Inuit flame attendant from Nunavut, participating in the event strengthened his identity as an Indigenous person living in Canada. "I am proud to be Inuit," he said, "but I felt very proud to be not just Inuit, but a Canadian Aboriginal. The experience really showed me that no matter where we're from, where we work or what we are, we're all the same."[49]

The Royal Bank of Canada (RBC) sponsored the torch relay and hired former national chief of the Assembly of First Nations Phil Fontaine as an adviser to its executive team in September 2009. The bank asked Fontaine to "ensure that the bank maximizes the involvement of the aboriginal community in the 2010 Olympic Torch Relay."[50] His partnership with RBC illustrates that sponsors of the Vancouver Olympics worked alongside games' organizers to involve Indigenous peoples in the decision-making process. RBC's partnership with Fontaine had two additional benefits. It strengthened the bank's brand by linking the company with a positive social value associated with the Vancouver Olympics (i.e., support for Indigenous inclusion in the games), and it helped RBC and VANOC garner positive publicity for the event and avoid the kind of criticism the Lubicon Lake Nation and their allies directed at Petro-Canada when the oil company sponsored the 1988 Calgary Olympic torch relay.

During the Vancouver Olympic opening ceremony, the FHFN logo was projected on the stage while representatives from the Líl̓wat (Lil'wat), xʷməθkʷəy̓əm (Musqueam), Sḵwx̱wú7mesh (Squamish) and Tsleil-Waututh First Nations delivered an official welcome. The logo shows four faces inside a circle and was designed by Sḵwx̱wú7mesh (Squamish) artist Jody Broomfield. According to Broomfield, "The rim of the logo represents the Creator and our ancestors, watching over a human face representing each of the four Nations. In the centre, four feathers point to the cardinal directions – north, south, east and west – inviting and welcoming the athletes and peoples of the world to come to the 2010 Winter Games in Vancouver. The feathers can also be seen to symbolize arms stretched up and open, welcoming and extending respect to all visitors. It is the tradition of the FHFN people to welcome visitors, or to compliment for something well done, by saying 'I hold my hands up to you'"[51] (figure 5.2).

The logo appears on a $75 gold coin which, according to the Mint, represents the FHFN's official welcome: the coin's "black-on-gold design

5.2 Logo of the Four Host First Nations.

welcomes you to Vancouver 2010 and the ancestral territories of the Four Host First Nations."[52] Pins featuring the FHFN logo were also available for sale.[53] These coins and pins brought a celebratory message about the FHFN's partnership with VANOC into a commercial realm. In other words, ideas conveyed through the opening ceremony about Indigenous inclusion in the Vancouver Olympics were also represented through material goods.

After the FHFN welcome, Indigenous youth danced in the opening ceremony "in their own traditional styles wearing their own traditional clothing and regalia representative of their unique and diverse Aboriginal cultures."[54] VANOC hired David Atkins Enterprises to create an implementation plan for the opening and closing ceremonies. The company consulted with over 200 members of the Canadian cultural community about the ceremonies through a series of symposia and "the importance of representing Aboriginal Canada, and specifically 'not in a token way'" emerged as an important theme.[55] In a likely unintentional reference to the Montreal Olympic closing ceremony and lacrosse coin, as well as the Calgary Olympic medal design, an Indigenous participant "pointed out she was over the whole 'head-dress and feathers' depiction of Aboriginality."[56]

The Indigenous youth who danced in the opening ceremony also attended the Vancouver 2010 Indigenous Youth Gathering, where they gained exposure to the Olympic Games and promoted "Aboriginal culture, heritage, protocols and languages."[57] Many participants spoke positively about their experiences and expressed hope for the future. One commented, "We showed the world our beauty, our diversity. Our generation is stepping into a world in which we will experience even more opportunity … and much more respect." Another said, "I'm definitely walking away feeling that we're on the right track," while a third hoped that the Vancouver Games have "inspired many Aboriginals and non-Aboriginals to learn and educate themselves [about] the First Peoples of Canada."[58] Indigenous cultures were also featured in the 2010 Olympic Aboriginal Pavilion hosted by the FHFN. It offered "a feast for the senses – Aboriginal cuisine, traditional and contemporary art, dramatic and musical performances, language and celebration," and received more than 200,000 visitors over the course of the Games.[59]

***

Indigenous groups benefited economically from the Vancouver Games in numerous ways. Artists sold their work through the Aboriginal Licensing and Merchandising Program and VANOC donated one-third of the royalties, amounting to $200,000, to the Aboriginal Youth Legacy Fund, which supports education, sport, and cultural programs for Indigenous youth across Canada.[60] FHFN CEO Tewanee Joseph praised the licensing and merchandising program for showcasing "the best Aboriginal artists from across Canada" to a global audience.[61] The commodities sold through the program offer alternatives to the objects representing a "'head-dress and feathers' depiction of Aboriginality" that circulated in the Montreal and Calgary Games.[62]

An Indigenous businessperson, Shain Jackson, criticized VANOC for including products in the Aboriginal Licensing and Merchandising Program that were not made in Canada, and for not including items distributed by Indigenous retailers. Jackson, who sells Indigenous art through a company called Spirit Works, circulated a petition calling on VANOC to stop describing the commodities sold through the program as authentic.[63] The committee did not submit to Jackson's request. It argued that "from the outset, the FHFN worked towards ensuring authenticity in its merchandise. In 2007, they co-hosted an Appropriate Use Roundtable, which resulted in the development of comprehensive Aboriginal merchandise guidelines."[64] VANOC's response illustrates that committee members believed an object's authenticity could be determined through a set of mutually agreed upon guidelines. Yet, for Jackson, these guidelines are flawed if they do not mandate that Indigenous peoples retain control over the design, production, distribution, and sale of Indigenous products. Such disagreements highlight an idea also reflected in Chief Poking Fire's sale of spoof products during the "Indian Days" celebration organized by the Kanien'kehá:ka (Mohawk) of Kahnawá:ke during the Montreal Olympics (discussed in chapter 1). Specifically, the process involved in defining a cultural object as authentic remains highly complex and contested.

The FHFN and other Indigenous groups worked closely with games organizers to ensure they would benefit from the tourism opportunities offered by the 2010 Winter Olympic Games. BC attorney general Geoff Plant said in a 2004 press release, "There are enormous openings emerging in aboriginal tourism as we prepare for the [Vancouver] Olympics and we are working to support these."[65] A few years later, in 2007, the chiefs of the FHFN, along with representatives from the provincial and federal governments, organized a 2010 Aboriginal Business Summit. It was sponsored by Tourism BC, VANOC, and the following Canadian corporations: the Hudson's Bay Company (HBC), RBC, and Rona. The conference program notes, "The 2010 Winter Games present Canada's Aboriginal peoples with a very real opportunity to … make the most of the international tourism potential that comes with hosting the world."[66] Another section reads, "In 2010, Canada, and in particular Vancouver, Whistler and British Columbia, will welcome the world. With some 14,000 media expected to attend the Vancouver 2010 Olympic and Paralympic Winter Games, Aboriginal tourism will have an international opportunity to capture the imagination of visitors and residents alike."[67]

One example of how Indigenous groups benefited from these tourism opportunities is the Shared Legacies Agreement signed by the Lil̓wat (Lil'wat) and Sḵwx̱wú7mesh (Squamish) First Nations with the VBC and province of BC. In the agreement, the province agrees to provide 300 acres of land for the Nations "to pursue economic development opportunities within their shared territories."[68] It also includes a funding commitment to cover a portion of the costs of constructing a Squamish Lil'wat cultural centre. The centre, it reads, will "showcase and celebrate the First Nations cultures" and "provide a Whistler base for outbound First Nations eco-cultural/tourism adventures that will add to the broader tourism pool of quality activities."[69] Whistler mayor Ken Melamed complimented the centre, saying, "The legacy of Aboriginal participation in the Games, including the Squamish Lil'wat Cultural Centre, enriches our community as a premier resort destination internationally."[70]

Plant and Melamed's comments illustrate that Indigenous communities in BC were not the only group to benefit from Indigenous-led tourism initiatives associated with the Vancouver Olympics. Rather, these initiatives enhanced various groups' efforts to increase tourism in the region. Tourism representatives from the cities of Vancouver, Victoria, Whistler, and Richmond, the province of BC, and the Canadian Tourism Commission (a federal Crown corporation) formed the Tourism 2010 Committee in the lead-up to the 2010 Winter Olympics. Its members committed to work "together, and with the media, Olympic sponsors/organizers and others, to leverage funds and ensure tourism opportunities are maximized for the province."[71] In addition, representatives from Tourism BC briefed the VANOC Sub-Committee on Ceremonies and Torch Relay about the province's brand identity in 2006. They emphasized the "overwhelming appeal" of the province's natural environment, noting, "mountains, oceans/coast and scenery are the main features that make BC an attractive travel destination."[72] Standout features of this environment, including mountains overlooking the ocean, are represented in the games' emblem design and "Landscape of a Dream" segment of the opening ceremony, which I discuss in detail later in this chapter.

* * *

By participating in the Vancouver Olympics, Indigenous peoples helped advance the aims of the provincial government's "New Relationship with Aboriginal People and Communities in British Columbia" (New Relationship). The BC Ministry of Aboriginal Relations and Reconciliation describes the New Relationship as "a vision for improved government-to-government relations founded on respect, reconciliation and recognition of First Nations rights and titles as cornerstones to strong, forward-looking relationships between the Province and First Nations."[73] As part of its commitment to the New Relationship, the province promised to increase consultation with First Nations on relevant public policy; ensure that First Nations share in the profits earned from resource extraction practices on their land; and establish a $100 million New Relationship Trust Fund.[74]

The Ministry of Aboriginal Relations and Reconciliation characterized the FHFN's involvement in the 2010 Games as a central achievement of the New Relationship. Its 2009–2010 Annual Report on Progress reads, as the first Indigenous hosts of the Olympic Games, FHFN members "achieved something historic, unprecedented and amazingly successful."[75] Furthermore, the Vancouver Olympic Aboriginal Pavilion revealed "why Aboriginal culture – First Nations, Inuit, and Métis – is an important part of BC's past, present and future."[76] The ministry also praised the 2010 Winter Games for increasing "support for the Aboriginal cultural tourism industry."[77]

Like the VBC's conceptualization of sustainability, which pairs economic growth with social progress, the BC government used the New Relationship to improve Indigenous-Settler relations while also strengthening the province's economy. After the *Delgamuukw* ruling, many foreign companies associated with BC's resource extraction industries became concerned that the government would no longer be able to protect their investments in the province. In this way, the uncertain status of Indigenous peoples' land rights in BC affected the region's economy, with Premier Glen Clark arguing in 1998 that this uncertainty, and its resulting financial implications, was the most important issue facing the province. Anti-logging protests staged in the 1990s that disrupted ongoing forestry projects compounded matters and made logging companies wary of starting new projects in the province.[78] The Business Council of BC encouraged Premier Campbell to establish the New Relationship by arguing that foreign investment in the province would decrease significantly if questions about land and resource ownership remained unresolved.[79]

Caitlyn Vernon interviewed government representatives, business operators, and Indigenous leaders about the New Relationship and they all "agreed that a major impetus to develop the New Relationship arose from the desire by the provincial government, industry, and some First Nations to secure access to lands and resources for economic development."[80] Vernon asserts that the 2010 Winter Games was one of the "political, economic, and legal pressures leading up to the New Relationship." The BC government, she argues, wanted to improve public perception of its relations with Indigenous peoples in the lead-up to the games.[81]

According to David Rossiter and Patricia Wood, politicians in BC adopted a neoliberal approach to treaty rights negotiations and Indigenous-Settler reconciliation by prioritizing Indigenous peoples' participation in capitalist-driven industry initiatives.[82] Rossiter and Wood also critique official discourses surrounding a referendum that Premier Campbell initiated in 2002 regarding First Nations treaty rights and land claim negotiations. The government did not recognize the history of Settler colonialism in Canada, attempting instead to "do away with the messy past and to recreate the province's spaces as 'neutral' and open for investment: as fantastic topographies."[83]

Rossiter and Wood identify two limitations of the approach BC politicians took to reconciliation that are equally applicable to the FHFN's involvement in the Vancouver Olympics and, more generally, representations of Indigenous cultures in the games. First, these practices ignore the historical and current Settler colonial context in which the games took place. Second, they pair a commitment to improving Indigenous-Settler relations with profit-oriented goals, goals which often benefit government and corporate actors more than participating Indigenous communities. These shortcomings limited the Vancouver Olympics' potential to create lasting and meaningful social change. Janice Forsyth makes this argument when she writes, "in spite of the increased visibility of Aboriginal people at the 2010 Games and the creation of the FHFN, the power relations sustaining historic inequities between Olympic organizers and Indigenous people have remained largely unchanged … Above all else, the Olympic industry relies on and perpetuates inequities by exploiting the commercial value of Indigenous lands, insignia, and labour while ignoring the broader needs and concerns of those same Indigenous groups. Governments and corporations alike have benefitted enormously from this exploitative condition."[84]

Politicians intended that the New Relationship would significantly reduce the socio-economic gap between Indigenous and non-Indigenous peoples living in BC. However, there is little evidence to suggest they achieved this goal. The Ministry of Aboriginal Relations and

Reconciliation compiled data on the following four priority areas in 2005/2006 and again in 2010/2011: education, housing and infrastructure, health, and economic opportunities. The ministry's findings show that the gap between Settlers' and Indigenous peoples' quality of life remained high during these years. For instance, the number of long-term drinking water advisories on Indigenous reserves in BC rose from nineteen in 2005 to twenty-five in 2011.[85] Moreover, the ministry recorded youth suicide in the province between 2001 and 2005 and 2006 and 2010. In both time periods, Indigenous youth were significantly more likely to commit suicide compared to non-Indigenous youth.[86]

The report also reveals that although the FHFN's involvement in the Vancouver Olympics brought significant attention to First Nations' cultures in the province, public perception of their cultures did not significantly improve in the years between 2007 and 2010. In 2010, 30 per cent of British Columbians surveyed described themselves as very aware "of the diversity of First Nations cultures" within the province, up only 4 per cent from 2007 when participants were asked the same question. Moreover, the percentage of British Columbians surveyed who strongly agreed with the statement "First Nations have made a wide range of valuable contributions to BC" increased only 4 per cent between 2007 and 2010, rising from 23 per cent to 27 per cent.[87]

The symbolic significance of the FHFN logo and related commodities (e.g., $75 gold coins marked with the logo) can be understood within this context. They are fetish objects that hold together competing ideas about the significance of Indigenous peoples' participation in the 2010 Winter Games. On one hand, the games offered the FHFN a historic opportunity to participate as equal partners in Olympic-related decision-making processes. On the other hand, their participation supported the aims of a government-led reconciliation process that did not lead to substantial improvements in the socio-economic status of Indigenous peoples living in BC.

* * *

VANOC argued that the FHFN's contributions to the Vancouver Games helped advance Olympic sustainability and legacy goals. The committee's *Sustainability Report* mentions its commitment to achieving "unprecedented Aboriginal participation" in the games seven times.[88] One passage reads, "Aboriginal Participation and Collaboration means working with our partners to achieve unprecedented Aboriginal participation in the planning and hosting of the Games and in the creation of Games legacies."[89] The report also includes a list of "Our Sustainability legacy and cumulative highlights/actions" that includes the following bullet point: "Recognition of Aboriginal peoples by the International Olympic Committee (IOC) as Games partners."[90]

It is unlikely that VANOC's dual emphasis on sustainability and legacy was accidental. The IOC began mandating that every Olympic Games leave a legacy in 2003, the same year Vancouver won its Olympic bid, and sustainability and legacy initiatives became increasingly interconnected in subsequent years. Legacies can be tangible (e.g., they can improve a host city's infrastructure and economy) or intangible (e.g., they can develop cultural values). Host cities can leave a legacy by meeting social, economic, and environmental sustainability goals. Conversely, they can contribute to sustainable development by leaving a legacy of changed attitudes and behaviours that lead to positive social change.[91]

VANOC advanced its Indigenous-related sustainability and legacy practices through the Vancouver Olympic Truce Northern Outreach Project. Although Olympic truce projects usually provide aid to groups living outside the host country, VANOC's project served remote Indigenous communities in the Yukon, Northwest Territories, and Nunavut. Between 4 January and 8 January 2010, a Canadian Forces plane transported sporting goods donated by Canadian NHL teams and the sporting goods company Nike to these communities, with the goal of increasing youth participation in sport. The communities received hockey sticks, soccer balls, baseballs, basketballs, and lacrosse gear. Individuals dressed as the Vancouver Olympic mascots, Canadian Olympians, and representatives from VANOC, Nike, and the United Nations Association in Canada, travelled to northern Canada on the Canadian Forces plane to deliver the gear.[92]

VANOC's description of the Aboriginal Licensing and Merchandising Program suggests that sustainability/legacy and business goals are compatible: "This program showcased excellence in Aboriginal arts, culture and enterprise in Canada. It also brought global attention to Aboriginal artists and businesses, and represented a clear investment in Canadian Aboriginal youth."[93] Organizers further argued that one way VANOC achieved its sustainability/legacy goals was through "physical and capacity-building legacies created from sustainability and/or corporate social responsibility (CSR) initiatives by Games partners and sponsors that leveraged the sustainability platform of the Games to 'scale up' value and impact."[94] Olympic sponsor Coca-Cola developed a CSR campaign associated with the Vancouver Games that complemented VANOC's Aboriginal Licensing and Merchandising Program and, in VANOC's words, "scaled up" the value and impact of this program. The company auctioned off bottles designed by Indigenous artists and donated proceeds to the Aboriginal Youth Legacy Fund, which also received some of the royalties from the Aboriginal Licensing and Merchandising Program.[95] Coca-Cola notably championed Olympic sustainability and legacy values (i.e., support for Indigenous communities in Canada) through a commercial practice while also commodifying symbols of Indigenous peoples' cultures.

According to a report from the IOC's Marketing Department, Indigenous artists used "the Coca-Cola contour bottle as their canvases" in order to create "unique pieces of art in celebration of their heritage and the Vancouver 2010 Olympic Winter Games."[96] The bottles were displayed at various Olympic locations prior to being auctioned. This initiative is an example of a "glocalized" promotional strategy. As Koji Kobayashi writes, "glocalization suggests that dominant cultures are not necessarily eradicating the local. Rather, global ideas, practices, and commodities are localized, leading to the renewal of local space, culture, and identity."[97] Transnational companies develop glocalized promotional strategies by incorporating national symbols into their marketing practices with the goal of developing an association between their brands and local cultures.[98] In the case of Coca-Cola's contour bottles, the company used Indigenous art to achieve this goal. It is not the only transnational company to include representations of Indigenous cultures in a glocalized promotional campaign. In 1999, Adidas designed an ad campaign featuring the *Ka Mate* haka, a Māori dance performed by the New Zealand All Blacks rugby team.[99]

Whereas the Adidas campaign reached audiences through television ads and billboards, Coca-Cola used its own packaging to establish a link between its brand, the Vancouver Olympics, and local Indigenous cultures. There are many layers to the commodification process associated with these specially designed bottles. While they contain the commodity that Coca-Cola sells (i.e., a beverage), the bottles themselves became a commodity, namely, a souvenir of the Vancouver Olympic Games. This souvenir, in turn, was an advertisement for the Coca-Cola brand. Thus, the bottles served three purposes. First, they contained a beverage; second, they were canvases for Indigenous art; third, they promoted the Coca-Cola brand.

The examples of VANOC's Aboriginal Merchandising and Licensing Program and Coca-Cola's "Aboriginal Art Bottle" initiative raise the question: Can profit-driven approaches to tackling social issues lead to meaningful, long-term social change? This question is central to Lyndsay Hayhurst and Courtney Szto's critique of Nike's N7 initiative, in which the company donates funds from the sale of Indigenous-specific Nike products to Indigenous health promotion programs. For Hayhurst and Szto, privatized social justice campaigns can never adequately address systemic social issues. Therefore, activism must be disentangled from corporate-led social justice initiatives.[100] This argument applies equally well to sustainability/legacy initiatives linked to the Vancouver Olympics. Anti-Olympic activists argued that the Vancouver Games would not address issues such as poor living conditions on Indigenous reserves; the high number of missing or murdered Indigenous women; and the overrepresentation of Indigenous peoples in the prison system compared to non-Indigenous peoples.[101] This argument is supported by statistics kept by the federal government. For instance, in 2010/2011 "27% of adults in provincial and territorial custody and 20% of those in federal custody involved Aboriginal people, about seven to eight times higher than the proportion of Aboriginal people (3%) in the adult population as a whole."[102]

Coca-Cola's "Aboriginal Art Bottle" initiative and VANOC's Aboriginal Licensing and Merchandising Program also reveal a limitation of privatized social justice campaigns not identified by Hayhurst and Szto. Specifically, these initiatives complement practices, such as the provincial government's development of the New Relationship, that celebrate contemporary Indigenous cultures while failing to acknowledge Canada's identity as a Settler colonial country. Indeed, the Vancouver Olympics were held on land that Indigenous peoples never ceded to the Crown through the signing of treaties. Although this reality went unacknowledged in the Vancouver Games, members of the activist group the Olympic Resistance Network (ORN) made it impossible to completely ignore through their popularization of the phrase "No Olympics on

Stolen Native Land." According to one anti-Olympic publication, the phrase "emphasizes the history of colonization in the province. It also reveals the fact that government and corporations are involved in theft (of land & resources), and therefore lack moral and legal authority to govern or conduct business."[103] Supporters of the "No Olympics on Stolen Native Land" campaign resisted the disavowal of Settler colonialism that many Olympic-related representational and commercial practices relied on for success. Christine O'Bonsawin, for instance, identifies how supporters "argued there was a pressing political reality in British Columbia *that could not be forgotten* in both the organizing and hosting of the 2010 Games, which was that the Games were being hosted on unceded and non-surrendered indigenous territories, or what some people considered to be stolen Native lands."[104]

* * *

VANOC's selection of an Inukshuk design for the Vancouver Games' emblem, discussed earlier in this chapter, is also significant in relation to the ideas activists promoted through their "No Olympics on Stolen Native Land" campaign. Specifically, the organizing committee continued the historical Settler practice of using symbols of Indigenous peoples' cultures to define a nation that was built on Indigenous land. Rivera MacGregor chose the emblem's colour scheme to symbolize various elements of the Canadian landscape: green for forests, blue for oceans, red for sunsets, and yellow for wheat fields. She called the emblem Ilanaaq, the Inuktitut word for "friend," and this emphasis on friendship was a key element of national identity that Olympic organizers sought to convey through the emblem.[105] A press release describes Ilanaaq as a "uniquely Canadian symbol of friendship, hospitality, strength, teamwork and the vast Canadian landscape." It continues by depicting the emblem as a "contemporary interpretation of the traditional Inukshuk, a stone sculpture used by Canada's Inuit people as directional landmarks across the northern Canadian lands of snow and ice. Over time, the Inukshuk has become a representation of hope, friendship and an external expression of the hospitality of a nation that warmly welcomes the people of the world with open arms."[106]

This statement affiliates positive qualities like hospitality and friendship with Canadian identity while also appearing to honour Inuit culture.

However, the phrase "*Canada's* Inuit people" exposes a Settler mentality of possession over Indigenous peoples that recalls statements made by organizers of previous Canadian-hosted Olympic and Commonwealth Games. Moreover, Norman Hallendy, an expert on Inuit stone configurations, suggested that a more accurate word to describe the logo would be "innunguaq." A *Globe and Mail* article paraphrases Hallendy, noting, "an *inukshuk* is a collection of stones assembled by the northern Inuit to serve as navigational beacons, and can take many shapes. Similar stone figures that resemble humans are called *innunguaq*."[107] The emblem attracted criticism from Indigenous leaders including Grand Chief Edward John of the First Nations Summit and Chief Stewart Philip, president of the Union of BC Indian Chiefs, for featuring the symbol of an Indigenous group located outside the host province.[108] Philip commented, "the first nations community at large is disappointed with the selection. The decision makers have decided not to reflect the first nations and the Pacific region in the design of the logo."[109] O'Bonsawin argues that VANOC adopted "a foreign symbol that has proven to be both geographically irrelevant and culturally offensive to the FHFN as well as the Inuit populations of Canada's northern regions."[110]

Whereas some Indigenous leaders argued that the Ilanaaq design was geographically inappropriate, Sḵwx̱wú7mesh (Squamish) First Nation chief Gibby Jacob defended VANOC's selection of the emblem design by suggesting it was intended to represent the host nation.[111] Similarly, an article published in the *Globe and Mail* argued, "as with the maple leaf, although the maple tree is only native to certain regions of Canada and cannot grow in others, the inuksuit may belong first and foremost to the Inuit but they have become a symbol for Canada."[112] The article represents the emblem as a synecdoche, part of something (i.e., a cultural symbol within Canada) that stands in for the entire thing (i.e., all of Canada).

This way of representing Canada is not new. Leanne Stuart Pupchek convincingly shows that "in many contexts, Inuit imagery has become a synecdoche, symbolic part-for-the-whole, of Canadian identity."[113] The market for Inuit art began thriving in the 1930s when the Women's Art Association of Montreal began selling arts and crafts created by Inuit artists. An artist and teacher named James Houston procured many of these items on his visits to Inukjuak (previously Port Harrison), located on the Ungava Peninsula of northern Quebec. The federal government began paying Houston to introduce art created by Inuit artists to a mass audience in 1949, and these works came to represent Canadian identity. According to Pupchek, Inuit art was uniquely positioned to serve this purpose because the federal government had criminalized much of the art produced by First Nations (including those living in the Northwest Coast of Canada). However, Inuit art production was legal.[114]

The Inukshuk has also been featured in popular media representations of Canadian identity. A 1994 "Heritage Minutes" video produced by Historica Canada and aired on the Canadian Broadcasting Corporation shows a Royal Canadian Mounted Police officer watching an Inuit family construct an Inukshuk. It ends with a boy translating a statement his mother makes in Inuktitut to the officer: "Now the people will know we were here."[115] By showing the family literally and figuratively fading into the background, the video depicts Indigenous peoples as part of the nation's past rather than its present or future.[116] Put another way, the Inukshuk featured in the video represented an Indigenous culture that was fading into a vanishing past. By contrast, the Inukshuk that appears on the Vancouver emblem represents a version of Canada that honours contemporary Inuit culture. In other words, it symbolizes Canadian identity but also retains its association with Inuit culture.

VANOC's depiction of the Ilanaaq emblem as a representation of Canadian culture both recognizes and disavows the nation's Settler colonial history. Because it contains a symbol of Inuit culture, the emblem design makes it impossible to completely ignore the fact that Settlers established a nation on Indigenous land and subsequently used Indigenous iconography to define this nation. Yet, the emblem also gives the appearance that this history has no bearing on contemporary Canadian society, where Indigenous peoples' cultures appear to be thriving. By depicting Canadian society in this way, the logo helped popularize a way of conceptualizing the nation that Prime Minister Harper promoted through his 2008 apology to Indian residential school students and their families and communities.

The apology began by depicting residential schools as "a sad chapter in our history" and concluded by expressing a commitment to improve relations between Indigenous peoples and Settler Canadians.[117] It followed a narrative of progress that problematically relegated injustices faced by Indigenous peoples to the past and, in doing so, failed to place residential schools within the Settler colonial context in which they operated.[118] Harper's apology did not include the word "colonialism," an absence that Jennifer Henderson and Pauline Wakeham argue enabled "a strategic isolation and containment of residential schools as a discrete historical problem of educational malpractice rather than one devastating prong of an overarching and multifaceted system of colonial oppression that persists in the present."[119] In 2009, one year after Harper delivered his official apology, he told a reporter that Canada has "no history of colonialism."[120] The ORN used the Vancouver Olympics as an opportunity to refute this statement. Activists distributed flyers that reprinted the prime minister's quote and asserted that the "Olympics are occurring on unceded & unsurrendered Indigenous lands" and asked rhetorically, "Really, no colonial history?"[121]

Activists also used the Vancouver Olympics as an opportunity to expose the fact that Harper's apology marked the beginning of a reconciliation process that is far from complete. Stella August published an article in a special anti-Olympic issue of the *Dominion* discussing this topic. August is part of the Downtown Eastside Power of Women Group, whose members include "women from all walks of life who are working poor, homeless or on social assistance" and describe themselves as living "in extreme poverty."[122] She is also a residential school survivor who, in her words, is "living proof of the residential school era. I was separated from my parents, my family and my culture. I lost my language. I was beaten and abused severely in residential school."[123] August writes that she, like many others, is "not satisfied with last year's formal apology from the federal government. The apology was supposed to start a new relationship with Indigenous peoples, one based on respect. But the 2010 Olympic Games represents just one of the many examples of the continuation of the same kind of colonial relationship: we are not consulted, are forcibly displaced, and endure increasing poverty for their benefit. This is not the start of a new relationship."[124]

August is not alone in her criticism. The TRC's 2015 final report found that "Aboriginal leaders identified a post-apology gap between the aspirational language of Canada's apology and Aboriginal peoples' continuing realities."[125] According to the report, "The promise of reconciliation, which seemed so imminent back in 2008 when the prime minister, on behalf of all Canadians, apologized to Survivors, has faded."[126] Understood in this context, the Ilanaaq emblem and related commodities hold together contradictory ideas about the nation. The emblem represents an idealized version of Canadian society that is untroubled by the nation's Settler colonial past, while at the same time it represents the reality that Canada continues to operate according to Settler colonial policies and practices that make reconciliation between Indigenous peoples and Settler Canadians impossible.

Several games-related cultural practices complemented the ideas about the nation represented by Ilanaaq by celebrating Canada's progressive values without acknowledging, in Henderson and Wakeham's words, the "overarching and multifaceted system of colonial oppression that persists in the present."[127] For instance, "For the first time ever at an Olympics, Pride Houses, where gay and lesbian supporters watched and celebrated these events, were set up in Vancouver."[128] Heather Sykes argues that discourses celebrating Indigenous and Two-Spirit peoples' participation in Pride House events were highly problematic. Specifically, they made it possible for participants to acknowledge Indigenous peoples' contributions to the initiative without confronting the Indigenous rights issues that anti-Olympic activists publicized through the games.[129] Moreover, one Pride House made legal support services available for people wishing to claim asylum in Canada based on their sexual orientation, gender identity, or HIV status. Although supporters of this initiative discussed it in patriotic terms and suggested it was an example of the inclusive values that underpin Canadian society, the legal services offered by the Pride House were based on Settlers' conceptualization of Canadian citizenship and helped to promote what Sykes characterizes as "a politics of imperialist settler homonationalism – that ignored and avoided indigenous notions of citizenship, nationhood and sovereignty."[130]

A cultural display included in the Vancouver opening ceremony called the "Landscape of a Dream" conveyed the idea that Canada has moved beyond the state's past mistreatment of Indigenous peoples. Consequently, it perpetuated a message conveyed through Harper's apology. In her writing on the apology, Eva Mackey argues, "In part through a choreographed official ritual of regret, over two hundred years of colonial violence, momentarily brought to the foreground through the apology process, become contained in the past so that the nation may move forward into a unified future."[131] The "Landscape of a Dream" sequence helped convey the idea that this unified future had arrived. Like Harper's apology, it was haunted by the fact that Canada remains a Settler colonial country.

VANOC decided that the domestic audience for the opening ceremony was its most important audience, reasoning that if the ceremony engaged Canadians from across the country, they would be more likely to support the games.[132] Twenty-three million Canadians, or 78 per cent of the country's total population, watched the opening ceremony.[133] The "Landscape of a Dream" sequence comes after the FHFN officially welcome spectators and visitors, and Indigenous dancers perform on stage. The sequence begins by celebrating the landscape of northern Canada. Actors representing Indigenous peoples and European Settlers appear on stage and wave to each other. They appear to be meeting for the first time and their exchange seems friendly. The Vancouver Olympic opening ceremony program reveals that organizers intended to represent early encounters between Indigenous peoples and European Settlers in this performance. The program includes the following description of the "Landscape of a Dream" sequence set in northern Canada: as a multicultural country, Canada "is a dynamic work-in-progress, rooted in the Aboriginal traditions of hospitality that helped the first Europeans survive their harsh and beautiful new home."[134]

The encounters between Indigenous peoples and European Settlers dramatized in the opening ceremony does not end happily. As they wave to each other, the ice upon which they are standing breaks apart. Individuals are separated from one another and the gap between them widens as the stadium grows dark. The ice breaking and darkness are highly symbolic features of this dramatization. I interpret them as representations of the following idea: Canada experienced a *dark period* in its past when harmonious relations between Indigenous peoples and Settler Canadians *broke down*. Coming after the FHFN welcome and followed by an upbeat sequence celebrating the beauty of the Canadian landscape, the overall impression given by the opening ceremony is that relations between Indigenous peoples and Settler Canadians are no longer fractured.[135]

This reading differs from Nathan Kalman-Lamb's interpretation of the opening ceremony, which he argues celebrated "hegemonic whiteness."[136] He writes, "The early emphasis on Indigeneity" in the ceremony "hammers home the multicultural legitimacy of Canadian national identity and gestures to the cultural roots of the nation. Yet this is not the nation that is actually being celebrated. As the ceremonies progress, viewers come to see that modern, athletic Canada is profoundly white."[137]

Kalman-Lamb's interrogation of whiteness in the opening ceremony is valuable. However, I am not entirely convinced by his argument that "the extreme emphasis on Indigenous origins at the ceremonies ... does not threaten the hegemony of whiteness because of the widely held – and mistaken – notion that Indigenous peoples were eradicated during the nation's colonial history and no longer have a significant place in discussions of the present moment."[138] I argue instead that the FHFN's welcome in the ceremony gave the appearance that Settler Canadians honour Indigenous peoples' cultures and traditions. The ceremony consigns the mistrust and discord between Indigenous peoples and Settler Canadians, rather than Indigenous peoples themselves, to the past. This interpretation aligns with Jennifer Adese's argument that the "perception of reconciliation gleaned from the ceremony ... allows for the nation to continue denying the ongoing and real impacts of colonialism on Indigenous peoples' lives."[139]

This interpretation of the opening ceremony also extends Glen Coulthard's critique of Harper's 2008 apology to residential school survivors. Coulthard creatively re-frames the words Harper used, writing, "'Forgiveness' and 'reconciliation' are posited as a fundamental step in transcending the painful 'legacy' that has hampered our collective efforts to '*move on*'; they are necessary to 'begin anew' so that Indigenous peoples can start to build 'new partnerships' together with non-Indigenous peoples on what is now unapologetically declared to be 'our land.'"[140] The Vancouver Olympics gives the impression that Canadians had successfully moved on from the nation's painful past. After the dramatization set in northern Canada, the "Landscape of a Dream" sequence shows salmon swimming in the Pacific Ocean and transforming into Northwest Pacific coastal totem poles; a ballet dance in a Canadian forest; a display of fiddling traditions amidst a backdrop of "the spectacular colours of a Canadian fall"; an aerial ballet performance above a wheat field; and skiers and snowboarders descending snowy mountains.[141] The sequence exposes viewers to the same elements of the Canadian landscape represented in the Vancouver Games' emblem through its colours, thus creating a connection between representations of the nation found in the emblem and the opening ceremony. Both representations celebrate, in Coulthard's words, features of what Settlers "now unapologetically declared to be 'our land.'"[142]

Mascots and Education Resources

Like the "Landscape of a Dream" sequence in the Vancouver Olympic opening ceremony, the design of the games' mascots helped convey the message that Canada is a progressive country that honours Indigenous peoples' cultures. VANOC identified young people aged three to fifteen as the mascots' target market. The committee's focus on this demographic is hardly surprising considering Olympic organizers use mascots to attract youth audiences to the Olympics and expose them to the movement's values, as well as the pleasures of consuming merchandise related to the games. In addition, mascots typically represent the identity of the Olympic host city and/or nation.[143] These three priorities are evident in VANOC's requirements for the games' mascots: organizers wanted them to "reflect considerations around inclusivity – i.e., gender, ethnicity, sustainability, etc." and "convey a distinctly Canadian character."[144] In addition, the design had to be easily reproduceable in commodity form: it should "allow for scalability (can it be produced on a lapel pin?)" and "address issues of mass production in various materials and forms (simplicity is key)."[145]

Vicki Wong and Michael Murphy, who own the company Meomi Design, used "local Aboriginal mythological creatures" as their inspiration for the mascots of the 2010 Winter Olympic and Paralympic Games.[146] Wong and Murphy designed a sea bear (part killer whale, part Kermode bear) named Miga and a sasquatch named Quatchi as the Olympic mascots (figure 5.3). They designed an animal spirit named Sumi as the Paralympic mascot and added a "special 'sidekick' character," a marmot named Mukmuk, which appeared with the other mascots in print and online.[147]

The mascots often made public appearances together, and they collectively helped to create an association between the games and Pacific Northwest Coast Indigenous cultures. By the time Vancouver bid to host the 2010 Winter Games, the IOC had begun requiring that cities include plans to host both the Olympics and Paralympics in their proposals.[148] The 1976 Summer Olympic and Paralympic games were held in different cities: Montreal (Olympics) and Toronto (Paralympics). The 1988 Winter Olympic and Paralympic games were held on different continents: Calgary, Canada (Olympics) and Innsbruck,

5.3 Miga and Quatchi, mascots of the 2010 Vancouver Olympics; Sumi, mascot of the 2010 Vancouver Paralympics; Mukmuk, mascot sidekick.

Austria (Paralympics). The 2010 Winter Paralympic Games were held in Vancouver shortly after the 2010 Winter Olympics ended, and facilities in the host city were used for both events. Thus, unlike the mascots for previous Canadian Olympic Games, those for the Vancouver Olympics and Paralympics were complementary.

A bilingual picture book called *Miga, Quatchi and/et Sumi: The Story of the Vancouver 2010 Mascots/L'Histoire des Mascottes de Vancouver* tells the story of how the creatures meet and eventually become the Olympic and Paralympic mascots. The narrative exposes readers to features of Northwest Coast Indigenous cultures reflected in Wong and Murphy's designs. The book notes that Miga's identity as a sea bear was "inspired by the legends of the Pacific Northwest First Nations, tales of orca whales that transform into bears when they arrive on land"; orcas are "honoured in the art and stories of West Coast First Nations, as travellers and guardians of the sea."[149] It describes Quatchi as a sasquatch, "a popular figure in local native legends of the Pacific West Coast. The sasquatch reminds us of the mystery and wonder that exist in the natural world."[150] Sumi, for his part, "lives in the mountains of British Columbia ... He wears the hat of the orca whale, flies with the wings of the mighty thunderbird and runs on the strong furry legs of the black bear. Sumi's name comes from the Salish word 'Sumesh' which means 'guardian spirit.'"[151]

Some individuals argued that VANOC's selection of Quatchi, Sumi, and Miga as the Olympic and Paralympic mascots was inappropriate. They criticized the organizing committee for "failing to consult with indigenous people about its use of indigenous symbols [in the mascot designs] and for exploiting indigenous symbols for self-promotion and economic gain."[152] VANOC and Olympic licensees certainly profited from the sale of Miga, Quatchi, and Sumi commodities, which included plush toys, pins, postage stamps, coins, key chains, pillows, backpacks, towels, slippers, bathrobes, and picture frames. Some of these commodities reinforced the mascots' link to Pacific Northwest Coast Indigenous cultures by showing the mascots stacked on top of one another, with Quatchi (the largest mascot) at the bottom and Sumi (the smallest mascot) at the top, to form a structure resembling a totem pole. The cover of the book *Miga, Quatchi and/et Sumi*, a pin, and a picture frame all show the mascots in this configuration.[153]

Miga, Quatchi and/et Sumi became a national bestseller and McDonald's Happy Meals included special mascot toys for a limited time.[154] Consumers bought more than 200,000 mascot-related commodities in 2007, the first year they were unveiled.[155] Journalist Ken MacQueen made a witty remark about the mascots' commercial appeal when he asked a fellow journalist, "Aren't they the cutest little profit centres you ever saw?"[156] VANOC designed a mascot portal that offered young people entertaining and interactive opportunities to learn about Miga, Quatchi, Sumi, and Mukmuk. For example, visitors could take a quiz titled "Which mascot are you like?" and play a game called "Quatchi's Shootout Shutout," where players helped Quatchi block Miga's and Sumi's slapshots. The portal received more than 1.8 million page views in its first year of operation and directed visitors to a VANOC website selling mascot commodities.[157] In addition, a married couple created a blog called "Quatchi Watch" which included news about the mascot, documented Quatchi's public appearances, and listed Quatchi merchandise available for purchase.[158] Glenn Street, president of the manufacturing company Street Characters Inc., observed that VANOC "has done a great job of making the character desirable. Every kid at school has a Quatchi backpack, a keychain, something."[159]

Rather than being turned off by VANOC's aggressive marketing of Miga, Quatchi and Sumi, some members of the public campaigned to bring Mukmuk into the same heavily commercialized realm as the official Olympic and Paralympic mascots. Although VANOC originally designed Mukmuk as a "mascot sidekick" who appeared only in virtual spaces and in print, Jeff Lee of the *Vancouver Sun* started a "Free Mukmuk" campaign. He argued that Mukmuk should be a full-fledged mascot and complained that the creature was not available in commodity form: "While his friends have their images plastered on everything from clothing to pins, and are created in effigy by the thousands, little Mukmuk doesn't get his face on so much as a key chain fob."[160]

Vancouver Sun readers rallied behind the "free Mukmuk" campaign. The newspaper received so many letters of support that it concluded, although fans "love the three official [Vancouver Olympic and Paralympic] mascots, they identify more with Mukmuk as a very real Canadian icon."[161] A pair of siblings aged five and nine wrote a letter to the newspaper arguing that Mukmuk should be freed "from siber jail" and commented that he must be very lonely.[162] About forty individuals organized a rally for Mukmuk, "demanding equal 2010 Games mascot status for the fuzzy furball."[163] VANOC did not turn the marmot into a full-fledged mascot, but it released a line of Mukmuk commodities including stuffed animals, t-shirts, hats, and pins in November 2008. VANOC's director of licensing and merchandising denied that the organizing committee had always planned to release a Mukmuk line of products just in time for the holiday season.[164] VANOC's original intentions notwithstanding, the organizing committee capitalized on the unexpected popularity of the "mascot sidekick" by timing the release of Mukmuk products to coincide with the heaviest gift-giving time of the year.

* * *

The Vancouver Olympic and Paralympic mascots appear alongside Mukmuk in an education resource the Canadian Olympic Committee (COC) produced for the games called "Brand Development and the

Vancouver 2010 Olympic Games." The COC included this resource in its Canadian Olympic Schools Program, an education initiative sponsored by RBC. The "Brand Development" case study describes Miga, Quatchi, Sumi, and Mukmuk as "the face of the 2010 Games for children around the world. Aside from plush toys, their images were found on a variety of merchandise ranging from pins to clothing. The mascots comprised a large portion of VANOC's merchandise sales. They reinforced Vancouver's warm, welcoming and safe qualities, while extending the brand to children around the world."[165] This statement teaches young people that the mascots represent the Vancouver Olympic brand while also providing a lucrative source of merchandising revenue for the organizing committee.

An activity included in the "Brand Development" resource emphasizes the fact that the mascots represent Indigenous cultures. Students are instructed to research the Olympic Winter Games' mascots and present an argument in favour of or against the following statement: "The mascots for the Vancouver 2010 Olympic Winter Games were a playful representation of Canada and its Aboriginal peoples' mythology."[166] Students could have argued in favour by referencing the fact that the mascots are creatures found in Pacific Northwest Indigenous legends; this idea was made explicit in texts about the mascots, such as the *Miga, Quatchi and/et Sumi* picture book. On the other hand, students could have argued against the statement by referencing an argument made by critics of the mascot, namely, that VANOC exploited Indigenous symbols by selecting Wong and Murphy's mascot design.[167]

It is also possible that students or teachers criticized the way the question was phrased by pointing out that it describes Indigenous cultures as belonging to Canada (i.e., the mascots "were a playful representation of *Canada and its* Aboriginal peoples' mythology"). The language of possession used in the question draws attention to an unacknowledged truth about the mascots' symbolic meaning. Specifically, their link to Pacific Northwest Indigenous cultures cannot be entirely separated from the fact that the federal government outlawed cultural practices of Indigenous peoples in this region in the nineteenth century.

Anti-Potlatch laws contributed to the federal government's efforts to assimilate Indigenous peoples into Settler society. Christian missionaries and Department of Indian Affairs officers argued that Indigenous peoples' participation in the Potlatch hindered efforts to integrate them into Settler society and convert them to Christianity.[168] Douglas Cole and Ira Chaikin argue, "Only the repression of native languages among Indian schoolchildren can compete with the Potlatch law as an example of the assault on indigenous culture."[169] Understood in this way, Wong and Murphy took inspiration for their design of the Vancouver Olympic and Paralympic mascots from Indigenous cultures whose practices the Canadian state criminalized through anti-Potlatch laws. Moreover, these mascots represent an event that was held on what the ORN characterized as "stolen land" that Indigenous peoples never surrendered to the Crown through a treaty.

The history and persistence of Settler colonialism in Canada haunted the information about the Vancouver Olympic and Paralympic mascots contained in the "Brand Development" resource. It also haunted educational resources that VANOC produced in partnership with the government of Canada and FHFN. The committee created a *Find Your Passion in Sport* poster series featuring Travis Jones, a Métis curler from BC; Sammy Kent, a First Nations alpine skier from Yukon; and Leah Sulyma, an Inuit ice hockey player from the Northwest Territories.[170] The federal government praised the series, stating that it offered "a unique opportunity to enhance awareness among Canadians of the sporting achievements of Aboriginal youth in Canada and to inspire young people through the power of sport."[171] VANOC collaborated with the BC Ministry of Education and Indigenous experts to create Vancouver 2010 Aboriginal Education Resources (AER), which included "lesson starters" based on the poster series.

One lesson starter called "When Aboriginal Athletes Meet the Press" was intended for middle school students (those in grades four to seven). It instructs them to brainstorm questions for Jones, Kent, and Sulyma and work in pairs to interview one another, alternatively playing the role of a journalist and one of the athletes. One of the learning outcomes listed in the lesson starter is: "knowledge and appreciation of the athlete's Aboriginal community and culture."[172] A lesson starter intended for high school students called "Understanding Traditional and Modern Plant Uses" also includes an activity intended to teach students about Indigenous peoples' cultures. It begins by instructing students to describe features of the natural environment included in the *Find Your Passion in Sport* poster series. Students should then "participate in a field trip to a local Aboriginal education/cultural centre, ecology centre or other local ecosystem" to learn about local plants and "how the selected plants have been used traditionally in the local Aboriginal culture(s)."[173] Like the education resource "AA en mas" created for the Victoria Commonwealth Games (discussed in chapter 4), these lessons expose young people to Indigenous peoples' perspectives and cultures. However, they fall short of the standard set by the "AA en mas" resource because they do not directly address the topic of Settler colonialism in Canada.

Conclusion

Symbols of Indigenous peoples' cultures appeared in representations of the nation featured in the 2010 Vancouver Olympics to an unprecedented degree compared to previous Olympic and Commonwealth Games hosted in Canada. Indigenous peoples participated in the opening ceremony and torch relay; commodities featuring Indigenous art and iconography were sold during the games; the Vancouver Olympic emblem and mascots included symbols of Indigenous cultures; and education resources taught young people about Indigenous athletes. The FHFN officially partnered with VANOC, and Indigenous peoples retained significant control over representations of their cultures. Moreover, Indigenous artists and communities profited from the sale of commodities featuring symbols of their cultures. They were not the only group to benefit from these representational and commercial practices. VANOC, the IOC, and Olympic sponsors used Indigenous-related sustainability/legacy initiatives to enhance the value of their brands. The BC government, meanwhile, strategically used the FHFN's involvement in the 2010 Games to advance the goals of the New Relationship.

The potential for Indigenous peoples to create meaningful social change through their involvement in the games was constrained, however, by a narrative about Canada that found expression in games-related cultural and commercial practices. Notably, this narrative aligned with, and built on, ideas about the nation that politicians had recently promoted through government-led reconciliation practices. Specifically, Vancouver Olympic organizers and sponsors gave the impression that Canada was a progressive country that honours and celebrates Indigenous peoples' cultures, and that conflicts between Indigenous peoples and

Settlers were a thing of the past. However, anti-Olympic activists used the Vancouver Olympics to expose truths about the history and persistence of Settler colonialism in Canada that were unacknowledged during the games. In doing so, they complicated the version of national identity and history circulating through the 2010 Winter Games and demonstrated that reconciliation between Indigenous peoples and Settlers is far from complete. Commodities sold through the games, ranging from Ilanaaq key chains to Miga, Quatchi, and Sumi stuffed animals, represent a nation that is haunted by these unacknowledged truths.

Conclusion

Red Mitten Nationalism and a History That Is Still Alive

Many Canadians turned their hands into miniature flags in advance of the 2010 Vancouver Olympics by wearing red mittens decorated with white maple leaves on the palms, specially designed for the games by the Hudson's Bay Company (HBC) (figure 6.1). As Clare Ogilvie observed in the *Vancouver Province* a few months before the games began, "It's hard to walk down the streets of Vancouver or Whistler these days and not see someone wearing a pair of woolly red Olympic mittens."[1] A few decades earlier, when Montreal hosted the 1976 Summer Olympics, few Canadians who attended the games brought flags to wave. In contrast, Canadians wore a national symbol, the maple leaf, on their bodies in the lead-up to the 2010 Winter Games.

In this concluding chapter, I analyze the symbolic significance of the HBC mittens and, more broadly, the company's sponsorship of the Vancouver Olympics. The mittens hold together the most complex and multidimensional symbolic meanings of any fetish object discussed in this book. The fusion of nationalism and commercialism in the Canadian-hosted Olympics reached a new level of sophistication and political significance through the promotion, circulation, and consumption of the mittens. I conclude this chapter – and the book as a whole – by situating the mittens within the broader context of the fusion of nationalism and commercialism in all the Canadian-hosted Olympic and Commonwealth games. I emphasize, as I have throughout this book, that commodities that symbolize the nation both represent and obscure Canada's identity as a Settler colonial nation.

6.1 Red mittens produced by the Hudson's Bay Company for the 2010 Vancouver Olympics.

Branded Nationalism and Commodity Nationalism in the Vancouver Olympics

HBC executives did not expect the company's red mittens to become an iconic commodity associated with the Vancouver Olympics. In fact, the company initially designed plain white gloves for the torch bearers to wear, to complement the white, blue, and green colour scheme VANOC had chosen for the games. However, Jeffrey Sherman, who became HBC president and CEO in 2008, decided to replace the white gloves with the now iconic red mittens. He wanted to give the torch bearers' outfits "something a little extra, something a little more distinctly Canadian, something that would give it a little colour pop."[2] For Sherman, the company's Vancouver Olympic clothing line displayed "a sense of history of what it means to be Canadian."[3] HBC vice-president of Olympics Mark Kinnin echoed this sentiment, remarking, "There's a great story around Canada and the history of Canada and the team and how we're getting ready for the Vancouver Games … Can we commercialize that? Absolutely, because sports is a business."[4]

These statements reveal that HBC intentionally designed the red mittens and other Olympic merchandise to represent national identity, and these objects helped the company create a link between its sponsorship of the Vancouver Games and its contribution to Canadian nation-building. HBC began establishing this association the moment it signed on as a domestic Olympic sponsor in 2005. George Heller, who preceded Sherman as president and CEO of HBC, made the following statement in a press release announcing HBC's partnership with VANOC: "Today, Hbc is continuing our 335 year long tradition of supporting Canadian priorities and interests … We are delighted to play our part in making the Vancouver 2010 Games a truly pan-Canadian celebration through our stores located in virtually every Canadian community."[5]

Heller had previously served as CEO of the Victoria Commonwealth Games Society, and a 2014 *Times Colonist* article claimed this experience inspired him to seek out sponsorship opportunities associated with the 2010 Winter Games: "Because of his Victoria experience, Heller became a big advocate for Canadian amateur athletes. Roots Olympic gear was all the rage, but you just knew when that deal was up, Heller would make it a priority for the Bay to land the rights to Canadian Olympic team clothing."[6] The company chose an opportune time to secure these rights. A 2005 Ipsos-Reid survey reported that seven in ten Canadians interviewed said they would feel better about an organization if they knew that it had sponsored the 2010 Games.[7]

One year prior to the 2010 Winter Olympics, HBC executives began emphasizing the company's history (it was founded in 1670) by using its full name, original crest, and trademark "point blanket" pattern in promotional material.[8] That same year, an ad for HBC's Olympic clothing line, which draws attention to the company's contributions to early nation-building activities in Canada, began airing on television. Titled "We Were Made for This," the ad shows Europeans arriving by boat to Canada for the first time and glorifies Settlers' ability to survive the harsh conditions. The narrator says, "We arrived 340 years ago to a land of rock, ice, and snow. We outfitted a nation of pioneers, explorers, and dreamers. We are the skiers, we are the sledders. We didn't just survive the elements. Together, we thrived in them."[9] This description of Canada as a nation of "pioneers, explorers, and dreamers" celebrates the first Europeans who settled in Canada, characterizing them as adventurous and hardy. It also depicts HBC's support of these Settlers as essential to Canada's development as a nation.

The ad does not acknowledge that Canada is a Settler colonial nation that was founded on Indigenous peoples' land, and it targets Settler Canadian viewers to the exclusion of Indigenous peoples by using the pronoun "we" (i.e., "*we* arrived 340 years ago"; "*we* are the skiers, *we* are the sledders"). This language encourages Settlers to identify with the history of European settlement in Canada without recognizing that Indigenous peoples lived in the country long before Europeans arrived. The ad also fails to recognize that Indigenous peoples' labour, knowledge, and skills were essential to HBC's success in the fur trade industry.

Audience response to the ad was mixed. Some individuals who viewed the ad on YouTube left admiring messages on the comment wall, such as "hbc is the best forever"; "i love this commercial"; and, simply, "EPIC!" Others criticized the version of history promoted in the ad. One person criticized it for excluding Indigenous peoples from its depiction of Canadian history: "no aboriginals or anything. Mhm. Completely uninhabited land." Another viewer described early European Settlers as "people who sought to assimilate First Nations people by placing them in residential schools where they were abused in every way possible." Someone defended the company's involvement in Canadian history by writing, "The Hudson's Bay company helped bridge relations with European settlers and the native population."

One commentator argued that the ad was "ironic" because it promoted "HBC's line of knockoff Cowichan sweaters originating from the aboriginal peoples of Vancouver Island."[10] Indeed, the ad closes with a model wearing an imitation of the knitted sweaters made by members of the Cowichan First Nation who live on Vancouver Island. HBC officials originally considered hiring Cowichan knitters, who pass on knitting skills from generation to generation, to produce the sweaters. However, the company ultimately concluded that the knitters would not be able to meet its production needs on time. Instead, HBC sold a product with a contemporary design that, in the company's words, "nods towards this icon of Canadian fashion."[11] Members of the Cowichan First Nation were unhappy with decision and the CEO of the FHFN raised the issue with VANOC. The organizing committee ultimately agreed to allow Cowichan knitters to sell their sweaters in the First Nations Pavilion and Olympic Superstore.[12]

A comparison between the "We Were Made for This" ad and the print ads HBC published in the *Edmonton Journal* in the lead-up to the 1978 Commonwealth Games, discussed in chapter 2, is instructive.

Both the television ad and print ads celebrate HBC's involvement in early Canadian nation-building enterprises, with one ad from 1978 boasting, "Our unique cloth bears the Hudson's Bay Seal of Quality, a standard for the world, and is marked with the lines that used to indicate the number of beaver skins required in trade for a blanket. If you're thinking of Canadian history … it's hard not to think of the Bay!"[13] However, HBC's 2009 television ad circulated in a different commercial environment. Specifically, organizers and sponsors of the 2010 Vancouver Olympics worked collaboratively to advance their priorities. HBC supported the organizing committee's goal of engaging Canadians across the country in the games. Vancouver Olympic organizers, for their part, created an ideal environment for companies like HBC to link their brand identity to national identity and pride.

VANOC endeavoured to "use the power of the Games to unite a country, to instill national pride."[14] It boasted that it "attained unprecedented domestic sponsorship levels – success that can be directly attributed to Canada's Games and its ability to leverage funding. This Canadian approach began early and extended to VANOC's domestic sponsorship program … By engaging companies from one end of the country to the other, all Canadians would be touched by the Games through these sponsors."[15] HBC, for its part, benefited from VANOC's efforts to depict corporate sponsorship of the Vancouver Olympics as a nationally significant practice in which only select companies could participate. VANOC CEO John Furlong publicly criticized a contest organized by Hockey Canada and Esso to send fans to the 2006 Torino Winter Olympics to "cheer on Canada." Furlong accused Esso of engaging in ambush marketing, which is the unauthorized use of Olympic-related material for promotional or marketing purposes. He also claimed that the company risked weakening the commercial value of the Vancouver Games: "How can we credibly appeal to Canadian companies to support our Games, our athletes and our nation-building ambitions if their competitors can either – deliberately or accidentally – undermine those investments?"[16] Furlong's comments show that VANOC officials protected a distinctively Canadian privilege associated with sponsoring the Vancouver Olympics, namely, appearing to contribute to a national cause.

* * *

The red mittens HBC produced for the Vancouver Olympics were so popular that public demand for them outpaced supply. Stores began stocking the items in October 2009 and sold out of the first shipment in less than a month. HBC set a target of selling one million pairs of mittens by the time the games ended in February 2010 but ended up selling more than three times that number.[17] Consumers mobbed stores when new shipments of the mittens arrived and one journalist compared consumers' rush to buy the objects to a "feeding frenzy."[18] The director of HBC's downtown Vancouver store, which housed the 2010 Olympic Superstore, had never before seen consumers act this way. Dana Hall said, "We don't even get time to take the mittens out of the box. People start swooping and surrounding them like piranhas."[19] When consumers could not find mittens in stores, they turned to eBay, where the $10 mittens were listed as high as $200.[20] HBC released the garments one year after the 2008 economic crisis, when many Canadians were struggling financially. A *Globe and Mail* article paraphrased Tod Hirsch, senior economist at ATB Financial, commenting that the mittens, "with their modest cost, are a perfectly priced item for tough times in the runup to Christmas."[21]

Consumers wanted to buy the mittens HBC designed for the Vancouver 2010 Paralympic torch relay even though they were not for sale. These mittens are identical to the ones worn by Vancouver Olympic torchbearers except they feature the Paralympic emblem, a stylized three-toned landscape representing forests, mountains, and the sky. BC cabinet minister Mary McNeil received a pair of the mittens when she ran as a torch bearer in the Paralympic torch relay, and she began wearing them out in public. McNeil told a journalist that people approached her asking where they could buy a pair: "I'm encouraging them [HBC] to produce them, because I think they're great."[22]

The 2010 Olympic Superstore opened in Vancouver in October 2009 and served over 10,000 customers every day for the duration of the games. HBC extended store hours to accommodate the high volume of shoppers, and it became an extension of public spaces, like sports arenas, where individuals came together to collectively share in the emotional experience of attending the games.[23] Journalist James Keller observed that HBC's downtown Vancouver store "has become an Olympic attraction in its own right, with thousands of locals and tourists flocking in for a chance to buy sweaters, scarves and the now-iconic red mittens."[24] He quotes Hall saying that shopping at the store "is definitely an experience – you can talk about it all you want, but until you get here, that's when you really feel it, this buzz, this excitement, there's people from all over the world."[25]

By the time the Vancouver Olympic torch relay began on 30 October 2009, the original batch of HBC mittens had been sold out and Olympic officials were spreading the message that Canadians could unite behind the games by purchasing and wearing them. A 2009 post on the Canadian Olympic Committee's (COC) website encouraged Canadians to "keep warm and show your support of Canadian athletes in their quest for gold at the 2010 Winter Games by wearing a pair of Vancouver 2010 Red Mittens. Wear your mittens at the rink, schoolyard or along the Olympic Torch Relay route when it comes to your community."[26] Another post on the committee's website from 2009 described the mittens as "the most visible illustration of Canada's excitement for 2010."[27]

An article in the *Prince George Citizen* from October 2009 quotes Canadian Olympian Veronica Brenner describing the COC's red mittens campaign as "a visible reminder that the wearers of the mittens believe in you as an athlete and are supporting your efforts to fulfill your dreams in 2010 and beyond."[28] These narratives promote red mitten nationalism by encouraging Canadians to express their patriotism by buying and wearing a material good. The article also quotes Furlong's claim that wearing the red mittens "is a way for every Canadian to feel a close, personal connection to Canada's Games and to each other by supporting our best Canadian winter athletes. We're hoping that everywhere the Olympic flame visits in Canada it will be greeted and cheered on its journey by a sea of red mittens waved proudly by Canadians in the crowd."[29] His statement reinforces the idea that the mittens represent Canadians' national pride, and that citizens can demonstrate their support for the nation through the mittens. Similarly, an article in Saskatoon's *Star Phoenix* quotes VANOC's director of licensing and merchandising, Dennis Kim, saying that buying and wearing the mittens is "a tangible way for the country to support the Games and be part of the excitement."[30]

These narratives functioned similarly to the ads that Petro-Canada released in the lead-up to the Calgary Olympic torch relay. Specifically, they instructed Canadians on how to act during the Vancouver

Olympic torch relay and, subsequently, the games. In the case of the 1988 Winter Olympics, Petro-Canada encouraged Canadians to enhance the relay's emotional resonance by cheering on torchbearers, and the company capitalized on the relay's success by selling commemorative glassware. In the case of the 2010 torch relay, the red mittens did not simply represent the national pride that many Canadians affiliated with the games. Rather, VANOC responded in a savvy way to the garments' popularity by using them to unite Canadians behind the games. In this way, consumers helped create an association between the Vancouver Olympics and national pride when they wore the red mittens in public.

An article in the *Prince George Citizen* notes that the red mittens helped create a singular branding experience around the torch relay. The mittens, it reads, functioned as "a unifying element that knit together Olympic torchbearers, Canadian athletes, Canadian fans and Olympic supporters around the world."[31] This article reveals that the meaning of the red mittens included, but also extended beyond, HBC's corporate identity to represent an Olympic-related national experience. This feature of the mittens differentiates them from other commodities produced by HBC.

***

A portion of the proceeds from sales of the red mittens went to Own the Podium (OTP), a program that provides financial and structural support for elite athletes training to compete in the Olympics. The origins of OTP date to 2004, when the COC formed a taskforce to study how Canada could maximize its medal count at the Vancouver Games. The subsequent "OTP – 2010 plan" was funded by a mix of public and private money. VANOC helped fund the initiative through income from corporate sponsorship, and sales of the HBC red mittens contributed to this privately sourced pool of money.[32]

Understood within the context of OTP, the act of consuming the red mittens was highly significant. Canadians who purchased the garment used their consumer dollars to buy a symbol of the nation while also making a financial contribution to a nationally important social cause, namely, support for high performance Canadian athletes. The COC president delivered a pair of red mittens to Prime Minister Stephen Harper in Parliament in December 2010 and an Olympian who attended the event, Adam Kreek, made a telling statement: "The Red Mittens are an amazing symbol of support for our athletes, both financially and emotionally … Now, Red Mittens have become a true Canadian Olympic symbol that everyone can share."[33] By describing the mittens as a symbol of Canadians' material and immaterial support for the nation's athletes, Kreek suggests that buying them is a nationally important act.

The idea that Canadians could make material as well as symbolic contributions to the nation by buying Olympic-related commodities was not new in 2010. Petro-Canada, for instance, associated this idea with the glassware it sold to commemorate the 1988 Calgary Olympic torch relay. The company donated a portion of the proceeds from sales of these items to the Torch Relay Legacy Fund, which provides financial support for elite athletes and coaches in Canada. An ad released by Petro-Canada in the lead-up to the Vancouver Olympics references the earlier games and the significance of consuming the glasses: "It was 1988, the Calgary Winter Games, when the country came together to support Olympic athletes with glasses from Petro-Canada. Isn't it time to do it again? Buy the glass. Support Canadian athletes. Only at Petro-Canada."[34] The ad shows glasses from the 1988 Calgary Games in unremarkable places in peoples' homes: sitting empty on a kitchen shelf, holding paint brushes on a table, filled with loose change on a coffee table, etc. These images convey the idea that the glasses have become integrated into Canadians' lives and are now commonplace and unremarkable household items.

Petro-Canada produced and distributed the 1988 Calgary Olympic commemorative glasses at a time when neoliberalism was on the rise in Canada. By the 2000s, neoliberalism had become an even more prominent feature of Canadian society. Jules Boykoff, however, argues that "the Olympics are less about neoliberalism and more about the dynamics of capitalism in general. The tenets of neoliberalism, as relevant as they are in some respects, do not take us the entire way in illuminating the five-ring juggernaut."[35] He proposes that the concept of "celebration capitalism" best describes the economic system that underpins recent Olympic Games, beginning with the 2004 Athens Olympics. Celebration capitalism strategically uses moments of collective, public euphoria to push the economy closer to a lopsided public-private partnership. Within this context, private companies benefit enormously from public funding of the games. Thus, according to Boykoff, a central tenet of neoliberalism, minimizing government spending, is not applicable to the Olympics because governments spend enormous sums of money on them.[36]

The Vancouver Olympics included key features of celebration capitalism. For instance, Canadians participated in "festive commercialism that inspires public support for the Games" by buying and wearing HBC red mittens.[37] In addition, the OTP initiative linked to the Vancouver Olympics is an example of a public-private partnership. Numerous organizations, including the Canadian Paralympic Committee, COC, National Sport Organizations, Sport Canada, VANOC, and VBC, helped create OTP.[38] Olympic sponsors, meanwhile, contributed funds to the program.[39] However, Boykoff's conceptualization of celebration capitalism does not capture the full significance of the interconnected web of relations between the groups involved in OTP, or the manifold ways these groups benefit from the program. In this regard, it remains important to consider how HBC's involvement in OTP occurred within a neoliberal context.

OTP is now a not-for-profit organization that, according to its website, "prioritizes and determines investment strategies for National Sport Organizations in an effort to deliver more Olympic and Paralympic medals for Canada."[40] It receives funding from the federal government, COC, the Canadian Olympic Foundation (the fundraising arm of the COC), and Canadian Paralympic Committee. HBC donates a portion of the sales from red mittens sold after the Vancouver Olympics – what the COC describes as "the next generation of its iconic Canadian Olympic Team Red Mittens" – to the Canadian Olympic Foundation.[41] HBC's association with OTP and the Canadian Olympic Foundation is an example of cause-related marketing, a practice in which companies support a social cause in their promotional activities and raise money for this cause, often through the sale of specially designed commodities.[42] Inger Stole situates this commercial practice within a neoliberal context, writing, "Cause marketing fills a function, not only as a promoter of products and producer of consumer goodwill, but as an important tool in the neoliberal struggle for greater privatization of welfare and social services."[43] In the case of the HBC red mittens, proceeds from the sale of these items reduced the burden placed on the federal government to fund high-performance athletics in Canada.

Furlong commented that Canadians who wore the HBC red mittens "wore their hearts on their hands."[44] Canadians embraced a commodified expression of nationalism and literally embodied their national identity when they turned their hands into miniature Canadian flags. In addition, when Canadians wore the red mittens, they advertised their support for OTP on their bodies. In doing so, they marked themselves as proud Canadians who used their consumer dollars to fund a nationally significant cause, namely, elite sport in Canada. This fact is particularly notable considering that the body has become a visual reflection of how well individuals conform to contemporary citizenship norms and expectations.[45]

One Olympic spectator from Vancouver Island, Scott Edwardson, praised Canadians for expressing their patriotism by wearing the red mittens: "It's about time. Other countries do it, and we lag behind. We're too polite."[46] John Wright, Gregory Millard, and Sarah Riegel argue that Canadians use the national flag to, paradoxically, loudly declare that they are quietly patriotic: "Waving the Canadian flag wherever one goes on grounds that it stands for the 'quiet North American,'" they write, "is like entering a library and loudly announcing one's silence."[47] Similarly, the red mittens were quietly loud symbols of Canadians' patriotism. By wearing these garments, individuals expressed their national pride without speaking a word.

* * *

As a symbol of Canadian nationalism, the red mittens rest on a fragile foundation, one that is predicated on a partial forgetting of Canada's Settler colonial past and a denial of the Settler colonial present. The Olympic Resistance Network (ORN) publicized this reality through a pamphlet showing the mittens dripping with blood. As mentioned in the introduction, "Blood on Your Hands" tells readers that HBC "took control over several areas of Canada, forcing their rules of trade, immigration, settlement and governance onto Indigenous people," "acted as the colonial government" in Canada, introduced alcohol and new diseases into Indigenous communities, and disrupted their traditional economies.[48]

The red mittens circulated during the Vancouver Olympics alongside representations of Indigenous peoples' cultures. News images often showed mitten-clad torch bearers holding the Olympic torch, which was designed with the games' Inukshuk emblem. The Vancouver

Olympic mascots Miga and Quatchi, whose designs were based on "local Aboriginal mythological creatures," sometimes made public appearances wearing red mittens with white maple leaves on the palm.[49] One fan knitted mini replicas of the mittens for her hand-made stuffed Quatchi, observing that the garments "are the most popular souvenir from the games so I thought it was fitting our little office mascot should have a pair of his own."[50] The mittens appeared in retail spaces such as the Vancouver Olympic Superstore alongside commodities of the Ilanaaq emblem and Olympic mascots.

The mittens became popular consumer items two years after Prime Minister Harper apologized to survivors of Indian residential schools, their families, and communities (I discuss the apology in chapter 5). Some individuals argued that the apology was adequate should have laid Indigenous grievances to rest. Keavy Martin critiques this perspective, observing that an over-emphasis on healing and reconciliation can "entail a fixation upon *resolution* that is not only premature but problematic in its correlation with *forgetting*."[51] Furthermore, the expectation that Indigenous peoples must move on from past traumas can lead to "an eventual forgetting, even as its processes ask us to remember."[52] A similar dynamic of remembering and forgetting Canada's Settler colonial history animates the symbolic meaning of the HBC mittens. The patriotism they represent relies on a disavowal of the reality that Canada was, and still is, a Settler colonial nation. However, reminders of this reality were impossible to entirely miss during the games and were even evident in HBC's "We Were Made for This" ad, which celebrates early European Settlement in Canada. To adapt Martin's words, using the red mittens to represent national pride through the Olympic Games can lead to an eventual *remembering* of Settler colonialism in Canada just as the commercial and cultural processes surrounding these mittens ask us to *forget about* it.

Evidence of Canada's Settler colonial history, and HBC's involvement in this history, was noticeable when the Olympic flame passed through Fort Langley, BC on 8 February 2010. HBC temporarily reopened a trading post in that location that had been closed for 124 years. Once filled with provisions for gold miners, the post was now stocked with Olympic merchandise, including HBC red mittens and mascot commodities. Justine Hunter wrote an article about the re-opened trading post for the *Globe and Mail*, in which she notes that the miners heading to the Fraser River in search of gold who visited the post in the nineteenth century "gave rise to the colony of British Columbia – and eventually allowed Canada to stretch from sea to shining sea."[53] She does not acknowledge that Indigenous peoples lived in Western Canada before Settlers arrived in the area in search of gold. However, animal pelts in the trading post were displayed alongside Olympic merchandise. These pelts serve as reminders that HBC was a key player in the early fur trade in Canada, and employees traded products like wool blankets for the furs procured by Indigenous trappers.

Facing a History That Is Still Alive

On cold days, Canadians still wear the original HBC red mittens, as well as later design iterations of the garments. The mittens join other commodities from the Canadian-hosted Olympic and Commonwealth games that fill private and public spaces in this country. Plush toys of the games' mascots decorate children's rooms or lie in boxes with other childhood keepsakes. Coins marked with the games' emblems mix with other circulating Canadian currency, while limited edition coins sit in display cases in peoples' homes. Special issue Olympic and Commonwealth games postage stamps fill drawers and join other stamps in philatelists' collections. Pins decorated with the Olympic and Commonwealth games emblems, as well as the Team Petroleum '88 logo, Echoing the Spirit logo, and Four Host First Nation logo, mix with costume jewelry stored in closets. Petro-Canada mugs from the Calgary and Vancouver Olympics take up space in kitchen cupboards and, as an ad the company released in the lead-up to the 2010 Games reminded viewers, serve as makeshift containers for objects like paint brushes and loose change. It is possible that somewhere in Canada, a Petro-Canada Olympic glass is filled with coins issued for the Montreal, Calgary, and Vancouver Olympics.

Many commodities sold through the Canadian-hosted Olympic and Commonwealth games have become familiar and ordinary parts of Canadians' everyday lives. However, their very ordinariness makes it easy to overlook their cultural importance. These objects lie at the juncture of sport, national identity, and commercialism. Their symbolic meanings were shaped by, and in turn helped shape, narratives about the nation that were communicated through the games opening and closing ceremonies; torch/Queen's baton relays; companies' promotional practices; educational initiatives associated with the games; and political initiatives aimed at improving Indigenous-Settler relations.

The authors of the Truth and Reconciliation Commission of Canada's (TRC) final report remind readers that in order for Indigenous peoples and Settler Canadians to establish and maintain a respectful relationship, "there has to be awareness of the past, acknowledgment of the harm that has been inflicted, atonement for the causes, and action to change behaviour."[54] For Paulette Regan, reconciliation requires the rejection of "a false hope that we can somehow compartmentalize the past without facing the history that is still alive."[55] This living history animates many commodities sold during the Canadian-hosted Olympic and Commonwealth games, ranging from mascot toys to coins marked with the games' emblems. As fetish objects, these commodities both represent and obscure Canada's Settler colonial past and present.

Indigenous activists contested dominant ideas about national identity that circulated in the Canadian-hosted Olympic and Commonwealth games. Their opposition often concentrated on the extraction of natural resources on Indigenous land. Protestors challenged the authority of private companies and the Canadian state to profit from resources like oil and lumber and, more broadly, to claim ownership over the land upon which these resources are found. In doing so, the protestors drew attention to the reality that Settler colonialism is, at heart, a land-based practice.[56] When Canadians used commodities sold during the Olympic and Commonwealth games to symbolize their national identity and pride, they disavowed the truths about the nation that Indigenous activists exposed. Re-interpreting the symbolic meanings of these commodities opens new ways of conceptualizing the nation.

Decolonization, however, is a long and challenging process that does not begin or end with consumer choices. The TRC's final report includes ninety-four calls to action targeting federal, provincial, and territorial governments as well as educational, legal, healthcare, religious, sporting, and cultural institutions. They cover a wide range of issues. To mention just a few, the TRC calls on all levels of government to close the health, education, and employment gaps between Indigenous and non-Indigenous peoples. The commission calls for the creation of mandatory primary and secondary school curriculum on residential schools, treaties, and Indigenous peoples' historical and contemporary contributions to Canada. Other calls to action urge companies to consult with Indigenous peoples and obtain their informed consent before proceeding with economic development projects on Indigenous land. In relation to sport, the TRC calls on all levels of government to tell the national story of Indigenous athletes from the past and support Indigenous athletes' development.[57] Canadians would do well to read, and commit to, these calls to action.

Settlers can also engage in direct action, such as participating in blockades impeding the flow of resources from one part of the country to another that advance Indigenous rights. Glen Coulthard acknowledges that this approach is more confrontational than formal negotiations between the government and Indigenous peoples. It will, he writes, "inevitably be very upsetting to some; it will be incredibly inconvenient to others. But it is what needs to happen if we are to create a more just and sustainable life in this country for the bulk of Indigenous communities, and for the majority of non-Indigenous people as well."[58] His words serve as important reminders of the power negative emotions can hold. The feel-good version of Canadian identity that many consumers associate with commodities like HBC red mittens does not leave opportunities for ambivalence or discomfort over what it means to live in the Settler colonial present in Canada. I urge Canadians to grapple with such a reality.

Notes

Introduction

1 Item – *The World's Biggest Potlatch – Aboriginal participation in the Vancouver 2010 Olympic and Paralympic Winter Games*, AM1550, Series 3, Box 819–C–7, VANOCF, CVA, 93.

2 For video footage of the ceremony, see "Complete Vancouver 2010 Opening Ceremony – Vancouver 2010 Winter Olympics," YouTube video, 3:09:47, Olympicvancouver2010, 11 April 2010, https://www.youtube.com/watch?v=MxZpUueDAvc; I am grateful to an insightful commentator at the 2012 *International Symposium on Olympic Research* who drew my attention to this image.

3 IOC Marketing Department, *Marketing Report Vancouver 2010*, 116; VANOC, *Vancouver 2010: Staging the Olympic Winter Games Knowledge Report*, 44, 63; Dana Flavelle, "A Red-Hot Happy Accident; American CEO of the Bay Thought Torch Bearer Outfit Needed Something Colourful and Distinctly Canadian," *Toronto Star*, 2 March 2010, B1.

4 Furlong quoted in "Red Mittens Support Athletes," *Prince George Citizen*, 5 October 2009, 12, italics added.

5 Tag attached to 2009-edition red mittens, author's personal collection.

6 "Blood on Your Hands," AM1519, Box 632–A–02, Item PAM 2010–37, CVPC, CVA.

7 Ibid.

8 A copy of *The Royal Charter, for Incorporating the Hudson's Bay Company, Granted by His Majesty King Charles the Second, in the Twenty-Second Year of His Reign. A.D. 1670* is available from the Edith and Lorne Pierce Collection of Canadiana housed at Queen's University in Kingston, Ontario.

A digital version is available at https://qspace.library.queensu.ca/bitstream/handle/1974/8862/royalcharterforioohuds.pdf?sequence=1.

9 HBC History Foundation, "Hudson's Bay Point Blanket," n.d., http://www.hbcheritage.ca/things/fashion-pop/hbc-point-blanket.

10 Wolfe, "Settler Colonialism and the Elimination of the Native," 389.

11 As I discuss later in this chapter, Anne McClintock describes the fetish as an "impassioned object." McClintock, *Imperial Leather*, 184.

12 See Roche, *Mega-Events and Modernity*, chap. 1.

13 Billings and Wenner, "The Curious Case of the Megasporting Event."

14 For a discussion of mega-events, nationalism, and politics, see Roche, *Mega-Events and Modernity.*

15 For a discussion of the history of the modern Olympic Games, see Barney, "The Olympic Games in Modern Times"; MacAloon, *This Great Symbol*; Roche, *Mega-Events and Modernity*, chaps. 2–4.

16 IOC, *Olympic Charter*, 8.

17 For a discussion of the concept of Olympism see Roche, *Mega-Events and Modernity*, 194–202.

18 For a discussion of exclusionary practices associated with early modern Olympic Games, see Barney, "The Olympic Games in Modern Times"; Brownell, "Introduction"; Forsyth and Wamsley, "Symbols without Substance"; Rahman and Lockwood, "How to 'Use Your Olympian'"; and Roche, *Mega-Events and Modernity*, chaps 2–4.

19 Moore, "Strange Bedfellows and Cooperative Partners," 117. See also Moore, "The Warmth of Comradeship"; Gorman, "Amateurism, Imperialism, Internationalism and the First British Empire Games."

20 Ibid.

21 See Gorman, "Amateurism, Imperialism, Internationalism and the First British Empire Games"; Moore, "Strange Bedfellows and Cooperative Partners"; and Moore, "The Warmth of Comradeship."

22 Gorman, "Amateurism, Imperialism, Internationalism and the First British Empire Games"; Gerald Redmond, "A Brief History of the Commonwealth Games," in *Edmonton'78: The Official Pictorial Record of the XI Commonwealth Games*,15–16.

23 Carstairs, "Roots Nationalism," 241.

24 See Belisle, *Retail Nation*, chap. 2 and epilogue.

25 Ibid.

26 Carstairs, "Roots Nationalism," 241.

27 Ibid., 249.

28 Harvey, *A Brief History of Neoliberalism*; Stole, "Philanthropy as Public Relations."

29 Somers, *Genealogies of Citizenship*, 73; Somers acknowledges that market

fundamentalism is similar to neoliberalism, but she prefers the former term because it highlights the idea that market fundementalists build a system of beliefs around a central idea: in this case, the notion that the market should operate in its natural state, free from external regulation (see 73n15).

30 Ibid., 73–81.

31 See Prince and Rice, "Governing through Shifting Social-Policy Regimes."

32 Ibid.

33 See Barney, Wenn, and Martyn, *Selling the Five Rings*, chap. 7.

34 James Christie and Miro Cernetig, "Notebook Commonwealth Games: Prince above Disabled Remarks," *Globe and Mail*, 18 August 1994, F8; "Games Good Product That Lacks Promotion, According to Official," *Ottawa Citizen*, 18 August 1994, C7.

35 Ibid.

36 Cleve Dheensaw, "15 Ways the Commonwealth Games Changed Us," *Times Colonist*, 17 August 2014, D5.

37 VANOC, *Vancouver 2010: Staging the Olympic Winter Games Knowledge Report*, 9.

38 Carstairs, "Roots Nationalism," 250.

39 Ibid., 236.

40 Cormack and Cosgrave, *Desiring Canada*, 91.

41 See Wagman, "Wheat, Barley, Hops, Citizenship"; "The Rant" can be viewed on YouTube: "I Am Canadian," YouTube video, 0:59, Vinko, 22 May 2006, https://www.youtube.com/watch?v=BRI-A3vakVg.

42 Castelló and Mihelj, "Selling and Consuming the Nation."

43 Ibid., 568.

44 Bruce Horovitz mentions where the mittens were produced in his article: Bruce Horovitz, "Olympics Fans Seeing – and Buying – Red: Mittens with Canada Maple Leaf are Big Hit and Big Seller," USA *Today*, 16 February 2010, 1B.

45 Carstairs, "Roots Nationalism," 250.

46 Ibid., 254.

47 Wright, Millard, and Riegel, "Here's Where We Get Canadian," 20.

48 Wolfe, "Settler Colonialism and the Elimination of the Native," 390–3.

49 Ibid., 388.

50 Voyageur, Newhouse, and Beavon, "Introduction," 4.

51 See Cole and Chaikin, *An Iron Hand upon the People*, chap. 1; Voyageur, Newhouse, and Beavon, "Introduction."

52 Voyageur, Newhouse, and Beavon, "Introduction," 5.

53 TRC, *Honouring the Truth, Reconciling for the Future*, 110.

54 See TRC, *Honouring the Truth, Reconciling for the Future*; TRC, *The Survivors Speak*.

55 Stephanie Scott, "Honouring 751 Innocent Lives by Showing the Full Picture of Residential Schools across Canada," 24 June 2021, https://nctr.ca/honouring-751-innocent-lives-by-showing-the-full-picture-of-residential-schools-across-canada.
56 TRC, *Honouring the Truth, Reconciling for the Future*, 92–107.
57 NCTR and the Indian Residential School History and Dialogue Centre at UBC. "Concerted National Action Overdue for All the Children Who never Came Home from Residential Schools," 2 June 2021, https://nctr.ca/concerted-national-action-overdue-for-all-the-children-who-never-came-home-from-residential-schools/.
58 Scott, "Honouring 751 Innocent Lives by Showing the Full Picture of Residential Schools Across Canada."
59 Ibid.
60 See Henderson and Wakeham, "Colonial Reckoning, National Reconciliation?"; Mackey, "The Apologizers' Apology."
61 See O'Bonsawin, "Indigenous Peoples and Canadian-Hosted Olympic Games," 37–8; Drees, "White Paper/Red Paper."
62 O'Bonsawin, "Indigenous Peoples and Canadian-Hosted Olympic Games," 38.
63 See O'Bonsawin, "Indigenous Peoples and Canadian-Hosted Olympic Games," 37–8; Drees, "White Paper/Red Paper."
64 Coulthard, *Red Skin, White Masks*, 4–5.
65 See Godlewska and Webber, "The *Calder* Decision, Aboriginal Title, Treaties, and the Nisga'a."
66 Coulthard, *Red Skin, White Masks*, 6, italics in original.
67 Ibid., 117.
68 See Goddard, *Last Stand of the Lubicon Cree*, chap. 13.
69 See Peach, "The Power of a Single Feather."
70 See Pertusati, *In Defense of Mohawk Land*, chap. 7.
71 RCAP, *Report of the Royal Commission on Aboriginal Peoples*, vol. 1, 12.
72 See Coulthard, *Red Skin, White Masks*, chap. 4; Jung, "Canada and the Legacy of the Indian Residential Schools"; Regan, *Unsettling the Settler Within*, chap. 4.
73 Coulthard, *Red Skin, White Masks* 121.
74 Jung, "Canada and the Legacy of the Indian Residential Schools"; see also Regan, *Unsettling the Settler Within*, chap. 4.
75 Jung, "Canada and the Legacy of the Indian Residential Schools."
76 "Indian Residential Schools Settlement Agreement," Crown-Indigenous Relations and Northern Affairs Canada (formerly Indigenous and Northern Affairs Canada), https://www.rcaanc-cirnac.gc.ca/eng/1100100015576/1571581687074.

77 For a full transcript of Harper's apology, see "Statement of Apology to Former Students of Indian Residential Schools," Crown-Indigenous Relations and Northern Affairs Canada (formerly Indigenous and Northern Affairs Canada), https://www.rcaanc-cirnac.gc.ca/eng/1100100015644/1571589171655.

78 TRC, *Honouring the Truth, Reconciling for the Future*, 264.

79 For detailed critiques of the federal government's reconciliation practices, see Dorrell, "From Reconciliation to Reconciling"; Henderson and Wakeham, "Colonial Reckoning, National Reconciliation?"; Henderson and Wakeham, "Introduction"; Mackey, "The Apologizers' Apology"; Martin, "Truth, Reconciliation, and Amnesia."

80 Simpson, *Mohawk Interruptus*, 7–8.

81 See Marx, *Capital*, chaps 26–32; Coulthard, *Red Skin, White Masks*, 6–15.

82 Coulthard, *Red Skin, White Masks*, 6–15.

83 Ibid.

84 Ibid., 14.

85 Marx, *Capital*, 125–77; Heinrich, *An Introduction to the Three Volumes of Karl Marx's Capital*, 39–44.

86 Ibid; see also Appadurai, "Introduction."

87 Appadurai, "Introduction," 17.

88 Ibid., 13–14.

89 Ibid.

90 Vancouver 2010 Officially Licensed Lapel Pins, Collector's Guides to Pins, Released January 2006–September 2007, AM1550, Series 1, Sub-Series 19, Box 819-D-6, File 3, VANOCF, CVA.

91 Flavelle, "A Red-Hot Happy Accident," *Toronto Star*, 2 March 2010.

92 McClintock, *Imperial Leather*, 181; Leiss et al., *Social Communication in Advertising*, 186–91.

93 Ibid., 181.

94 Marx, *Capital*, 164.

95 Marx, *Capital*, 125–77; Leiss et al., *Social Communication in Advertising*, 186–91.

96 McClintock, *Imperial Leather*, 184.

97 For this argument I am indebted to Donica Belisle's application of McClintock's writing on fetish to the Canadian context: Belisle, "Toward a Canadian Consumer History," 185.

98 Billig, "Commodity Fetishism and Repression," 313.

99 Ibid., 326.

100 Trunnell and Holt, "The Concept of Denial or Disavowal," 769–84; Cohen, *States of Denial*, chap. 2.

101 Gordon, *Ghostly Matters*, 24.

102 Ibid., 17, 21.
103 Rosenberg, Dean, and Granzow, "Centennial Hauntings," 405.
104 Ibid.
105 Ibid.
106 Freud, *The Uncanny*, 132.
107 Ibid., 132; see also Francis, *Creative Subversions*, 6–14.
108 Gordon, *Ghostly Matters*, 50.
109 Ibid., 23.
110 RCAP, *Highlights from the Royal Commission on Aboriginal Peoples*, https://www.rcaanc-cirnac.gc.ca/eng/1100100014597/1572547985018; Emilie Cameron links this passage in the RCAP report to Gordon's theory of haunting. See Cameron, "Indigenous Spectrality and the Politics of Postcolonial Ghost Stories," 386.
111 Alicia Elliott, "This Entire Country Is Haunted," *Maclean's*, 12 July 2021, https://www.macleans.ca/opinion/this-entire-country-is-haunted/, italics added.
112 Cindy Blackstock, "Screaming into Silence," *Maclean's*, 30 June 2021, https://www.macleans.ca/opinion/residential-schools-survivors-cindy-blackstock/.
113 Ibid.
114 Rosenberg, Dean, and Granzow, "Centennial Hauntings," 400.
115 Ibid., 400–1.
116 Cameron, "Indigenous Spectrality and the Politics of Postcolonial Ghost Stories," 390.
117 Elliott, "This Entire Country Is Haunted."
118 Forsyth, "Tee-pees and Tomahawks."

Chapter One

1 Olympic Games 1976: Invitation to Montreal, metropolis of Canada, E46, Series 204, Box 1981-06-009\485, File Exposition de Lausanne, FCOJO, BAnQ.
2 Ibid.
3 This transformation reached its height in the 1960s, but some argue that it began earlier. See Bothwell, *Canada and Quebec*, chap. 5; Cuccioletta and Lubin, "The Quebec Quiet Revolution."
4 See Bothwell, *Canada and Quebec*, chap. 5, Cuccioletta and Lubin, "The Quebec Quiet Revolution."
5 Kidd, "The Culture Wars of the Montreal Olympics," 154.
6 McKenna and Purcell, *Drapeau*, 265.
7 See Kidd, "The Culture Wars of the Montreal Olympics," 156; McKenna and Purcell, *Drapeau*, 266–7.

8 Worrall, *My Olympic Journey*, 144.

9 COJO, *The Official Report of the XXI Olympiad Montréal 1976*, 59. The first Olympic postage stamps were created for the 1896 Athens Games and the first Olympic coins were issued for the 1952 Helsinki Winter Olympics. The Olympic lottery that Germany established in the lead-up to the 1972 Munich Summer Olympics, called the "GlücksSpirale," raised significant funds used to organize the games, demonstrating the value of Olympic-related lotteries. See Preuss, *Economics of the Olympic Games*, 167–83.

10 Letter from the Commissioner General for the 1976 Olympic Games and President of COJO to W.A. Kennett, Re: remittance to the COJO of the Olympic coin revenue, 2 January 1974, E46, Series 24, Box 1981-06-009\1969, Binder Marketing Advisory Committee #3, FCOJO, BANQ.

11 Barney, Wenn, and Martyn, *Selling the Five Rings*, 2.

12 Jim Kearney Column, *Vancouver Sun*, 5 March 1974, 22.

13 COJO, *The Official Report of the XXI Olympiad Montréal 1976*, 58–9; all funds in Canadian dollars unless otherwise indicated.

14 Ibid., 59.

15 Centre D'Accueil, Manuel de Base de L'Hôtesse, E46, Series 50, Box 1981-06-009/1568, FCOJO, BANQ, i. The handbook is in French. Unless otherwise indicated, all translations are my own. The original reads, "Les fonctions d'hôtesses et de guides aux Jeux Olympiques de Montréal 1976 feront de vous des représentants, non seulement du Comité organisateur (le Cojo), mais encore de la ville de Montréal, du Québec et du Canada tout entier."

16 Ibid., 1–2. The original reads, "C'est, toutefois, aux Français, qui laissèrent une empreinte durable, que nous devons le charactère distinctif du Canada, la double culture qui imprègne encore de nos jours, la vie quotidienne de ses citoyens."

17 Ibid., 1–15. The original reads, "Le Québec représente l'un des deux camps de la dualité culturelle et ethnique du Canada. Il compte plus de six millions d'habitants, dont plus de 80p. cent sont francophones. Les neuf autres États de la fédération comptent chacun un groupe minoritaire francophone de plus ou moins grande importance, formant une population totale de quelque 1,3 millions d'habitants. C'est pourquoi de Québec ressent avec une acuité accrue sa vocation naturelle de point d'appui des Canadiens de langue française."

18 Ibid., 1–16. The original reads, "Or en raison de cette majorité de cinq millions d'habitants d'origine et de langue françaises, et dans la mesure où celle-ci a éprouvé des difficultés à participer à l'activité du pouvoir central, le Québec a toujours recherché un maximum d'autonomie à l'intérieur de la Confédération."

19 See Bothwell, *Canada and Quebec*, 116–17, 129–32; Cohen-Almagor, "The Terrorists' Best Ally"; Mills, *The Empire Within*, 175–86.

20 Centre D'Accueil, Manuel de Base de L'Hôtesse, E46, Series 50, Box 1981–06–009/1568, FCOJO, BANQ, 1–17. The original reads, "le Canada a-t-il assisté, de février 1968 à juin 1971, à quatre grandes conférences sur les questions constitutionnelles réunissant les premiers ministres des 10 États fédérés, sous la présidence du chef du gouvernement fédéral. La dernière, convoquée à Victoria (Colombie-Britannique), comportait une charte contenant les propositions fédérales qui, eût-elle été acceptée à l'unanimité, aurait transformé la constitution canadienne. Cependant, eu égard à ses positions fondamentales, le Québec n'a pu y souscrire."

21 Lalonde, as told to Bothwell, *Canada and Quebec*, 133.

22 Centre D'Accueil, Manuel de Base de L'Hôtesse, E46, Series 50, Box 1981–06–009/1568, FCOJO, BANQ, 1–46, 1–47. The original reads, "'Si l'on considère le Québec comparativement au reste du Canada, on remarque certaines particularités, pourriez-vous en spécifier une?'; 'En quelle année le Français, fut-il proclamé langue officielle du Québec et par qui?'; 'Le Québec est une province très prolifique dans le domaine des arts. Nommez un(e) artiste québécois(e) connu(e) au delà des frontières canadiennes et mentionnez quel est son mode d'expression?'"

23 Latouche, "Montreal 1976," 253.

24 Kidd, "The Culture Wars of the Montreal Olympics," 157, 161n4.

25 Drapeau, quoted in McKenna and Purcell, *Drapeau*, 271.

26 Ibid., 271; Kidd discusses this statement in his article "The Culture Wars of the Montreal Olympics," 156.

27 COJO, *The Official Report of the XXI Olympiad Montréal 1976*, 314, italics added.

28 Centre D'Accueil, Manuel de Base de L'Hôtesse, E46, Series 50, Box 1981–06–009/1568, FCOJO, BANQ, 2–43; COJO, *The Official Report of the XXI Olympiad Montréal 1976*, 314; International Marketing Programmes, COJO, Revenue Division, E46, Series 24, Box 1981–06–009\1967, File 24, FCOJO, BANQ.

29 Ibid., 1–15. For the original, see note 17 above.

30 COJO, *The Official Report of the XXI Olympiad Montréal 1976*, 282.

31 Ibid., 285–6.

32 Latouche, "Montreal 1976," 252.

33 Ibid.

34 COJO, *The Official Report of the XXI Olympiad Montréal 1976*, 300.

35 James Christie, "Standing Ovation for Canadian Athletes: Hope and Harmony Theme Emphasized at Games Opening," *Globe and Mail*, 19 July 1976, S1, italics added.

36 COJO, *The Official Report of the XXI Olympiad Montréal 1976*, 306.

37 Younging, *Elements of Indigenous Style*, 55–6.

38 Ibid., 55. Italics in original.
39 Olympic Games 1976: Invitation to Montreal, metropolis of Canada, E46, Series 204, Box 1981-06-009\485, File Exposition de Lausanne, FCOJO, BANQ.
40 Centre D'Accueil, Manuel de Base de L'Hôtesse, E46, Series 50, Box 1981-06-009/1568, FCOJO, BANQ, 1–12. The original reads, "Les uns, devenus ce que les Européens ont appelé les Indiens, se sont fixés au Sud; les autres, les Esquimaux, arrivés plus récemment, ont essaimé au Nord jusqu'au Groenland. Cependant l'histoire du Québec, qui peut se mesurer chronologiquement, dont on connaît bien la continuité, commence en 1534."
41 Ibid., 1–1. The original reads, "la France et l'Angleterre luttait non seulement contre les Indiens, mais encore l'un contre l'autre pour la suprématie dans le Nouveau Monde."
42 Bromont: Site of Equestrian Competitions, E46, Series 16, Box 1981-06-009/1879, FCOJO, BANQ.
43 Ibid.
44 Note de Service, "Object: Official Launching of COJO Mascot," E46, Series 16, Box 1981-06-009\2441, File Mascotte, FCOJO, BANQ; "This Will Be One Busy Beaver," *Globe and Mail*, 26 September 1974, 44.
45 COJO, *The Official Report of the XXI Olympiad Montréal 1976*, 354.
46 Press Release, "Beaver Chosen as Montréal Games' Mascot," 25 September 1974, E46, Series 16, Box 1981-06-009\2441, File Mascotte, FCOJO, BANQ.
47 Ibid.
48 See Francis, *Creative Subversions*, 31–5; Miller, *Skyscrapers Hide the Heavens*, 37–9.
49 Francis, *Creative Subversions*, 33.
50 Magdalinski, "Cute, Loveable Characters," 79.
51 Ibid., 80.
52 Ibid., 83.
53 Note de service (Memorandum) from Richard Gareau to Georges Huel, Suject: Mascotte, 21 November 1973, E46, Series 16, Box 1981-06-009\2441, File Mascotte, FCOJO, BANQ. The original reads, "Sur le côté commercial, il va sans dire que nous pouvons profiter énormément d'une mascotte qui peut s'adapter facilement à toutes sortes de marchandises (bandes dessinées, publications générales, jouets, casse-tête, bijoux, foulards, cravates, chapeaux, etc.)"
54 Note de service (Memorandum) from Georges Huel, Directeur général du graphisme et du design to Raymond Beauchemin, Directeur general des Communications, Subject: Nom de la Mascotte, 9 December 1974, E46, Series 121, Box 1981-06-009\2441, File Mascotte, FCOJO, BANQ. The original reads, "Nous croyons que le but premier de la création d'une

mascotte est de donner l'occasion à des licenciés officiels de produire des souvenirs de celle-ci."

55 List of official licensees for the 1976 Games as of 13 November 1975, E46, Series 121, Box 1981-06-009\1968, FCOJO, BANQ.

56 James Christie, "Plug on Quebec Cars: Plates to Carry Olympic Logo," *Globe and Mail*, 2 October 1975, 60.

57 Francis, *Creative Subversions*, 34.

58 "I Am Canadian," YouTube video, 0:59, Vinko, 22 May 2006, https://www.youtube.com/watch?v=BRI-A3vakVg.

59 COJO, *The Official Report of the XXI Olympiad Montréal 1976*, 354.

60 Ibid., 354, 49; the line on p. 49 reads, Amik "means beaver in Algonquian [*sic*], the basic language spoken by the tribes who greeted the first Settlers in the country."

61 Jancewicz, "Related-Language Translation," 136n13.

62 O'Bonsawin, "Indigenous Peoples and Canadian-Hosted Olympic Games," 40.

63 Langevin, quoted in TRC, *Honouring the Truth, Reconciling for the Future*, 61.

64 Indian Affairs, "Programme of Studies for Indian Schools," quoted in ibid., 83.

65 Scott, quoted in ibid., 2–3.

66 Ibid., 83–7.

67 RCAP, *Report of the Royal Commission on Aboriginal Peoples*, vol. 1, 317.

68 Moses, quoted in TRC, *The Survivors Speak*, 105.

69 Wolfe, "Settler Colonialism and the Elimination of the Native," 388.

70 Cardinal, quoted in Miller, *Skyscrapers Hide the Heavens*, 236–7.

71 TRC, *Honouring the Truth, Reconciling for the Future*, 3.

72 Wolfe, "Settler Colonialism and the Elimination of the Native," 389.

73 COJO, *The Official Report of the XXI Olympiad Montréal 1976*, 47.

74 Ibid., 68.

75 Ibid.

76 Ibid., 71.

77 Downey, *The Creator's Game*, 20; as part of this discussion, Downey records a creation story told by Ga·yo·go·ho:nq'(Cayuga) Faithkeeper Dao Jao Dre, Delmor Jacobs, 3–12.

78 Downey, *The Creator's Game*, 44–8; Fisher, *Lacrosse*, 24.

79 Downey, *The Creator's Game*, 20; Fisher, *Lacrosse*, 24.

80 Downey, *The Creator's Game*, 56–7; Fisher, *Lacrosse*, 30–1; Poulter, *Becoming Native in a Foreign Land*, 118.

81 Beers, quoted in Robidoux, "Imagining a Canadian Identity through Sport," 215.

82 Downey, *The Creator's Game*, 48.

83 See ibid., 57–69.

84 Ibid.

85 Aiontonnis, quoted in ibid., 67, italics added by Downey.
86 Poulter, *Becoming Native in a Foreign Land*, 125–33.
87 Ibid., 128–9.
88 Forsyth, "Tee-pees and Tomahawks," 72; Closing ceremony of the Games of the XXI Olympiad Montréal 1976, E46, Series 117, Box 1981-06-009\944, FCOJO, BANQ, 14; COJO, *The Official Report of the XXI Olympiad Montréal 1976*, 306; the report describes the Indigenous performers erecting "wigwams," but Jennifer Adese describes them as tepees: Adese, "Colluding with the Enemy?" 287.
89 COJO, *The Official Report of the XXI Olympiad Montréal 1976*, 309.
90 Adese, "Colluding with the Enemy?" 488.
91 O'Bonsawin, "Indigenous Peoples and Canadian-Hosted Olympic Games," 37.
92 Ibid., 37.
93 See Wolfe, "Settler Colonialism and the Elimination of the Native."
94 Ibid., 389.
95 Francis, *Creative Subversions*, 142.
96 Forsyth, "Tee-pees and Tomahawks," 72.
97 Ibid.
98 Laura Robinson, "After 32 Years, Native Runners Completed Their Dream," *Vancouver Sun*, 3 November 2003, D7; the runners names are Russell Abraham, Charlie Bittern, Patrick Bruyere, William Chippeway, David Courchene Jr, Fred Harper, Milton Mallette, William Merasty, John Nazzei, and Charlie Nelson.
99 Forsyth, "Tee-pees and Tomahawks," 72–3.
100 Ibid., 71.
101 Ibid., 73.
102 Ibid.
103 Ibid.
104 See COJO, *The Official Report of the XXI Olympiad Montréal 1976*, 15–16; Howell, *The Montreal Olympics*, chap. 7; Kidd, "The Culture Wars of the Montreal Olympics," 157; McKenna and Purcell, *Drapeau*, 308–22.
105 See King, *Pink Ribbons, Inc.*, chap. 1; Stole, "Philanthropy as Public Relations."
106 COJO, *The Official Report of the XXI Olympiad Montréal 1976*, 55.
107 Memo, from J. Neil Asselin, Director-General, Marketing to G.M. Snyder, Vice-President, Revenue, Marketing Plan – Olympic Coins, National Olympic Funds Proposal (Appendix D), 7 December 1973, E46, Series 24, Box 1981-06-009\1969, Binder Marketing Advisory Committee #1, FCOJO, BANQ.
108 Marketing Advisory Committee Meeting Minutes, Olympic Coin Program, 10 February 1975, E46, Series 24, Box 1981-06-009\1969, Binder Marketing Advisory Committee #4, FCOJO, BANQ.

109 Postmaster General, quoted in COJO, *The Official Report of the XXI Olympiad Montréal 1976*, 72.

110 Ibid. The first American postage stamp that raised funds for a cause, breast cancer research, was released over a decade later, in 1998. Corporate social responsibility campaigns had become widespread in the United States by that time, and funding breast cancer research was already one of the most popular causes in the country. See King, *Pink Ribbons, Inc.*, chap. 3.

111 Olympic Games Semi-Postal 1974, Pamphlet issued by Canada Post, E46, Series16, Box 1981–06–009\2441, File Timbres, FCOJO, BANQ.

112 Castelló and Mihelj, "Selling and Consuming the Nation," 563.

113 COJO, *The Official Report of the XXI Olympiad Montréal 1976*, 74.

114 Ibid.

115 Letter to go to head of Canadian companies, Marketing plan for corporate relations by Alfred Warkentin, 26 July 1973, E46, Series 24, Box 1981–06–009\1967, FCOJO, BANQ, 27.

116 Marketing plan for corporate relations by Alfred Warkentin, 26 July 1973, E46, Series 24, Box 1981–06–009\1967, FCOJO, BANQ, 11.

117 Ibid., 12.

118 Ibid., 11, 12.

119 Ibid., 12.

120 COJO, *The Official Report of the XXI Olympiad Montréal 1976*, 55.

121 Ibid., 67.

122 Special Analysis of September 28, 1975, Olympic Lottery Draw Telecast Prepared for Trilocan Inc., A.C. Nielsen Company of Canada Limited, E45, Series 23, Box 1981–06–009/1912, FCOJO, BANQ.

123 See Campbell, "Canadian Gambling Policies"; Campbell, "Under the Halo of Good Causes"; and Campbell and Smith, "Gambling in Canada – From Vice to Disease to Responsibility." Many provinces interpreted the term "lottery schemes" to include games of chance, like roulette and blackjack, in addition to lotteries.

124 COJO, *The Official Report of the XXI Olympiad Montréal 1976*, 71.

125 Ibid., 74. The report cites the combined income from sales of coins and stamps at $115 million. Sales of coins reached $386 million, but $278.7 million represented the face value of the coins, which must be held in reserve. Related expenditures were $8 million, which the report includes in the $115 million figure but which they leave out of the $100 million they cite as the income raised from sales. From these figures, I concluded that the income from the stamps was approximately $7 million.

126 A Preliminary report on price sensitivity for Olympic Coins, 11 April 1974, E46, Series 24, Box 1981–06–009\1969, Binder Marketing Advisory Committee #3, FCOJO, BANQ.

127 Case, "Serial Collecting as Leisure, and Coin Collecting in Particular"; Belk, "Collectors and Collecting," 317–26; Bryant, "Stamp and Coin Collecting," 1329–65.
128 Meeting with Royal Canadian Mint, 22 December 82, PR-90, Records of the Marketing Group, Series I, Box 3, File Coin Program Royal Canadian Mint Correspondence, 1981–1987, XVWGI, CCA.
129 Ibid.
130 Memo from Richard Gareau, Director – licensing and legal affairs, to G.M. Snyder, Vice-President, finance, "Ultimate Goal – $350,000,000," 17 May 1973, E46, Series 16, Box 1981-06-009\2441, File Revenu – Notes de Service, FCOJO, BANQ.
131 Howell, *The Montreal Olympics*, 17.
132 Ross Macnab, Report: Canada at the Olympic Youth Camp, prepared by Cat. J.A. Murray, Canadian Delegation Leader, 4 August 1976, E46, Series 68, Box 1981-06-009/1297, FCOJO, BANQ.
133 Ibid., italics added.
134 A. Gay Kirkpatrick, "Letters to the Editor: Olympics," *Globe and Mail*, 21 July 1976, 6.
135 Peter J. Fletcher, "Irked by Olympic French? Just 'Turn the Box Around,'" *Globe and Mail*, 23 July 1976, 7, italics added.
136 Goyens, quoted in Lawrence Martin, "Canadians Lag in Another League, Fans' Cheering not Medal Calibre," *Globe and Mail*, 22 July 1976, 51.
137 Unnamed COJO official, quoted in ibid.
138 COJO, *The Official Report of the XXI Olympiad Montréal 1976*, 60, 353.
139 Hubert Bauch, "Final Deficit on 'Modest' Olympics to be $221 Million, Organizers Say," *Globe and Mail*, 10 July 1975, 1.
140 COJO, *The Official Report of the XXI Olympiad Montréal 1976*, 60; Hubert Bauch, "Drapeau's 'Modest' Games to Cost $1 Billion: Quebec to Take Over Financing, Construction of Olympics as $600 million Deficit Seen," *Globe and Mail*, 15 November 1975, 10.
141 Kidd, "The Culture Wars of the Montreal Olympics," 152.
142 Latouche, "Montreal 1976," 247, italics added.

Chapter Two

1 Olive Elliott, "The Mood in Munich," in *Let the Games Begin*! 61–2.
2 "The Mascot," XI Commonwealth Games, Edmonton 1978; Students' workbook issued by the XI Commonwealth Games Canada (1978) Foundation, PR 74, Series 109, VCGSF, CVICA, 2. Although this document is related to the Edmonton Commonwealth Games, a copy is held in the City of Victoria archives; I am grateful to Michael Dawson who generously shared this find with me.

3 *The Friendly Games: The XI Commonwealth Games, Edmonton, Alberta, Canada, August 3–12, 1978*, 163, 184.
4 "City's Bill Could Put Games in Red," *Globe and Mail*, 18 May 1979, 36; according to the article, the XICGCF closed its books with an "accumulative budget surplus of more than $318,00 to the end of 1978." However, the City of Edmonton claimed that the foundation owed it approximately $2.5 million for games-related expenses.
5 Brian Butters, "Edmonton Games Likely to Be Spared Montreal-Type Mess," *Globe and Mail*, 24 January 1976, 8; "Commonwealth Games Won't Be in the Red: Montreal Followed Design, Edmonton Followed the Budget," *Globe and Mail*, 25 June 1976, 11; "Commonwealth Games: Doing Things Better," *Globe and Mail*, 20 August 1977, 8.
6 Summary Report, Marketing Division, XI Commonwealth Games Canada (1978) Foundation, September 1978, RG–78, Series 2, Sub-Series 16, File 25, CGF, CEA.
7 *The Friendly Games*, 225; see also the Commonwealth Games Federation, "Cardiff, 1958," https://thecgf.com/games/cardiff-1958.
8 Ceremonial Division Meeting, 19 February 1976, RG–78, Series 2, Sub-Series 4, File 12, CGF, CEA.
9 Letter from Dr. M.L. Van Vliet, President, XICGCF to Commissioner S.M. Hodgson, Government of the Northwest Territories, 26 April 1976, RG–78, Series 2, Sub-Series 4, File 26, CGF, CEA.
10 *The Friendly Games*, 225.
11 Ceremonial Division Meeting, 30 September 1976, RG–78, Series 2, Sub-Series 4, File 13, CGF, CEA.
12 Pupchek, "True North."
13 Pupchek, "True North," 195; Moray, *Unsettling Encounters*, 7–11.
14 Moray, *Unsettling Encounters*, 9.
15 Ibid., 11.
16 Poulter, "Snowshoeing and Lacrosse," 246, italics added.
17 Downey, *The Creator's Game*, 200–3.
18 "Authenticity," *Edmonton Journal*, 16 September 1977, cited in Downey, *The Creator's Game*, 201.
19 "Lacrosse Show Exclusion 'Bloody Insult' to Natives," *Edmonton Journal*, 8 March 1978.
20 "Native Lacrosse Players Reject Token Role," *Edmonton Journal*, 7 March 1978, cited in Downey, *The Creator's Game*, 201.
21 Dan Powers, XI Commonwealth Games Edmonton 1978 column, *Edmonton Journal*, 25 February 1978, 26.
22 Downey, *The Creator's Game*, 202–3.

23 Allen Abel, "Brave Warriers Are Covered by Hokum," *Globe and Mail*, 12 August 1978, cited in Downey, *The Creator's Game*, 203.
24 Downey, *The Creator's Game*, 201.
25 Ibid.
26 James Christie, "259 Canadians Hailed Amidst Games Pageantry: Blazer Troupe Troops Colors before Queen," *Globe and Mail*, 4 August 1978, 27.
27 Memo from J. Peter Swann to Dr Van Vliet, 2 June 1977, RG–78, Series 2, Sub-Series 4, File 22, CGF, CEA.
28 XICGCF Opening/Closing Ceremonies Committee, Minutes of Meeting, 5 May 1977, RG–78, Series 2, Sub-Series 4, File 14, CGF, CEA.
29 Letter from K.S. Duncan, Hon. Secretary, Commonwealth Games Federation to Don McColl, Commonwealth Games Foundation, 11 October 1977, RG–78, Series 2, Sub-Series 4, File 23, CGF, CEA.
30 Helen Corbett, "More Than Simply Sport: Art, Music, Dancing and Folklore; It's All Together in Festival 78," *Let the Games Begin*! 15–16, italics added.
31 *The Friendly Games*, 14.
32 HBC ad "Eskimo Carvings Unique Art from Canada's North," *Edmonton Journal*, 1 August 1978, A16.
33 Ibid.
34 Ibid.
35 Ibid.
36 Monod, "Bay Days," 191.
37 HBC ad, "World Famous Hudson's Bay Coats," *Edmonton Journal*, 2 August 1978, A19–A20.
38 HBC ad, "Eskimo Carvings Unique Art from Canada's North," *Edmonton Journal*, 1 August 1978, A16.
39 For a discussion of the logic of elimination, see Wolfe, "Settler Colonialism and the Elimination of the Native."
40 Kathy Kohut, "Buckskin Carpet for Queen at Indian Village," *Edmonton Journal*, 2 August 1978, B2.
41 Ibid.
42 Ibid.
43 Bouvette, quoted in Dan Powers, XI Commonwealth Games Edmonton 1978 column, *Edmonton Journal*, 25 February 1978, 26.
44 "Natives to Stage Cultural Display," *Edmonton Journal*, 3 August 1978, A7.
45 HBC ad, "World Famous Hudson's Bay Coats," *Edmonton Journal*, 2 August 1978, A19–A20.
46 Memo from Mr Konye, Solicitor, Legal Department, to H.L. Pawson, PR Director, RG–78, Series 2, Sub-Series 16, File 9, CGF, CEA.
47 Creighton, *The Forked Road*, 128–9.

48 Mackey, *The House of Difference*, 68–71.
49 Ibid., 69.
50 "Education Committee," *The Friendly Games*, 233.
51 "What Is a Commonwealth Country?" XI Commonwealth Games, Edmonton 1978; Students' workbook issued by the XI Commonwealth Games Canada (1978) Foundation, PR 74, Series 109, VCGSF, CVicA, 4, italics added.
52 Ibid., underline in original.
53 Ibid., underline in original.
54 Wolfe, "Settler Colonialism and the Elimination of the Native," 389.
55 "The Mascot," XI Commonwealth Games, Edmonton 1978; Students' workbook issued by the XI Commonwealth Games Canada (1978) Foundation, PR 74, Series 109, VCGSF, CVicA, 2.
56 Licensees (no date), RG–78, Series 2, Sub-Series 4, File 13, CGF, CEA.
57 "The Mascot," XI Commonwealth Games, Edmonton 1978; Students' workbook issued by the XI Commonwealth Games Canada (1978) Foundation, PR 74, Series 109, VCGSF, CVicA, 2.
58 Ibid., 3.
59 Ahenakew, ed., *Nêhiyawêwin Masinahiķan Michif/Cree Dictionary.*
60 Ibid.
61 Goddard, *Last Stand of the Lubicon Cree*, 48–52.
62 This term was coined by Hannah Arendt: Arendt, *The Origins of Totalitarianism*, 297.
63 See Blackburn, "Differentiating Indigenous Citizenship."
64 Arendt, *The Origins of Totalitarianism*, 297.
65 Ibid., 293.
66 List of Suppliers and Licensees, 6 September 1978, RG–78, Series 2, Sub-Series 16, File 24, CGF, CEA.
67 Wolfe, "Settler Colonialism and the Elimination of the Native."
68 "Brothers Canning Reeking Crude Oil to Be Sold as Souvenirs of Province," *Edmonton Journal*, 3 July 1964, 39.
69 Kostyshyn, quoted in ibid.
70 For a list of contributors, see *The Friendly Games*, 396–403.
71 Pawson, "Edmonton: Host City," in *Edmonton'78*, 11.
72 *Vth British Empire and Commonwealth Games: Official Souvenir Book and Programme of Events: Vancouver, Canada, July 30–August 7, 1954*, AM172, Box 513–B–4, File Publications, BECGSF, CVA, 31.
73 Ibid., 34, 46.
74 Lougheed, quoted in Wood, *The Lougheed Legacy*, 147.
75 See Chastko, *Developing Alberta's Oil Sands*, 147–56.

76 See Chastko, *Developing Alberta's Oil Sands*, 147–56; Wood, *The Lougheed Legacy*, 148–9.
77 Trudeau, quoted in Paul Palango, "PM Urges New Relationship as Queen Warns of Dangers," *Globe and Mail*, 7 August 1978, 1.
78 Lougheed, quoted in Damian Inwood, "Queen Stresses the Need for a United Canada," *Edmonton Journal*, 3 August 1978, C2.
79 The stamps can be viewed on the Postage Stamp Guide website: Postage Stamp Guide, "Edmonton XI Commonwealth Games," https://postagestampguide.com/stamps/16067/edmonton-1978-canada-postage-stamp-xi-commonwealth-games.
80 Altaf Jina, "Stamp," *Globe and Mail*, 7 August 1978, 6.

Chapter Three

1 King, *It's How You Play the Game*, 85.
2 Ibid.
3 Ibid., 103.
4 Olympic organizing committees can no longer pay for the games entirely through private fundraising initiatives. The IOC now mandates that host cities rely on a mix of public and private funds.
5 See Barney, Wenn, and Martyn, *Selling the Five Rings*, chaps 7–10; Tomlinson, "The Commercialisation of the Olympics."
6 King, *It's How You Play the Game*, 127–32.
7 Barney, Wenn, and Martyn, *Selling the Five Rings*, 206.
8 Ibid., 205–7; see also King, *It's How You Play the Game*, 135–41.
9 OCO'88, *XV Olympic Winter Games*, 81, 327, 341; King, *It's How You Play the Game*, 175.
10 OCO'88, *XV Olympic Winter Games*, 657.
11 Ibid., 329.
12 OCO'88, *XV Olympic Winter Games*, 329; Team Petroleum'88 – Objectives, 11/07/86, PR-90, Records of the Communications Group Part II, Series XVIII, Sub-Series General Files, Box 6, File Team Petroleum'88, 1986, XVWGI, CCA.
13 IOC, "The Olympic Partner Programme," n.d., https://olympics.com/ioc/partners.
14 King, *It's How You Play the Game*, 253.
15 Letter to Mr. Joynt, Senior Vice President Communications OCO'88 and Ms. Jackson-Dover, Vice President Culture OCO'88 from W.A. Calder, Director, Social Policy Coordination, Constitutional Affairs and Social Policy Coordination, Alberta Federal and Intergovernmental Affairs,

31 October 1985, PR–90, Records of the Communications Group Part II, Series: XV, Sub-Series Arts Festival, Box 25, File Native Ad Hoc Committee 1985–1986, XVWGI, CCA.

16 Letter distributed to 3M's European journalist group by Sykes F. Powderface, coordinator, Native Liaison, 21 September 1987, PR–90, Records of the Communications Group Part I, Series II, Sub-Series General Files, Box 4, File Natives, 1985–1987, XVWGI, CCA.

17 King, *It's How You Play the Game*, 57.

18 Ibid., 50.

19 Ibid., 75.

20 Ibid., 62.

21 Letter from Ralph Klein and Frank King to William McKnight, minister of Indian Affairs and Northern Development, 14 October 1987, PR–90, Records of the Communications Group Part I, Series II, Sub-Series General Files, Box 4, File Natives, 1985–1987, XVWGI, CCA.

22 King, *It's How You Play the Game*, 85.

23 Ibid., 86.

24 Mackey, *The House of Difference*, 15–16.

25 Ibid., 14–15.

26 Ibid.

27 Ibid., 15.

28 See Daschuk, *Clearing the Plains*, chap. 7.

29 For a discussion of the logic of elimination, see Wolfe, "Settler Colonialism and the Elimination of the Native."

30 Letter distributed to 3M's European journalist group by Sykes F. Powderface, coordinator, Native Liaison, 21 September 1987, PR–90, Records of the Communications Group Part I, Series II, Sub-Series General Files, Box 4, File Natives, 1985–1987, XVWGI, CCA.

31 Ibid.

32 Ibid.

33 Wamsley and Heine, "Don't Mess With the Relay – It's Bad Medicine," 173.

34 O'Bonsawin, "Indigenous Peoples and Canadian-Hosted Olympic Games," 50, italics in original.

35 King, *It's How You Play the Game*, 270.

36 Frank King writes in his book that Tlen sang the anthem in Cree, but Jennifer Adese and Jeanne Ferguson indicate that the language was Southern Tutchone, not Cree: Adese, "Colluding with the Enemy?" 290; Jeanne Ferguson, "Shäwthän Dän, Shäwthän Kwänjè," 166; King, *It's How You Play the Game*, 272. An article posted on the "WhatsUpYukon" website by Peter Jickling, which quotes Tlen discussing his experience singing the national anthem in Southern Tutchone, corroborates Adese and Ferguson's account: Peter Jickling, "Keeping His Culture Strong," Whats Up Yukon, 2009,

https://whatsupyukon.com/Yukon-Lifestyle/Yukon-people/keeping-his-culture-strong/.

37 Adese, "Colluding with the Enemy?" 488–9.

38 Ibid., 489.

39 OCO'88, *XV Olympic Winter Games*, 293.

40 OCO'88 Theme, 17 September 1986, PR–90, Records of the Communications Group Part I, Series II, Sub-Series General Files, Box 3, File OCO'88 Theme, 1986, XVWGI, CCA.

41 OCO'88, *XV Olympic Winter Games*, 53.

42 Gary Kingston, "Not Another Snowflake," Salute to 2010 Special Edition, *Vancouver Sun*, 23 April 2005, located in AM1550, Series 1, Sub-Series 18, Box 820–F–2, File 4, VANOCF, CVA, 7.

43 Official licensees, 2 July 1987, PR–90, Records of the Communications Group Part I, Series X, Sub-Series Youth Department General Files, Box 21, File Marketing Licenses, 1987, XVWGI, CCA; Coca-Cola's pin collectors guide of the 1988 Olympic Winter Games, PR–90, Records of the Communications Group Part III, Series XXIII, Sub-Series General Publications, Box 2, File Coca-Cola Company Presents the Pin Collectors Guide of the 1988 Olympic Winter Games, XVWGI, CCA.

44 "OCO'88 Official Mascots Make Olympic History," 16 December 1983, PR–90, Records of the Governing Boards and Executive Group, Series XII, Sub-Series 1983–1985, Box 1, File Mascot, 1983–1984, XVWGI, CCA; "Mascot Program," Memo from Frances Jackson to Bill Pratt and Bill Wardle re: Mascot Copyright and Trademark, 4 October 1983, PR–90, Records of the Governing Boards and Executive Group, Series XII, Sub-Series 1983–1985, Box 1, File Mascot, 1983–1984, XVWGI, CCA.

45 IOC, "Calgary 1988: The Mascot," https://www.olympic.org/calgary-1988-mascots.

46 OCO'88, *XV Olympic Winter Games*, 259.

47 Ibid., 259.

48 OCO'88 Theme, 17 September 1986, PR–90, Records of the Communications Group Part I, Series II, Sub-Series General Files, Box 3, File OCO'88 Theme, 1986, XVWGI, CCA.

49 "Hidy and Howdy: The Calgary 1988 Olympic Winter Games Mascots," in "Come Together …" Junior High Resource Kit (7–9), ed. Deanna Binder, PR–90, Records of the Communications Group Part I, Series X, Sub-Series Educational Resources and Kits, Box 44, XVWGI, CCA, 10.

50 "Calgary: You're Going to Love it Here" reading card in "Come Together … The Olympics and You," Elementary Resource Kit, ed. Deanna Binder, PR–90, Records of the Communications Group Part I, Series X, Sub-Series Educational Resources and Kits, Box 43, XVWGI, CCA, theme V–15.

51 Ibid.

52 Goodstriker, "Introduction," 9.
53 OCO'88 Theme, 17 September 1986, PR–90, Records of the Communications Group Part I, Series II, Sub-Series General Files, Box 3, File OCO'88 Theme, 1986, XVWGI, CCA.
54 Ibid.
55 OCO'88, *XV Olympic Winter Games*, 499.
56 King, *It's How You Play the Game*, 247–8; OCO'88, *XV Olympic Winter Games*, 259; Hidy and Howdy Corporate Appearances, PR–90, Records of the Marketing Group, Series I, Box 10, File Mascots, Hidy & Howdy, 1987–1988, XVWGI, CCA.
57 OCO'88, *XV Olympic Winter Games*, 259.
58 "Mascot Program," Memo from Frances Jackson to Bill Pratt and Bill Wardle re: Mascot Copyright and Trademark, 4 October 1983, PR–90, Records of the Governing Boards and Executive Group, Series XII, Sub-Series 1983–1985, Box 1, File Mascot, 1983–1984, XVWGI, CCA.
59 Magdalinski, "Cute, Loveable Characters," 79.
60 "Canadians and the Olympic Games: Interacting with an Institution; Station B: Symbols," in "Come Together …" Junior High Resource Kit (7–9), ed. Deanna Binder, PR–90, Records of the Communications Group Part I, Series X, Sub-Series Educational Resources and Kits, Box 44, XVWGI, CCA, 25.
61 "Social Studies; Games People Play: A Comparison of Competition in Pre-Industrial and Industrial Cultures; Focus on the Issue: Compare the Games," in "Come Together …" Junior High Resource Kit (7–9), ed. Deanna Binder, PR–90, Records of the Communications Group Part I, Series X, Sub-Series Educational Resources and Kits, Box 44, XVWGI, CCA, 3–5.
62 Ibid.
63 Goddard, *Last Stand of the Lubicon Cree*, 7–13.
64 Ibid., 21–31.
65 Ibid., 75–6.
66 Ibid., 76–7.
67 Ibid., chap. 10; See Ominayak v. Norcen Energy Resources Lt. et al., Alberta Court of Queen's Bench, 1983.
68 The journal *Native Studies Review* published an edited version of Fulton's discussion paper: Fulton, "Document One: The Fulton Report"; see also Goddard, *Last Stand of the Lubicon Cree*, chap. 11. The federal government established a reserve for the Lubicon Lake Band in October 2018 on 246 square kilometres near Little Buffalo. The band also signed a $113 million Indigenous Title settlement with the federal and provincial governments that year. However, the agreement was signed by the Lubicon Lake *Band*, not the *Nation*. A letter the Lubicon Lake Nation submitted to the *Peace River Record Gazette* explains the difference: "The Nation is the traditional governance

structure of the Lubicon Cree people, which has functioned for hundreds of years and is separate from the Lubicon Lake Band #453, which was only recently created by Canada under the authority of the Indian Act in 1973 and revived in 2013." See Joanna McQuarrie, "Lubicon Lake Nation Raises Concerns; Issues Remain Unresolved, Said Chief Bernard Ominayak," *Peace River Record Gazette*, 21 November 2018, A9.

69 Ominayak, quoted in Martin-Hill, *The Lubicon Lake Nation*, 90.

70 Ominayak, quoted in ibid., 93.

71 Unnamed woman, quoted in Goddard, *Last Stand of the Lubicon Cree*, 132.

72 Ibid., 153–4; see also Daschuk, *Clearing the Plains*.

73 Ominayak, quoted in Goddard, *Last Stand of the Lubicon Cree*, 142.

74 Donna Spencer, "Frank King, Who Brought the 1988 Winter Olympic Games to Calgary, Dies at 81," *Canadian Press*, 10 May 2018. According to Turbo Resource's 1979 Annual Report, it is an "integrated resource company" that is involved in a number of businesses including drilling and servicing oil and gas wells, selling gasoline and lubricant, and exploring and producing oil and gas. A copy of the report is available through McGill University's Digital Library: https://digital.library.mcgill.ca/hrcorpreports/pdfs/6/631106.pdf.

75 King, *It's How You Play the Game*, 5.

76 Press release, "Flagship of '88 Olympics Arts Festival Launched by Glenbow Today," 15 April 1986, PR–90, Records of the Communications Group Part II, Series XV, Sub-Series Arts Festival, Box 22, File Glenbow Museum, 1985–1987, XVWGI, CCA.

77 Goddard, *Last Stand of the Lubicon Cree*, 157; O'Bonsawin, "Indigenous Peoples and Canadian-Hosted Olympic Games," 46.

78 Harrison, "'The Spirit Sings' and the Future of Anthropology," 8.

79 MacLeod, quoted in press release, "Flagship of '88 Olympics Arts Festival Launched by Glenbow Today," 15 April 1986, PR–90, Records of the Communications Group Part II, Series XV, Sub-Series Arts Festival, Box 22, File Glenbow Museum, 1985–1987, XVWGI, CCA.

80 Lennarson, quoted in Goddard, *Last Stand of the Lubicon Cree*, 144.

81 Wamsley and Heine, "Don't Mess With the Relay – It's Bad Medicine," 175.

82 Wamsley and Heine discuss Smith's views in their article on the Calgary Olympics, ibid., 173.

83 "1988 Olympic Medals Delivered to Host City of XV Olympic Winter Games," *Business Wire*, 21 January 1988.

84 O'Bonsawin, "Indigenous Peoples and Canadian-Hosted Olympic Games," 50.

85 "Prince and the Paupers Go Head-To-Head in Bobsledding," *Toronto Star*, 24 February 1988, F4.

86 Oberhoffner, quoted in ibid.

87 Ibid.
88 Norton, quoted in Kevin Cox, "Native Groups Want Artifacts Pulled from Show," *Globe and Mail*, 15 January 1988, A4.
89 Howard Witt, "Tiny Band of Indians Fights for Land, Survival," *Chicago Tribune*, 5 July 1987, 18; see also O'Bonsawin, "Indigenous Peoples and Canadian-Hosted Olympic Games," 44.
90 O'Bonsawin, "Indigenous Peoples and Canadian-Hosted Olympic Games," 45.
91 Minutes from the 30 May 1986 Scientific Committee Meetings of 30, 31 May and 1 June 1986, PR–90, Records of the Communications Group Part II, Series XV, Sub-Series Arts Festival, Box 22, File Glenbow Museum Contract, 1985–1986 File 2 of 2, XVWGI, CCA.
92 Ibid.
93 Ibid.
94 King, quoted in press release, "Flagship of '88 Olympics Arts Festival Launched by Glenbow Today," 15 April 1986, PR–90, Records of the Communications Group Part II, Series XV, Sub-Series Arts Festival, Box 22, File Glenbow Museum, 1985–1987, XVWGI, CCA, italics added.
95 Arnold Edinborough, "Glenbow Exhibit Shows Rich Tradition of Native Artistry," *Financial Post*, 11 April 1988, 22, italics added.
96 Moray, *Unsettling Encounters*, 9.
97 OCO'88, *XV Olympic Winter Games*, 243.
98 Ibid., 241; in addition to the Canadians selected through the lottery, OCO'88 invited individuals who had made outstanding contributions to the nation to participate in the relay as torch bearers.
99 King, *It's How You Play the Game*, 3.
100 Letter from Jim Hunter to Jerry Joynt, Subject: Positive Position of OCO on O.T.R. [Olympic Torch Relay], 27 August 1987, PR–90, Records of the Communications Group Part I, Series III, Sub-Series General Files, Box 1, File Petro-Canada, XVWGI, CCA.
101 Lakusta, quoted in The Olympic Torch Relay Media Guide, PR–90, Records of the Communications Group Part III, Series XXIII, Sub-Series General Publications, Box 4, File Petro-Canada Olympic Torch Relay: Media Guide, 1987, XVWGI, CCA, 3.
102 The ad can be viewed on YouTube: "Petro-Canada – Share the Flame (1987)," YouTube video, 1:00, RW–TV: RetroWinnipeg, 21 October 2009, https://www.youtube.com/watch?v=zOANKlwdJyk.
103 Ibid. A recording of the song is also available on YouTube: "Winter Games – Calgary 1988 – Can't you feel it?" 4:35, tomexsofter, 28 September 2010, https://www.youtube.com/watch?v=Rfo-ltRXAC4.

104 The ad can be viewed on YouTube: "Petro-Canada – Share the Flame (version #2, 1987)," YouTube video, 0:29, RetroWinnipeg, 21 October 2009, https://www.youtube.com/watch?v=T6kcgZMKGVg.
105 Shawna Richer, "Canada's First Winter Olympics: Now and Then How Great Was '88?" *Globe and Mail*, 30 October 2009, O12.
106 Ibid.
107 Hobson, *Share the Flame*, 14.
108 Ibid., 207.
109 Ibid., 163–4.
110 Goddard, *Last Stand of the Lubicon Cree*, 156
111 Rudy Platiel, "Native Leaders See Glimmer of Hope on Self-Rule," *Globe and Mail*, 29 December 1987, 3.
112 James Davidson, "Canada's Torch Song," *Globe and Mail*, 5 December 1987, E1, italics added.
113 Canadian Alliance in Solidarity with Native Peoples, "Support the Lubicon – Defend Native Rights," PR–90, Records of the Communications Group Part I, Series II, Sub-Series General Files, Box 4, Folder Natives, 1985–1987, XVWGI, CCA, underline in original.
114 Ibid., underline in original.
115 Coon-Come, quoted in Wamsley and Heine, "Don't Mess With the Relay," 175, italics added; this quotation was originally reported in the *Calgary Herald*, 15 January 1988.
116 Ted Williamson and Beverly Williamson, "Letter: Hard Life for Indians," *Globe and Mail*, 10 December 1987, A6, italics added.
117 John Duncanson, "Native Rights Protesters Forced to Leave Square," *Globe and Mail*, 24 December 1987, A15.
118 Herbert H. Denton, "Indian Band Protests in Calgary; Battle for Land Rights Threatens to Mar City's World Image," *Washington Post*, 27 February 1988, A10.
119 OCO'88, *XV Olympic Winter Games*, 189.
120 Kevin Cox, "The Frenzy Begins," *Globe and Mail*, 6 February 1988, A15.
121 Michael Valpy, "Bits and Pieces from Alberta," *Globe and Mail*, 2 March 1988, A8.
122 King, *It's How You Play the Game*, 235.
123 Wamsley and Heine, "Don't Mess With the Relay," 176.
124 Ibid.
125 Ibid.
126 David Ebner, "Countown to 2010 Olympic Marketing: Petrocan Hopes Its Glasses Will Strike Gold Again," *Globe and Mail*, 26 January 2009, A1.
127 Churton, quoted in ibid.

128 Ibid.

129 King, quoted in Hobson, *Share the Flame*, 9, italics added.

130 The ad can be viewed on YouTube: "Petro-Canada – Olympic Torch Relay Legacy Fund (1988)," 0:30, RetroWinnipeg, 3 July 2010, https://www.youtube.com/watch?v=TcO-rda-qjo, italics added.

131 Ibid.

132 McClintock, *Imperial Leather*, 184.

133 "Calgary 1988; Background; Calgary as Olympic Host; Torch Relay Announced: A Press Release," in "Come Together ... The Olympics and You," Senior High Resource Kit (10–12), ed. Deanna Binder, PR–90, Records of the Communications Group Part I, Series X, Sub-Series Educational Resources and Kits, Box 44, XVWGI, CCA, 10.

134 Somers, *Genealogies of Citizenship*, 63–117.

135 For a detailed discussion of marketization, see ibid., chap. 2.

136 Remarks by Frank King, Chairman of the XV Olympic Games Organizing Committee, Launch of Royal Canadian Mint's 1988 Olympic Coin Series, 16 September 1985, PR–90, Records of the Communications Group Part III, Series XXIII, Sub-Series General Publications, Box 5, File Royal Canadian Mint, The Pursuit of Excellence, Olympic Coin Program, XVWGI, CCA.

137 Remarks by the Hon. Harvie Andre, Associate Minister of National Defence and Former Minister Responsible for the Royal Canadian Mint, Launch of Royal Canadian Mint's 1988 Olympic Coin Series, 16 September 1985, PR–90, Records of the Communications Group Part III, Series XXIII, Sub-Series General Publications, Box 5, File Royal Canadian Mint, The Pursuit of Excellence, Olympic Coin Program, XVWGI, CCA.

138 Ibid.

139 Castelló and Mihelj, "Selling and Consuming the Nation," 568.

140 Remarks by the Hon. Otto Jelinek, Federal Minister of State, Fitness and Amateur Sport and Multiculturalism, Launch of Royal Canadian Mint's 1988 Olympic Coin Series, 16 September 1985, PR–90, Records of the Communications Group Part III, Series XXIII, Sub-Series General Publications, Box 5, File Royal Canadian Mint, The Pursuit of Excellence, Olympic Coin Program, XVWGI, CCA, italics added.

141 Ibid., italics added.

142 Team Petroleum '88 Banquet – Suggestions to Speakers, 6 August 1987, PR–90, Records of the Marketing Group, Series VI, Sub-Series General Files, Box 1, File Team Petroleum'88 Banquet, XVWGI, CCA.

143 Fisher, quoted in Canadian Western Natural Gas Company News Release, 26 May 1987, PR–90, Records of the Communications Group Part I, Series II, Sub-Series General Files, Box 2, File Canadian Western Natural Gas, 1985–1988, XVWGI, CCA.

144 Team Petroleum'88 – Objectives, 11 July 1986, PR–90, Records of the Communications Group Part II, Series XVIII, Sub-Series General Files, Box 6, File Team Petroleum'88, 1986, XVWGI, CCA.

145 ISL Marketing – TOP, An Opportunity for Worldwide Sponsorship of the Olympic Movement, PR–90, Records of the Communications Group Part III, Series XXIII, Sub-Series General publications, Box 3, File TOP Marketing, TOP: An Opportunity for Worldwide Sponsorship of the Olympic Movement CA 1985, XVWGI, CCA, 25.

146 Volunteer Training Manual, cited in Kevin Wamsley and Michael Heine, "Tradition, Modernity, and the Construction of Civic Identity," 86.

147 King, *It's How You Play the Game*, 249.

148 Volunteer Training Manual, cited in Wamsley and Heine, "Tradition, Modernity, and the Construction of Civic Identity," 86.

149 Whitson, "Olympic Hosting in Canada," 39.

150 "Selling Calgary" in "Come Together … The Olympics and You," Senior High Resource Kit (10–12), ed. Deanna Binder, PR–90, Records of the Communications Group Part I, Series X, Sub-Series Educational Resources and Kits, Box 44, XVWGI, CCA.

151 See Anholt, *Competitive Identity*; Kavaratzis, "From City Marketing to City Branding," 58–73.

152 Aronczyk, *Branding the Nation*, 28.

153 Aronczyk, "Living the Brand," 54; see also Aronczyk, *Branding the Nation*, chap. 3.

154 OCO'88, *XV Olympic Winter Games*, 441; King, *It's How You Play the Game*, 197–8.

155 "Volunteer Training Manual," cited in Wamsley and Heine, "Tradition, Modernity, and the Construction of Civic Identity," 85.

156 Ibid., 85–6.

157 The unnamed person made this statement while participating in a focus group about the Olympic Games in Canada: Female, 50–64, Calgary "Volunteering," Charlton Strategic Research Inc., "Report to VANOC, Olympic Connectors, Qualitative Focus Groups Research, Part 1 Emotional Connectors," 33, September 2006, AM1550, Series 1, Sub-Series 14, Box 820 E–7, File 17, VANOCF, CVA.

158 Male, 35–49, Calgary "Volunteering," cited in ibid.

159 Chastko, *Developing Alberta's Oil Sands*, 173–86.

160 Ibid., 184.

161 Ibid., 173–95.

162 Ibid., 199–202.

163 See Chastko, *Developing Alberta's Oil Sands*, chap. 8; Fossum, *Oil, the State, and Federalism*, chap. 6.

164 Denton, "Indian Band Protests in Calgary; Battle for Land Rights Threatens to Mar City's World Image," *Washington Post*, 27 February 1988, A10.

165 "Indians Hope to Dent the Good-Guy Image of Calgary's Cowboys," *Sydney Morning Herald*, 29 February 1988, 9.

166 Valk, quoted in Goddard, *Last Stand of the Lubicon Cree*, 148.

167 Wamsley and Heine, "Don't Mess With the Relay – It's Bad Medicine," 175.

Chapter Four

1 "Canada Bids for Commonwealth Games," PR *Newswire Europe*, 14 March 1988; "Victoria Awarded 1994 Games over India's Capital," *Toronto Star*, 15 September 1988, B3.

2 "Victoria Awarded 1994 Games over India's Capital."

3 Alex Strachan, "Yes, Victoria, the Game's Afoot: City Prepares to Welcome 3,200 Athletes," *Vancouver Sun*, 21 July 1994, A1; Corporate Partners' Handbook, 1992, PR–74, Series 141, File 1, VCGSF, CVicA, 66.

4 Craig McInnes, "Victoria Games Big Winner Commonwealth Event Nets $4.6-Million Surplus," *Globe and Mail*, 9 November 1994, A4.

5 Heller, quoted in Corporate Partners' Handbook, 1992, PR–74, Series 141, File 1, VCGSF, CVicA, 66.

6 Christie and Cernetig paraphrase Heller in their article: James Christie and Miro Cernetig, "Notebook Commonwealth Games: Prince Above Disabled Remarks," *Globe and Mail*, 18 August 1994, F8.

7 VANOC, *Vancouver 2010: Sustainability Report 2009–10*, 10, 11, 23, 76, 78.

8 Report Summary of the Native Participation Committee Business Plan, PR–74, Series 187, VCGSF, CVicA; "Games – Natives," *Canadian Press*, 4 June 1992; Backgrounder on BC First Nations Gathering, PR–74, Series 187, VCGSF, CVicA.

9 "3 Nations Gathering: Salish, Swagiulth and Nuu-Chah-Nulth Nations," PR–74, Series 187, VCGSF, CVicA.

10 Ibid.

11 Moira Farrow, "Fleet of War Canoes Ends Historic Journey: Let the Games Begin," *Vancouver Sun*, 19 August 1994, A3.

12 Seymour, quoted in ibid.

13 Smith, quoted in Alex Strachan, "Commonwealth Games Helping Native Indians Introduce Their Culture to World at Large," *Vancouver Sun*, 12 August 1994, B4.

14 Harcourt, VCGS, *Official Souvenir Magazine of the XV Commonwealth Games*, 11, italics added.

15 Ibid.

16 "XV Commonwealth Games Featured on Commemorative Stamps," *Canada NewsWire*, 5 May 1994.
17 VCGS, *Official Souvenir Magazine of the XV Commonwealth Games*, 119.
18 Alex Strachan, "Totem Pole for Games to Be Tallest in World," *Vancouver Sun*, 19 July 1994, A3; see also Moira Farrow, "Coastal Bands Carving World's Tallest Totem Pole to Welcome Athletes in '94," *Vancouver Sun*, 20 July 1993, A3.
19 CBC, "Broadcasters Handbook," 1–6.
20 Strachan, "Totem Marking Games Symbolizes Hope of a People," *Vancouver Sun*, 23 July 1994, A1.
21 Francis, *The Imaginary Indian*, 186.
22 Ibid., 183–6.
23 Strachan, "Totem Pole for Games to Be Tallest in World."
24 Strachan, "Totem Marking Games Symbolizes Hope of a People."
25 Vickers, quoted in ibid.
26 CBC, "Broadcasters Handbook," 1–4.
27 "XV Commonwealth Games Featured on Commemorative Stamps," *Canada NewsWire*, 5 May 1994; Moira Farrow, "Natives Plan Multitude of Events at 1994 Games," *Vancouver Sun*, 14 October 1993, B2.
28 Ki-Ke-in, quoted in Moira Farrow, "Medals Unveiled at Day of Healing," *Vancouver Sun*, 4 May 1994, A3.
29 Ki-Ke-in, quoted in ibid.
30 "Games – Natives," *Canadian Press*, 30 July 1993.
31 Ibid.
32 Sam, quoted in "Games – Natives," *Canadian Press*, 29 October 1993; see also "Games – Natives," *Canadian Press*, 4 June 1992.
33 Lemay, quoted in CBC, "Broadcasters Handbook," 1–3.
34 Penikett, *Reconciliation*, 89.
35 Harcourt, quoted in Farrow, "Fleet of War Canoes Ends Historic Journey."
36 D.B. Smith, "Clayoquot Sound Battle Escalates," *Windspeaker*, 16 August 1993, R1.
37 "Totem-Games," *Canadian Press*, 1 April 1993.
38 Strachan, "Totem Marking Games Symbolizes Hope of a People."
39 "Clayoquot Demonstrators Set Up Protest Camp," *Canadian Press*, 1 August 1994.
40 Alex Strachan, "Logging Foes Told Get Out or Face Action," *Vancouver Sun*, 3 August 1994, B2; "Clayoquot Protesters Vacate Park, Find New Home," *Canadian Press*, 6 August 1994.
41 MacMillan Bloedel ad "Forest Tours … An Event You Shouldn't Miss!"in VCGS, *Official Souvenir Magazine of the XV Commonwealth Games*, 62.

42 Province of BC ad "Where Dreams Run Wild" in ibid., 2.
43 Michael Smyth, "Hidden Clarion Call for Natives in Commonwealth Games Artwork," *Canadian Press*, 14 August 1994.
44 Elliott, quoted in ibid.
45 Ibid.
46 Paul, quoted in "Games – Natives," *Canadian Press*, 4 June 1992.
47 CBC, "Broadcasters Handbook," 1–5.
48 Alex Strachan, "Pin Trading Whole Point for Many at Event," *Vancouver Sun*, 1994, B4.
49 CBC, "Broadcasters Handbook," 1–1.
50 Ibid., 1–5.
51 Pageantry Letter, 9 September 1993, PR–74, Series 142, File 57, VCGSF, CVicA.
52 Pierre Berton, "Is Victoria the Commonwealth's Last Refuge?" *Toronto Star*, 27 August 1994, H3.
53 Executive Summary: Logo Design Selection Process, prepared for: Victoria Commonwealth Games Society, Prepared by: Jane Hall, January 1990, PR–74, Series 138, File 24, VCGSF, CVicA.
54 Ibid.
55 Ibid.
56 Naming of Mascot Entry, PR–74, Series 138, File 24, VCGSF, CVicA.
57 Carr, *Klee Wyck*, 36.
58 Petch, quoted in news release, "Our Commonwealth Games Orca Mascot Has a Name!" 23 August 1990, PR–74, Series 138, File 24, VCGSF, CVicA, italics added.
59 Arnold Edinborough, "Glenbow Exhibit Shows Rich Tradition of Native Ancestry," *Financial Post*, 11 April 1988, 22.
60 Initial recommendations of the XV Commonwealth Games Mascot Steering Committee, 14 June 1991, PR-74, Series 138, File 24, VCGSF, CVicA.
61 Ibid.
62 Ibid.
63 Tippett, *Emily Carr, a Biography*, 32; Crabtree, *Klee Wyck*; the description of Crabtree's documentary film on the National Film Board's website reads, "When Carr visited the Ucluelet Indian Reserve on Vancouver Island in 1898, the Nuu-chah-nulth people gave her the name Klee Wyck, meaning 'Laughing One,'" https://www.nfb.ca/film/klee_wyck/.
64 Tanner, "Kleewyck," 458; the entry in the dictionary lists the name as one word, but the description below lists the name as two words (i.e., Kleewyck vs. Klee Wyck).
65 Ibid.
66 Merchandise Catalogue, March 1994, PR–74, Series 141, File 6, VCGSF, CVicA.

67 Initial recommendations of the XV Commonwealth Games Mascot Steering Committee, 14 June 1991, PR–74, Series 138, File 24, VCGSF, CVicA.
68 Bridge, "Introduction," 10.
69 First Nations: AA En Mas "Come and Compete," First Nations Learning Resource, XV Commonwealth Games, PR–74, Series 185, VCGSF, CVicA, xiii.
70 Ibid., 16.
71 Ibid., xiii.
72 Ibid., 18, italics added.
73 Ibid., 16.
74 Ibid., xi.
75 Ibid., 65.
76 Ibid., 71–3.
77 Ibid., 73.
78 Ibid., 16.

Chapter Five

1 VBC, *The Sea to Sky Games: Vancouver 2010 Candidate City/Ville Candidate Bid Book*, vol. 1, 63.
2 Ibid., 3.
3 Ibid., 17.
4 Item – *The World's Biggest Potlatch – Aboriginal participation in the Vancouver 2010 Olympic and Paralympic Winter Games*, AM1550, Series 3, Box 819–C–7, VANOCF, CVA, 71.
5 Item – Opening ceremony of the XXI Olympic Winter Games Media Guide, AM1550, Series 3, Box 819–A–2, VANOCF, CVA, 29.
6 VANOC, *Vancouver 2010: Sustainability Report 2009–10*, 6, 81.
7 Jeff Lee, "Vancouver Olympics Generated $2.5 billion; Games Themselves Broke Even," *Calgary Herald*, 18 December 2010, A16.
8 IOC Marketing Department, *Marketing Report Vancouver 2010*, 120; VANOC, *Vancouver 2010: Staging the Olympic Winter Games Knowledge Report*, 43–4, 66.
9 Poole, quoted in VANOC, *Vancouver 2010: Bid Report*, 12; Christine O'Bonsawin discusses this quotation in her article on Indigenous representation in the Vancouver Olympics: O'Bonsawin, "The Conundrum of 'Ilanaaq.'"
10 Ibid., 12, 27.
11 Dunn, "Aboriginal Partnerships for Sustainable 2010 Olympic and Paralympic Winter Games," 81.
12 VANOC, *Vancouver 2010 Bid Report*, 21.
13 Ibid., 12.

14 O'Bonsawin, "Indigenous Peoples and Canadian-Hosted Olympic Games," 52–4.
15 VANOC, *Vancouver 2010 Bid Report*, 9–13.
16 IOC, *Olympic Movement's Agenda 21*, 17.
17 Ibid., 45.
18 Strategy and Positioning Development Discussion Paper (Draft), 10 April 2000, AM1581, Series 10, File Fundraising Plan, VBCF, CVA.
19 IOC, *Olympic Charter*, 8.
20 See Mallon, "The Olympic Bribery Scandal."
21 VANOC, *Vancouver 2010 Bid Report*, 8.
22 Ibid., 8.
23 See Maguire et al., "'Celebrate Humanity' or 'Consumers'?"; Maguire, "Branding and Consumption in the IOC's 'Celebrate Humanity' Campaign."
24 Nelson, quoted in Laura Robinson, "After 32 Years, Native Runners Completed Their Dream," *Vancouver Sun*, 3 November 2003, D7.
25 Godlewska and Webber, "The *Calder* Decision, Aboriginal Title, Treaties, and the Nisga'a," 19–20; Dunn, "Aboriginal Partnerships for Sustainable 2010 Olympic and Paralympic Winter Games; McKee, *Treaty Talks in British Columbia.*
26 Letter from Chief Ernest Campbell, Musqueam Indian Band to Jack Poole, President and CEO, Vancouver Whistler 2010 Bid Corporation, Re: Board of Directors – Vancouver/Whistler 2010 Bid Corporation, 11 February 2002, AM1581, Series 5, Sub-Series 4, Box 821–C–02, File Band Secretariat, VBCF, CVA.
27 Alfred, *Wasáse*, 41–2.
28 VANOC, *Vancouver 2010 Bid Report*, 22.
29 No Games 2010 Coalition, "Olympics: Fantasies and Facts," AM1581, Series 7, Sub-Series 1, Box 821–D–07, File Business and Professional Groups, VBCF, CVA; Green Party of BC, "Vote 'No' to Seven Years of Pain for 17 Days of Games," AM1581, Series 7, Sub-Series 1, Box 821–D–07, File Business and Professional Groups, VBCF, CVA.
30 No Games 2010 Coalition, "Olympics: Fantasies and Facts," AM1581, Series 7, Sub-Series 1, Box 821–D–07, File Business and Professional Groups, VBCF, CVA.
31 "Answering the NO side," AM1581, Series 7, Sub-Series 4, Box 822–C–01, File No Games Coalition, VBCF, CVA.
32 Ibid.
33 VANOC, *Vancouver 2010 Bid Report*, 8.
34 Press release: 20 CIBC Youth ambassadors selected to join 2010 Winter Games bid, Vancouver, 16 July 2002, AM1581, Series 2, Sub-Series 1, Box 822–C–02, File General, VBC, CVA.
35 Campbell, quoted in CIBC 20 For 10 Youth Bid Ambassadors Biographies, AM1581, Series 2, Sub-Series 1, Box 822–C–02, File General, VBCF, CVA.

36 TRC, *Honouring the Truth, Reconciling for the Future*, 348.
37 Item – *The World's Biggest Potlatch – Aboriginal participation in the Vancouver 2010 Olympic and Paralympic Winter Games*, AM1550, Series 3, Box 819-C-7, VANOCF, CVA, 102.
38 Corrine Hunt, Proposal for Olympic and Paralympic Medal Design, AM1550, Series 1, Sub-Series 18, File 11, Box 819-D-07, VANOCF, CVA.
39 Ibid.
40 News Release, "Introducing ILANAAQ: Vancouver 2010 Olympic Winter Games emblem celebrates Canada," 23 April 2005, AM1550, Series 1, Sub-Series 14, File 14, Box 820-E-7, VANOCF, CVA.
41 Ibid.
42 Letter from BC Premier Gordon Campbell to Nunavut Premier Paul Okalik, 21 March 2005, AM1550, Series 1, Sub-Series 18, Box 820-F-2, File 4, VANOCF, CVA.
43 Ibid.
44 Letter from John A. Furlong VANOC CEO to the Honourable Paul Okalik, Premier of Nunavut, 6 May 2005, AM1550, Series 1, Sub-Series 18, Box 820-F-2, File 4, VANOCF, CVA; in the letter, Furlong writes, "I wanted to express the deep appreciation of the entire team at VANOC for your personal support of our new emblem and for your in person attendance in Vancouver as Ilanaaq was introduced to our country and to the world."
45 Simon, quoted in Item – *The World's Biggest Potlatch – Aboriginal participation in the Vancouver 2010 Olympic and Paralympic Winter Games*, AM1550, Series 3, Box 819-C-7, VANOCF, CVA, 125.
46 Paul Irish, "Olympic Gear Helps Vancouver Games," *Toronto Star*, 20 November 2008, U4; Susan Lazaruk, "Olympic Merchandise Hits Shelves," *Vancouver Province*, 19 July 2005, A3.
47 Adriana Barton, "Today's Pavilion: Royal Canadian Mint Pavilion," *Globe and Mail*, 28 February 2010, S2.
48 VANOC, *Vancouver 2010: Staging the Olympic Winter Games Knowledge Report*, 13, 68, 58.
49 Putulik, quoted in Item – *The World's Biggest Potlatch – Aboriginal participation in the Vancouver 2010 Olympic and Paralympic Winter Games*, AM1550, Series 3, Box 819-C-7, VANOCF, CVA, 82.
50 Tara Perkins, "Guess Who's Coming to Bay Street? Fontaine Signs on with Royal Bank," *Globe and Mail*, 2 September 2009, B1.
51 Broomfield, quoted in Item – *The World's Biggest Potlatch – Aboriginal participation in the Vancouver 2010 Olympic and Paralympic Winter Games*, AM1550, Series 3, Box 819-C-7, VANOCF, CVA, 49.
52 "$75 Gold Coloured Coin – Four Host First Nations (2008)," Royal Canadian Mint, http://www.mint.ca/store/coin/75-gold-coloured-coin-four-host-first-nations-2008-prod260004.

53 Official Vancouver 2010 Licensed Lapel Pins, 2006–2009 releases, AM1550, Series 1, Sub-Series 19, Box 819-D-6, File 19, VANOCF, CVA.
54 Item – *The World's Biggest Potlatch – Aboriginal participation in the Vancouver 2010 Olympic and Paralympic Winter Games*, AM1550, Series 3, Box 819-C-7, VANOCF, CVA, 93.
55 David Atkins Enterprises, Symposium Report Executive Summary, AM1550, Series 1, Sub-Series 12, Box 819-B-3, File 17, VANOCF, CVA.
56 David Atkins Enterprises, Youth Symposium Creative Report, AM1550, Series 1, Sub-Series 12, Box 819-B-3, File 17, VANOCF, CVA.
57 Item – *The World's Biggest Potlatch – Aboriginal participation in the Vancouver 2010 Olympic and Paralympic Winter Games*, AM1550, Series 3, Box 819-C-7, VANOCF, CVA, 85.
58 Indigenous Youth Games participants, quoted in ibid., 158–9.
59 Opening Ceremony Programme of the 122nd Session of the International Olympic Committee, AM1550, Series 3, Box 819-D-5, Item Opening ceremony of the IOC 122nd session: Program and invitation, VANOCF, CVA; VANOC, *Vancouver 2010: Staging the Olympic Winter Games Knowledge Report*, 58.
60 IOC Marketing Department, *Marketing Report Vancouver 2010*, 51; VANOC, *Vancouver 2010: Staging the Olympic Winter Games Knowledge Report*, 58; VANOC, *Vancouver 2010: Sustainability Report 2009–10*, 6, 81.
61 Joseph, quoted in IOC Marketing Department, *Marketing Report Vancouver 2010*, 116.
62 David Atkins Enterprises, Youth Symposium Creative Report, AM1550, Series 1, Sub-Series 12, Box 819-B-3, File 17, VANOCF, CVA.
63 Mark Hume, "Native Artist Attacks VANOC over Authenticity of Handcrafts," *Globe and Mail*, 14 January 2010, A2.
64 VANOC, *Vancouver 2010: Sustainability Report 2009–10*, 81.
65 Rossiter and Wood quote the press release in their article "Fantastic Topographies," 364: Press Release, BC Ministry for Advanced Education and Treaty Negotiations Office, 12 March 2004, "BC boosts tourism training, jobs for First Nations."
66 Tourism British Columbia 2010 Aboriginal Business Summit Conference Program, 21 January–2 February 2007, AM1550, Series 3, Box 819-E-1, File 30, VANOCF, CVA.
67 Ibid.
68 "Partners Creating Shared Legacies From the 2010 Olympic and Paralympic Winter Games: Agreement Between the Squamish and Lil'Wat Nations, the Vancouver 2010 Bid Corporation, and the Province of British Columbia," 22 November 2002; for a copy of the agreement, see Appendix C, Dunn, "Aboriginal Partnerships for Sustainable 2010 Olympic and Paralympic Winter Games."

69 Ibid.
70 Item – *The World's Biggest Potlatch – Aboriginal participation in the Vancouver 2010 Olympic and Paralympic Winter Games*, AM1550, Series 3, Box 819–C–7, VANOCF, CVA, 9.
71 Tourism Industry Association of Canada, Canadian Sport Tourism Alliance, 2010 Olympics – A Call to Action for the Canadian Tourism Industry, Ottawa, July 2004, AM1550, Series 1, Sub-Series 20, Box 820–F–5, File 12, VANOCF, CVA.
72 Tourism BC Draft 21 December, AM1550, Series 1, Sub-Series 12, Box 820–E–5, File Ceremonies – Vancouver Opening and closing ceremonies briefing, 2006, VANOCF, CVA.
73 BC Ministry of Aboriginal Relations and Reconciliation, *New Relationships with Aboriginal People and Communities in British Columbia, Annual Report on Progress 2009–2010*, 10.
74 Ibid., 5.
75 Ibid., 7.
76 Ibid.
77 Ibid., 31.
78 See Blackburn, "Searching for Guarantees in the Midst of Uncertainty"; Woolford, "Negotiating Affirmative Repair."
79 Penikett, *Reconciliation*, 257.
80 Vernon, "What New Relationship?" 282.
81 Ibid., 283.
82 Rossiter and Wood, "Fantastic Topographies."
83 Ibid., 358.
84 Forsyth, "The Illusion of Inclusion," 24.
85 BC Ministry of Aboriginal Relations and Reconciliation, *New Relationships with Aboriginal People and Communities in BC: Measuring Outcomes, 2011–2012*, 8.
86 Ibid. The report defined youth as aged fifteen to twenty-four years old. Between 2001 and 2005, the ratio of Indigenous to non-Indigenous youth suicides in the province (expressed as the number of suicides per 10,000 people) was 3.8 to 0.8. Between 2006 and 2010, that ratio was 3.0 to 0.7. While any reduction in the number of youth suicides is a step in the right direction, these numbers remain alarmingly high.
87 Ibid.
88 VANOC, *Vancouver 2010: Sustainability Report 2009–10*, 10, 11, 23, 76, 78; the report includes the phrase "unprecedented Aboriginal participation" twice on pages 76 and 78.
89 Ibid., 10.
90 Ibid., 11.
91 See Gold and Gold, "Bring It Under the Legacy Umbrella."

92 Allan Besson, "Olympic Program Promotes Sport to Far North," *Ottawa Citizen*, 6 January 2010, B7; "Vancouver 2010 Olympic Truce Initiative to Bring Olympic Spirit to Canada's Far North," *Canada NewsWire*, 4 January 2010.

93 VANOC, *Vancouver 2010: Sustainability Report 2009–10*, 81.

94 VANOC, *Vancouver 2010: Staging the Olympic Winter Games Knowledge Report*, 52.

95 IOC Marketing Department, *Marketing Report Vancouver 2010*, 51.

96 Ibid.

97 Kobayashi, "Corporate Nationalism and Glocalization of Nike Advertising in 'Asia,'" 44.

98 Ibid. See also Silk and Andrews, "The Spatial Logics of Global Sponsorship."

99 Jackson and Hokowhitu, "Sport, Tribes, and Technology."

100 Hayhurst and Szto, "Corporatizating Activism through Sport-Focused Social Justice?"

101 "Anti-2010: Information Against the Olympic Industry: No Olympics on Stolen Native Land," AM1519, Item PAM 2010–21, CVPC, CVA, 7–8.

102 Mia Dauvergne, "Adult Correctional Statistics in Canada, 2010/2011," Statistics Canada, 2012, http://www.statcan.gc.ca/pub/85-002-x/2012001/article/11715-eng.htm#r11.

103 "Anti-2010: Information Against the Olympic Industry: No Olympics on Stolen Native Land," AM1519, Item PAM 2010–21, CVPC, CVA, 10.

104 O'Bonsawin, "Indigenous Peoples and Canadian-Hosted Olympic Games," 51–2, italics added. See also O'Bonsawin, "No Olympics on Stolen Native Land."

105 News Release, "Introducing ILANAAQ: Vancouver 2010 Olympic Winter Games emblem celebrates Canada," 23 April 2005, AM1550, Series 1, Sub-Series 14, File 14, Box 820–E–7, VANOCF, CVA.

106 Ibid.

107 Jane Armstrong, "The Friend Nobody Likes," *Globe and Mail*, 27 April 2005, A1, italics in original.

108 Jim Morris, "BC Natives Criticize Olympic Logo Choice," *Globe and Mail*, 26 April 2005, A9.

109 Philip, quoted in ibid.

110 O'Bonsawin, "The Conundrum of 'Ilanaaq,'" 391–2.

111 Morris, "BC Natives Criticize Olympic Logo Choice."

112 "Olympic Medals: The Aboriginal Aesthetic," *Globe and Mail*, 19 October 2009, A16.

113 Pupchek, "True North," 191.

114 Ibid., 198.

115 This video can be viewed on YouTube: "Heritage Minutes: Inukshuk," YouTube video, 1:00, Historica Canada, 9 March 2016, https://www.youtube.

com/watch?v=JD7rAD_S-fE; see also "Heritage Minutes," Historica Canada, https://www.historicacanada.ca/heritageminutes.

116 For a discussion of the ad, see Ruhl, "Iconification and the Nationalized Inukshuk," 8–10.

117 For a full transcript of Harper's apology, see "Statement of Apology to Former Students of Indian Residential Schools," Crown-Indigenous Relations and Northern Affairs Canada (formerly Indigenous and Northern Affairs Canada), https://www.rcaanc-cirnac.gc.ca/eng/1100100015644/1571589171655.

118 See Dorrell, "From Reconciliation to Reconciling."

119 Henderson and Wakeham, "Colonial Reckoning, National Reconciliation?" 2.

120 Harper, quoted in "Harper Drops the 'C-Bomb' on G20," *Winnipeg Free Press*, 3 October 2009, A19; Henderson and Wakeham discuss the significance of his statement: Henderson and Wakeham, "Colonial Reckoning, National Reconciliation?" 1–2.

121 "Do you hate the Olympics?" AM1519, Box 538-G-02, Item PAM 2010-7, CVPC, CVA.

122 Stella August and Phillipa Ryan, "In our own words: Women living in the Downtown Eastside weigh in on the Olympics," *The Dominion: News from the grassroots: A special report on the winter Olympics*, 2009, Issue #64, AM1519, Item PAM 2009-14, CVPC, CVA, 28.

123 August, contribution in ibid.

124 Ibid.

125 TRC, *Honouring the Truth, Reconciling for the Future*, 268.

126 Ibid., 8.

127 Henderson and Wakeham, "Colonial Reckoning, National Reconciliation?" 2.

128 Sykes, *The Sexual and Gender Politics of Sport Mega-Events*, 33; according to Sykes, Pride House organizers acknowledged that they could have done more to support Two-Spirited, trans, and queer youth.

129 Ibid., 39.

130 Ibid., 59.

131 Mackey, "The Apologizers' Apology," 49.

132 VANOC, *Vancouver 2010: Staging the Olympic Winter Games Knowledge Report*, 15.

133 Kalman-Lamb, "A Portrait of This Country," 6.

134 "Hymn to the North," Vancouver 2010 Olympic Winter Games Opening Ceremony (program), AM1550, Series 3, Box 822-G-1, VANOCF, CVA.

135 For video footage of the ceremony, see "Complete Vancouver 2010 Opening Ceremony – Vancouver 2010 Winter Olympics," YouTube video, 3:09:47, Olympicvancouver2010, 11 April 2010, https://www.youtube.com/watch?v=MxZpUueDAvc.

136 Kalman-Lamb, "A Portrait of This Country," 12.

137 Ibid., 19.
138 Ibid.
139 Adese, "Colluding with the Enemy" 496–7.
140 Coulthard, *Red Skin, White Masks*, 125, italics added.
141 Item – Opening ceremony of the XXI Olympic Winter Games Media Guide, AM1550, Series 3, Box 819–A–02, VANOCF, CVA, 47–69.
142 Coulthard, *Red Skin, White Masks*, 125.
143 Magdalinski, "Cute, Loveable Characters," 79.
144 "Vancouver 2010 Olympic Mascot – Creative Brief," 29 November 2006, AM1550, Series 1, Sub-Series 18, Box 819–E–01, File 14, VANOCF, CVA.
145 Ibid.
146 IOC Marketing Department, *Marketing Report Vancouver 2010*, 132.
147 Ibid.
148 Gold and Gold, "Access for All," 139.
149 Miga "Mascot Profile," in Wong and Murphy, *Miga, Quatchi and/et Sumi.*
150 Quatchi "Mascot Profile" in ibid.
151 Sumi "Mascot Profile" in ibid.
152 O'Bonsawin, "Indigenous Peoples and Canadian-Hosted Olympic Games," 55.
153 Wong and Murphy, *Miga, Quatchi and/et Sumi*; Official Vancouver 2010 Licensed Merchandise, AM1550, Series 1, Sub-Series 19, Box 819–D–7, File 21, VANOCF, CVA; Official Vancouver 2010 Licensed Lapel Pins 2006–2009 Releases, AM1550, Series 1, Sub-Series 19, Box 819–D–6, File 19, VANOCF, CVA.
154 Official Vancouver 2010 Licensed Merchandise, AM1550, Series 1, Sub-Series 19, Box 819–D–7, File 21, VANOCF, CVA; Wong and Murphy, *Miga, Quatchi and/et Sumi*; Bruce Constantineau, "Olympic Merchandise Bucks Sliding Retail Trend," *Vancouver Sun*, 27 February 2009, A8; "Making Mascot Merchandise Plush Job," *Star Phoenix*, 23 February 2009, C4; Steve Mandich and Eliza Truitt, "Quatchi Watch," 31 January 2010 and 30 April 2010 posts, https://quatchiwatch.wordpress.com/.
155 Rod Mickleburgh, "Mukmuk No Longer on the Sidelines," *Globe and Mail*, 28 November 2008, A13; "Mascot Mukmuk Gets Sprung from Cyberspace," *Vancouver Sun*, 28 November 2008, A6.
156 MacQueen, quoted in Pete McMartin, "Ta-Da … Meet the Four Profits," *Vancouver Sun*, 28 November 2007, A1.
157 "Mascot Mukmuk Gets Sprung from Cyberspace," *Vancouver Sun*, 28 November 2008, A6.
158 Mandich and Truitt, "Quatchi Watch," https://quatchiwatch.wordpress.com/.
159 Street, quoted in Shawna Richer, "We Love You, Quatchi. Oh Yes We Do. We Don't Love Anyone as Much as You," *Globe and Mail*, 20 February 2010, F3.

160 Jeff Lee, "Mukmuk's Identity Crisis: Marmot or Gofer?" *Vancouver Sun*, 12 February 2008, A4.

161 Jeff Lee, "People Want Mukmuk Unshackled," *Vancouver Sun*, 17 March 2008, B3.

162 "Readers Plead for Mukmuk," *Vancouver Sun*, 17 March 2008, B3.

163 Sam Cooper, "MukMuk Supporters Urge Mucky-Mucks to Heed Their Calls,'" *Vancouver Province*, 24 February 2010, A9.

164 Mickleburgh, "Mukmuk No Longer on the Sidelines."

165 Canadian Olympic School Program, "Brand Development and the Vancouver 2010 Olympic Winter Games," https://olympic.ca/education/resources.

166 Ibid.

167 O'Bonsawin, "Indigenous Peoples and Canadian-Hosted Olympic Games," 55.

168 Cole and Chaikin, *An Iron Hand upon the People*, 2.

169 Ibid., 1.

170 "The Government of Canada Encourages Aboriginal Youth Across Canada to Find Their Passion in Sport," Government of Canada, 2009, https://www.canada.ca/en/news/archive/2009/03/government-canada-encourages-aboriginal-youth-across-canada-find-their-passion-sport.html?=undefined&.

171 Ibid.

172 VANOC, "When Aboriginal Athletes Meet the Press … ," http://www.vancouver2010.com.

173 VANOC, "Understanding Traditional and Modern Plant Uses," http://www.vancouver2010.com.

Conclusion

1 Clare Ogilvie, "Clothes That Show Your Support," *Vancouver Province*, 24 November 2009, C13.

2 Dana Flavelle, "A Red-Hot Happy Accident; American CEO of the Bay Thought Torch Bearer Outfit Needed Something Colourful and Distinctly Canadian," *Toronto Star*, 2 March 2010, B1.

3 Sherman, quoted in Marina Strauss, "Hudson's Bay Goes for the Gold," *Globe and Mail*, 2 October 2009, A13.

4 Kinnin, quoted in Marina Strauss, "After Beijing Flop, Bay Goes All-Canadian," *Globe and Mail*, 17 June 2009, B3.

5 Heller, quoted in News Release, "Hudson's Bay Company and Vancouver 2010 announce eight-year partnership," 2 March 2005, AM1550, Series 1, Sub-Series 14, Box 820-E-7, File 14, VANOCF, CVA.

6 Cleve Dheensaw, "15 Ways the Commonwealth Games Changed Us," *Times Colonist*, 17 August 2014, D5.

7 Ipsos-Reid, "Canadian and Provincial Olympic Perceptions Summary Results," 17 May 2005, Series 1, Sub-Series 14, Box 820-E-7, File 17, VANOCF, CVA, 23.
8 Marina Strauss, "Bay Sees Store's Future in Its Past," *Globe and Mail*, 23 January 2009, B2.
9 The ad can be viewed on YouTube: Vancouverite1989, "HBC 2010: We Were Made for This (Vancouver 2010 Olympics)," YouTube video, 1:00, Vancouverite1989, 18 January 2010, https://www.youtube.com/watch?v=dLsFkZKj63U.
10 These comments can be viewed below the YouTube video, ibid.
11 HBC statement, quoted in Mark Hume, "The Bay, Cowichan Leaders Hope to Settle Sweater Row," *Globe and Mail*, 27 October 2009, A8.
12 Ibid. See also Brennan Clarke, "Cowichan Tribes, Bay Reach Deal on Sweaters," *Globe and Mail*, 25 January 2010, S1; Christine O'Bonsawin, "Indigenous Peoples and Canadian-Hosted Olympic Games," 56–7.
13 HBC ad "World Famous Hudson's Bay Coats," *Edmonton Journal*, 2 August 1978, A19–A20.
14 VANOC, *Vancouver 2010: Staging the Olympic Winter Games Knowledge Report*, 8.
15 Ibid., 9.
16 John Furlong speaking notes, 27 October, AM1550, Series 1, Sub-Series 14, Box 820-E-7, File 14, VANOCF, CVA.
17 IOC Marketing Department, *Marketing Report Vancouver 2010*, 116; Flavelle, "A Red-Hot Happy Accident."
18 Shelley Fralic, "Priceless Memories Don't Come Cheap," *Vancouver Sun*, 16 February 2010, E1.
19 Hall, quoted in Rod Mickleburgh, "Red Mitten Fever Has Gone National," *Globe and Mail*, 10 December 2009, A3.
20 Andrea Woo, "Olympic Mittens Still a Red-Hot Commodity," *Vancouver Sun*, 6 March 2010, A15.
21 Mickleburgh, "Red Mitten Fever Has Gone National."
22 McNeil, quoted in James Keller, "Good Luck Getting Your Paws in These Mitts: Paralympic Mittens a Rare Souvenir," *Canadian Press*, 12 March 2010.
23 IOC Marketing Department, *Marketing Report Vancouver 2010*, 88, 119.
24 James Keller, "On Your Mark … Get Set … Shop!," *Kamloops Daily News*, 20 February 2010, B1.
25 Hall, quoted in ibid.
26 COC, "Athletes CAN – Supporting the Voices of 2010 and Beyond," Canadian Olympic Team Official Website, 19 November 2009, http://olympic.ca/2009/11/19/athletescan-supporting-the-voices-of-2010-and-beyond/.

27 COC, "As Red mittens Fly off Shelves, Olympic Spirit Builds," Canadian Olympic Team Official Website, 21 December 2009, http://olympic.ca/2009/12/21/as-red-mittens-fly-off-shelves-olympic-spirit-builds/.
28 Brenner, quoted in "Red Mittens Support Athletes," *Prince George Citizen*, 5 October 2009, 12.
29 Furlong, quoted in ibid.
30 Kim, quoted in "Smitten with Mittens," *Star Phoenix*, 21 December 2009, C4.
31 "Red Mittens Support Athletes."
32 Kikulis, "Contemporary Policy Issues in High Performance Sport," 116.
33 Kreek, quoted in COC, "Stephen Harper Receives Holiday Gift from Canadian Olympic Team," 7 December 2010, https://olympic.ca/2010/12/07/stephen-harper-receives-holiday-gift-from-canadian-olympic-team-2/.
34 This ad can be viewed on YouTube: "Petro-Canada Vancouver 2010 Glassware Commercial," YouTube video, 0:30, Petro-Canada, 29 November 2013, https://www.youtube.com/watch?v=4yx7aXrcKro&list=PLWMRezgdS5q5ofZzQU2_uM82ltVSbJdx4.
35 Boykoff, *Celebration Capitalism and the Olympic Games*, 3.
36 Ibid., chap. 1.
37 Ibid., 5.
38 Kikulis, "Contemporary Policy Issues in High Performance Sport," 114–19.
39 Ibid., 116.
40 "About Own the Podium," Own the Podium, https://www.ownthepodium.org/en-CA/Notre-organisation.
41 COC, "New Red Mittens Unveiled: Helping Canadian Athletes Go For Gold in London 2012," 29 September 2011, https://olympic.ca/2011/09/29/red-mittens-2012/; see also Kikulis, "Contemporary Policy Issues in High Performance Sport," 114–19.
42 Stole, "Philanthropy as Public Relations," 26.
43 Ibid., 33. See also King, *Pink Ribbons, Inc.*
44 Furlong, quoted in IOC Marketing Department, *Marketing Report Vancouver 2010*, 115.
45 See Wright, "Biopower, Biopedagogies and the Obesity Epidemic"; Halse, "Bio-Citizenship."
46 Edwardson, quoted in Keller, "On Your Mark…Get Set…Shop!"
47 Wright, Millard, and Riegel, "Here's Where We Get Canadian," 21.
48 "Blood on Your Hands," AM1519, Box 632-A-02, Item PAM 2010-37, CVPC, CVA.
49 IOC Marketing Department, *Marketing Report Vancouver 2010*, 132. Photos showing the mascots visiting communities in Northern Canada as part of the Vancouver Olympic Truce Northern Outreach Project are posted

on the Quatchi Watch blog: Steve Mandich and Eliza Truitt, "Get in the Plane: Quatchi on Tour#2," Quatchi Watch, 2010, https://quatchiwatch.wordpress.com/2010/02/02/get-in-the-plane-quatchi-on-tour-2/.

50 "Hello from Quatchi," Life at Periwinkle, 2010, http://lifeatperiwinkle.blogspot.ca/2010/03/hello-from-quatchi.html. The creator of the website PogKnits posted a knitting pattern for the mittens on her website. See "Mini Olympic Red Mittens," PogKnits, 9 January 2010, http://pogknits.blogspot.com/2010/01/mini-olympic-red-mittens.html.

51 Martin, "Truth, Reconciliation, and Amnesia," 49, italics in original.

52 Ibid., 57.

53 Justine Hunter, "They Came for a Pelt and Left with a Quatchi," *Globe and Mail*, 9 February 2010, A3.

54 TRC, *Honouring the Truth, Reconciling for the Future*, 6.

55 Regan, *Unsettling the Settler Within*, 116.

56 Wolfe, "Settler Colonialism and the Elimination of the Native."

57 See TRC, *Honouring the Truth, Reconciling for the Future*, "The Legacy," 183–236, and "The Challenge of Reconciliation," 237–382.

58 Coulthard, *Red Skin, White Masks*, 168.

Bibliography

Archives

Bibliothèque et Archives nationales du Québec (BANQ), Montreal
Fonds Comité organisateur des Jeux olympiques de 1976 (FCOJO), E46
City of Calgary Archives (CCA)
XV Olympic Winter Games Inventories (XVWGI), PR-90
City of Edmonton Archives (CEA)
Commonwealth Games Fonds, 1967–1981 (CGF), RG-78
City of Vancouver Archives (CVA)
City of Vancouver Pamphlet Collection (CVPC), AM1519
Vancouver: British Empire and Commonwealth Games, Canada (1954) Society Fonds (BECGSF), AM172
Vancouver Bid Corporation Fonds (VBCF), AM1581
Vancouver Organizing Committee for the 2010 Olympic and Paralympic Winter Games Fonds (VANOCF), AM1550
City of Victoria Archives (CVicA)
Victoria Commonwealth Games Society Fonds (VCGSF), PR74

Newspapers, Magazines, and Wires

Business Wire
Calgary Herald
Canada Newswire
Canadian Press
Chicago Tribune
Edmonton Journal
Financial Post
Globe and Mail
Kamloops Daily News
Maclean's

Ottawa Citizen
Peace River Record Gazette
PR *Newswire Europe*
Prince George Citizen
Star Phoenix
Sydney Morning Herald
Times Colonist
Toronto Star
USA *Today*
Vancouver Province
Vancouver Sun
Washington Post
Windspeaker
Winnipeg Free Press

Works Cited

Adese, Jennifer. "Colluding with the Enemy? Nationalism and Depictions of 'Aboriginality' in Canadian Olympic Moments." *American Indian Quarterly* 36, no. 4 (2012): 479–502.

Ahenakew, Vince, ed. *Nêhiyawêwin Masinahiķan Michif/Cree Dictionary*. Saskatoon: Saskatchewan Indian Cultural Centre, 1998.

Alfred, Taiaiake. *Wasáse: Indigenous Pathways of Action and Freedom*. Peterborough: Broadview Press, 2005.

Anholt, Simon. *Competitive Identity: The New Brand Management for Nations, Cities and Regions*. London: Palgrave Macmillan, 2007.

Appadurai, Arjun. "Introduction: Commodities and the Politics of Value." In *The Social Life of Things: Commodities in Cultural Perspective*, edited by Arjun Appadurai, 3–63. Cambridge: Cambridge University Press, 1986.

Arendt, Hannah. *The Origins of Totalitarianism*. New York: Harcourt, Brace & World, 1968.

Aronczyk, Melissa. *Branding the Nation: The Global Business of National Identity*. Oxford: Oxford University Press, 2013.

– "'Living the Brand': Nationality, Globality and the Identity Strategies of Nation Branding Consultants." *International Journal of Communication* 2 (2008): 41–65.

Barney, Robert K. "The Olympic Games in Modern Times." In *Onward to the Olympics: Historical Perspectives on the Olympic Games*, edited by Gerald P. Schaus and Stephen R. Wenn, 221–42. Waterloo: Wilfrid Laurier University Press, 2007.

Barney, Robert K., Stephen R. Wenn, and Scott G. Martyn. *Selling the Five Rings: The International Olympic Committee and the Rise of Olympic Commercialism*. Utah: University of Utah Press, 2002.

BC Ministry of Aboriginal Relations and Reconciliation. *New Relationships with Aboriginal People and Communities in British Columbia, Annual Report on Progress 2009–2010*. Victoria, 2010.

– *New Relationships with Aboriginal People and Communities in BC: Measuring Outcomes, 2011–2012*. Victoria, 2012.

Belisle, Donica. *Retail Nation: Department Stores and the Making of Modern Canada*. Vancouver: UBC Press, 2011.

– "Toward a Canadian Consumer History." *Labour/Le Travail* 52 (2003): 181–206.

Belk, Russell W. "Collectors and Collecting." In *Interpreting Objects and Collections*, edited by Susan M. Pearce, 317–26. London and New York: Routledge, 1994.

Billig, Michael. "Commodity Fetishism and Repression: Reflections on Marx, Freud and the Psychology of Consumer Capitalism." *Theory & Psychology* 9, no. 3 (1999): 313–29.

Billings, Andrew C., and Lawrence A. Wenner. "The Curious Case of the Megasporting Event: Media, Mediatization and Seminal Sports Events." In *Sport, Media and Mega-Events*, edited by Lawrence A. Wenner and Andrew C. Billings, 3–18. London and New York: Routledge, 2017.

Blackburn, Carole. "Differentiating Indigenous Citizenship: Seeking Multiplicity in Rights, Identity, and Sovereignty in Canada." *American Ethnologist* 36 no. 1 (2009): 66–78.

– "Searching for Guarantees in the Midst of Uncertainty: Negotiating Aboriginal Rights and Title in British Columbia." *American Anthropologist* 107, no. 4 (2005): 586–96.

Bothwell, Robert. *Canada and Quebec: One Country, Two Histories*. Vancouver: University of British Columbia Press, 1995.

Boykoff, Jules. *Celebration Capitalism and the Olympic Games*. London and New York: Routledge, 2014.

Bridge, Kathryn. "Introduction: The Lost Klee Wyck." In *Klee Wyck*, 1–15. Vancouver/Toronto: Douglas & McIntyre, 2003.

Brownell, Susan. "Introduction: Bodies before Boas, Sport before the Laughter Left." In *The 1904 Anthropology Days and Olympic Games: Sport, Race, and American Imperialism*, edited by Susan Brownell, 1–58. Lincoln: University of Nebraska Press, 2008.

Bryant, John. "Stamp and Coin Collecting." In *Handbook of American Popular Culture*, edited by M. Thomas Inge, 1329–65. New York: Greenwood Press, 1989.

Cameron, Emilie. "Indigenous Spectrality and the Politics of Postcolonial Ghost Stories." *Cultural Geographies* 15, no. 3 (2008): 383–93.

Campbell, Colin S. "Canadian Gambling Policies." In *Casino State: Legalized Gambling in Canada*, edited by Thomas R. Klassen and James F. Cosgrave, 69–90. Toronto: University of Toronto Press, 2009.

– "Under the Halo of Good Causes." In *Gambling: Public Policies and the Social Sciences*, edited by William R. Eadington and Judy A. Cornelius, 607–20. Reno: Institute for the Study of Gambling and Commercial Gaming, 1997.

Campbell, Colin S., and Garry J. Smith. "Gambling in Canada – From Vice to Disease to Responsibility: A Negotiated History." *Canadian Bulletin of Medical History* 20, no. 1 (2003): 121–49.

Carr, Emily. *Klee Wyck*. Vancouver/Toronto: Douglas & McIntyre, 2003.

Carstairs, Catherine. "Roots Nationalism: Branding English Canada Cool in the 1980s and 1990s." *Histoire sociale/Social History* 39, no. 77 (2006): 235–55.

Case, Donald O. "Serial Collecting as Leisure, and Coin Collecting in Particular." *Library Trends* 57, no. 4 (2009): 729–52.

Castelló, Enric, and Sabina Mihelj. "Selling and Consuming the Nation: Understanding Consumer Nationalism." *Journal of Consumer Culture* 18, no. 4 (2018): 558–76.

CBC. *Broadcasters Handbook: XV Commonwealth Games: Victoria, BC, Canada, August 18–28, 1994*. Victoria: Fleming Printing Ltd., 1994.

Chastko, Paul. *Developing Alberta's Oil Sands: From Karl Clark to Kyoto*. Calgary: University of Calgary Press, 2004.

Cohen, Stanley. *States of Denial: Knowing about Atrocities and Suffering*. Cambridge: Polity Press, 2001.

Cohen-Almagor, Raphael. "The Terrorists' Best Ally: The Quebec Media Coverage of the FLQ Crisis in October 1970." *Canadian Journal of Communication* 25, no. 2 (2000): 251–84.

COJO. *The Official Report of the XXI Olympiad Montréal 1976*. Ottawa, 1978.

Cole, Douglas, and Ira Chaikin. *An Iron Hand upon the People: The Law against the Potlatch on the Northwest Coast*. Vancouver/Toronto: Douglas & McIntyre, 1990.

Cormack, Patricia, and James F. Cosgrave. *Desiring Canada: CBC, Contests, Hockey Violence, and Other Stately Pleasures*. Toronto: University of Toronto Press, 2013.

Coulthard, Glen Sean. *Red Skin, White Masks: Rejecting the Colonial Politics of Recognition*. Minneapolis: University of Minnesota Press, 2014.

Crabtree, Grant. *Klee Wyck*. National Film Board of Canada, 1946.

Creighton, Donald Grant. *The Forked Road: Canada 1939–1957*. Toronto: McClelland and Stewart, 1976.

Cuccioletta, Donald, and Martin Lubin. "The Quebec Quiet Revolution: A Noisy Evolution." *Québec Studies* 36 (2003): 125–38.

Daschuk, James W. *Clearing the Plains: Disease, Politics of Starvation, and the Loss of Aboriginal Life*. Regina: University of Regina Press, 2013.

Dorrell, Matthew. "From Reconciliation to Reconciling: Reading What 'We Now Recognize' in the Government of Canada's 2008 Residential Schools Apology." *English Studies in Canada* 35, no. 1 (2009): 27–45.

Downey, Allan. *The Creator's Game: Lacrosse, Identity, and Indigenous Nationhood*. Vancouver: UBC Press, 2018.

Drees, Laurie Meijer. "White Paper/Red Paper: Aboriginal Contributions to Canadian Politics and Government." In *Hidden in Plain Sight: Contributions of Aboriginal Peoples to Canadian Identity and Culture*, 2nd ed., vol. 2, edited by Cora J. Voyageur, David R. Newhouse, and Dan Beavon, 282–99. Toronto, 2011.

Dunn, Catharine Hilary. "Aboriginal Partnerships for Sustainable 2010 Olympic and Paralympic Winter Games: A Framework for Cooperation." Master's thesis, Simon Fraser University, 2007.

Ferguson, Jeanne. "Shäwthän Dän, Shäwthän Kwänjè: Good People, Good Words: Creating a Dän k'è Speech Community in an Elementary School." *Current Issues in Language Planning* 11, no. 2 (2010): 152–72.

Fisher, Donald M. *Lacrosse: A History of the Game*. Baltimore: Johns Hopkins University Press, 2002.

Forsyth, Janice. "The Illusion of Inclusion: Agenda 21 and the Commodification of Aboriginal Culture in the Vancouver 2010 Olympic Games." *Public* 27, no. 53 (2016): 22–34.

– "Tee-pees and Tomahawks: Aboriginal Cultural Representation at the 1976 Olympic Games." In *The Global Nexus Engaged: Past, Present, Future Interdisciplinary Olympic Studies: Sixth International Symposium for Olympic Research*, edited by Robert K. Barney, Scott G. Martyn, and Kevin B. Wamsley, 71–6. London: Centre for Olympic Studies, 2002.

Forsyth, Janice, and Kevin B. Wamsley. "Symbols without Substance: Aboriginal Peoples and the Illusions of Olympic Ceremonies." In *Global Olympics: Historical and Sociological Studies of the Modern Games*, edited by Kevin Young and Kevin B. Wamsley, 227–48. Amsterdam: Elsevier JAI, 2005.

Fossum, John Erik. *Oil, the State, and Federalism: The Rise and Demise of Petro-Canada as a Statist Impulse*. Toronto: University of Toronto Press, 1997.

Francis, Daniel. *The Imaginary Indian: The Image of the Indian in Canadian Culture*. Vancouver: Arsenal Pulp Press, 1992.

Francis, Margot. *Creative Subversions: Whiteness, Indigeneity, and the National Imaginary*. Vancouver: UBC Press, 2011.

The Friendly Games: The XI Commonwealth Games, Edmonton, Alberta, Canada, August 3–12, 1978. Edmonton: Koala Books of Canada, 1978.

Freud, Sigmund. *The Uncanny*. Translated by David McLintock. London: Penguin Books, 1953.

Fulton, John. "Document One: The Fulton Report." *Native Studies Review* 4, nos 1–2 (1988): 181–201.

Goddard, John. *Last Stand of the Lubicon Cree*. Vancouver/Toronto: Douglas & McIntyre, 1991.

Godlewska, Christina, and Jeremy Webber. "The *Calder* Decision, Aboriginal Title, Treaties, and the Nisga'a." In *Let Right Be Done: Aboriginal Title, the Calder Case, and the Future of Indigenous Rights*, edited by Hamar Foster, Heather Raven, and Jeremy Webber, 1–33. Vancouver: UBC Press, 2007.

Gold, John R., and Margaret M. Gold. "Access for All: The Rise of the Paralympic Games." *Journal of The Royal Society for the Promotion of Health* 127, no. 3 (2007): 133–41.

– "'Bring It under the Legacy Umbrella': Olympic Host Cities and the Changing Fortunes of the Sustainability Agenda." *Sustainability* 5 (2012): 3526–42.

Goodstriker, Wilton. "Introduction: Otsistsi Pakssaisstoyiih Pi (The Year when the Winter Was Open and Cold." In *The True Spirit and Original Intent of Treaty 7*, by Treaty 7 Elders and Tribal Council with Walter Hildebrandt, Dorothy First Rider, and Sarah Carter, 3–27. Montreal & Kingston: McGill-Queen's University Press, 1996.

Gordon, Avery. *Ghostly Matters: Haunting and the Sociological Imagination*. Minneapolis: University of Minnesota Press, 2008.

Gorman, Daniel. "Amateurism, Imperialism, Internationalism and the First British Empire Games." *International Journal of the History of Sport* 27, no. 4 (2010): 611–34.

Halse, Christine. "Bio-Citizenship: Virtue Discourses and the Birth of the Bio-Citizen." In *Biopolitics and the "Obesity Epidemic": Governing Bodies*, edited by Jan Wright and Valerie Harwood, 45–59. London and New York: Routledge, 2009.

Harrison, Julia. "'The Spirit Sings' and the Future of Anthropology." *Anthropology Today* 4, no. 6 (1988): 6–9.

Harvey, David. *A Brief History of Neoliberalism*. Oxford: Oxford University Press, 2005.

Hayhurst, Lyndsay M.C., and Courtney Szto. "Corporatizating Activism through Sport-Focused Social Justice?: Investigating Nike's Corporate Responsibility Initiatives in Sport for Development and Peace." *Journal of Sport & Social Issues* 40, no. 6 (2016): 522–44.

Heinrich, Michael. *An Introduction to the Three Volumes of Karl Marx's Capital*. Translated by Alexander Locascio. New York: Monthly Review Press, 2012.

Henderson, Jennifer, and Pauline Wakeham. "Colonial Reckoning, National Reconciliation?: Aboriginal Peoples and the Culture of Redress in Canada." *English Studies in Canada* 35, no. 1 (2009): 1–26.

– "Introduction." In *Reconciling Canada: Critical Perspectives on the Culture of Redress*, edited by Jennifer Henderson and Pauline Wakeham, 3–30. Toronto: University of Toronto Press, 2013.

Hobson, Alan. *Share the Flame: The Official Retrospective Book of the Olympic Torch Relay*. Vancouver: Murray/Love Productions, 1998.

Howell, Paul Charles. *The Montreal Olympics: An Insider's View of Organizing a Self-Financing Games*. Montreal & Kingston: McGill-Queen's University Press, 2009.

IOC. *Olympic Charter*. Lausanne: International Olympic Committee, 2021.

– *Olympic Movement's Agenda 21: Sport for Sustainable Development*. Lausanne: International Olympic Committee, 1999.

IOC Marketing Department. *Marketing Report Vancouver 2010*. Lausanne: International Olympic Committee, 2011.

Jackson, Steven J., and Brendan Hokowhitu. "Sport, Tribes, and Technology: The New Zealand All Blacks *Haka* and the Politics of Identity." *Journal of Sport & Social Issues* 26, no. 2 (2002): 125–39.

Jancewicz, Bill. "Related-Language Translation: Naskapi and East Cree." In *Born in the Blood: On Native American Translation*, edited by Brian Swann, 109–37. Lincoln: University of Nebraska Press, 2011.

Jung, Courtney. "Canada and the Legacy of the Indian Residential Schools: Transitional Justice for Indigenous Peoples in a Non-Transitional Society," 2009. https://ssrn.com/abstract=1374950 or http://dx.doi.org/10.2139/ssrn.1374950.

Kalman-Lamb, Nathan. "'A Portrait of This Country': Whiteness, Indigeneity, Multiculturalism and the Vancouver Opening Ceremonies." *Topia* 27 (2012): 5–27.

Kavaratzis, Michalis. "From City Marketing to City Branding: Towards a Theoretical Framework for Developing City Brands." *Place Branding and Public Diplomacy* 1, no. 1 (2004): 58–73.

Kidd, Bruce. "The Culture Wars of the Montreal Olympics." *International Review for the Sociology of Sport* 27, no. 2 (1992): 151–62.

Kikulis, Lisa M. "Contemporary Policy Issues in High Performance Sport." In *Sport Policy in Canada*, edited by Lucie Thibault and Jean Harvey, 97–145. Ottawa: University of Ottawa Press, 2013.

King, Frank W. *It's How You Play the Game: The Inside Story of the Calgary Olympics*. Calgary: Script: The Writer's Group, 1991.

King, Samantha. *Pink Ribbons, Inc.: Breast Cancer and the Politics of Philanthropy*. Minneapolis: University of Minnesota Press, 2006.

Kobayashi, Koji. "Corporate Nationalism and Glocalization of Nike Advertising in 'Asia': Production and Representation Practices of Cultural Intermediaries." *Sociology of Sport Journal*, 29 no. 1 (2012): 42–61.

Latouche, Daniel. "Montreal 1976." In *Olympic Cities: City Agendas, Planning, and the World's Games, 1896–2016*, 2nd ed., edited by John R. Gold and Margaret M. Gold, 247–67. London and New York: Routledge, 2011.

Leiss, William, Stephen Kline, Sut Jhally, Jacqueline Botterill, and Kyle Asquith. *Social Communication in Advertising*. 4th ed. New York and London: Routledge, 2005.

Let the Games Begin! Souvenir Magazine, XI Commonwealth Games Edmonton, Canada, Edmonton Journal, 2 August 1978.

MacAloon, John J. *This Great Symbol: Pierre de Coubertin and the Origins of the Modern Olympic Games*. Chicago: University of Chicago Press, 1981.

Mackey, Eva. "The Apologizers' Apology." In *Reconciling Canada: Critical Perspectives on the Culture of Redress*, edited by Jennifer Henderson and Pauline Wakeham, 47–62. Toronto: University of Toronto Press, 2013.

– *The House of Difference: Cultural Politics and National Identity in Canada*. London and New York: Routledge, 1999.

Magdalinski, Tara. "'Cute, Loveable Characters': The Place and Significance of Mascots in the Olympic Movement." OLYMPIKA: *The International Journal of Olympic Studies* 13 (2004): 75–92.

Maguire, Joseph A. "Branding and Consumption in the IOC's 'Celebrate Humanity' Campaign." *Sport in Society* 14 no. 7/8 (2011): 1056–68.

Maguire, Joseph, Sarah Barnard, Katie Butler, and Peter Golding. "'Celebrate Humanity' or 'Consumers'?: A Critical Evaluation of a Brand in Motion." *Social Identities* 41, no. 1 (2008): 63–76.

Mallon, Bill. "The Olympic Bribery Scandal." *Journal of Olympic History* May (2000): 11–27.

Martin, Keavy. "Truth, Reconciliation, and Amnesia: Porcupines and China Dolls and the Canadian Conscience." *English Studies in Canada* 35, no. 1 (2009): 47–65.

Martin-Hill, Dawn. *The Lubicon Lake Nation: Indigenous Knowledge and Power*. Toronto: University of Toronto Press, 2009.

Marx, Karl. *Capital*. Vol. 1. Translated by Ben Fowkes. New York: Vintage Books, 1977.

McClintock, Anne. *Imperial Leather: Race, Gender and Sexuality in the Colonial Contest*. London and New York: Routledge, 1995.

McKee, Christopher. *Treaty Talks in British Columbia: Building a New Relationship*. Vancouver: UBC Press, 2000.

McKenna, Brian, and Susan Purcell. *Drapeau*. Toronto/Vancouver: Clarke, Irwin & Company, 1980.

Miller, J.R. *Skyscrapers Hide the Heavens: A History of Indian-White Relations in Canada*. 3rd ed. Toronto: University of Toronto Press, 2000.

Mills, Sean. *The Empire Within: Postcolonial Thought and Political Activism in Sixties Montreal*. Montreal & Kingston: McGill-Queen's University Press, 2010.

Monod, David. "Bay Days: The Managerial Revolution and the Hudson's Bay Company Department Stores, 1912–1939." *Historical Papers/Communications historiques* 21, no. 1 (1986): 173–96.

Moore, Katharine E. "Strange Bedfellows and Cooperative Partners: The Influence of the Olympic Games on the Establishment of the British Empire Games." In *The 1984 Olympic Scientific Congress Proceedings*, vol. 7 of *Sport and Politics*, edited by Gerald Redmond, 117–21. Champaign: Human Kinetics Publishers, 1986.

– "'The Warmth of Comradeship': The First British Empire Games and Imperial Solidarity." *International Journal of the History of Sport* 6, no. 2 (1989): 242–51.

Moray, Gerta. *Unsettling Encounters: First Nations Imagery in the Art of Emily Carr*. Vancouver: UBC Press, 2006.

O'Bonsawin, Christine M. "The Conundrum of 'Ilanaaq': First Nations Representation and the 2010 Vancouver Olympics." In *Cultural Imperialism in Action: Critiques in the Global Olympic Trust: Eighth International Symposium for Olympic Research*, edited by Nigel Crowther, Robert Barney, and Michael Heine, 387–94. London: International Centre for Olympic Studies, 2006.

– "Indigenous Peoples and Canadian-Hosted Olympic Games." In *Aboriginal Peoples and Sport in Canada: Historical Foundations and Contemporary Challenges*, edited by Audrey R. Giles and Janice Forsyth, 35–63. Vancouver: UBC Press, 2013.

– "'No Olympics on Stolen Native Land': Contesting Olympic Narratives and Asserting Indigenous Rights within the Discourse of the 2010 Vancouver Games." *Sport in Society* 13, no. 1 (2010): 143–56

OCO'88. *XV Olympic Winter Games: Official Report*. Calgary, 1988.

Peach, Ian. "The Power of a Single Feather: Meech Lake, Indigenous Resistance and the Evolution of Indigenous Politics in Canada." *Review of Constitutional Studies/Revue d'etudes constitutionnelles* 16, no. 1 (2011): 1–29.

Penikett, Tony. *Reconciliation: First Nations Treaty Making in British Columbia*. Vancouver/Toronto: Douglas & McIntyre, 2006.

Pertusati, Linda. *In Defense of Mohawk Land: Ethnopolitical Conflict in Native North America*. Albany: State University of New York Press, 1997.

Poulter, Gillian. "Snowshoeing and Lacrosse: Canada's Nineteenth-Century 'National Games.'" In *Ethnicity, Sport, Identity: Struggles for Status*, edited by J.A. Mangan and Andrew Ritchie, 235–58. London and New York: Routledge, 2004.

– *Becoming Native in a Foreign Land: Sport, Visual Culture, & Identity in Montreal, 1840–85*. Vancouver: UBC Press, 2009.

Preuss, Holger. *Economics of the Olympic Games: Hosting the Games 1972–2000*. Petersham: Walla Walla Press, 2000.

Prince, Michael J., and James J. Rice. "Governing through Shifting Social-Policy Regimes: Brian Mulroney and Canada's Welfare State." In *Transforming the Nation: Canada and Brian Mulroney*, edited by Raymond B. Blake, 164–77. Montreal & Kingston: McGill-Queen's University Press, 2007.

Pupchek, Leanne Stuart. "True North: Inuit Art and the Canadian Imagination." *American Review of Canadian Studies* Spring/Summer (2001): 191–208.

Rahman, Momin, and Sean Lockwood. "How to 'Use Your Olympian': The Paradox of Athletic Authenticity and Commercialization in Contemporary Olympic Games." *Sociology* 45, no. 5 (2011): 815–29.

RCAP. *Report of the Royal Commission on Aboriginal Peoples*. Vol. 1, *Looking Forward, Looking Back*. Ottawa, 1996.

Redmond, Gerald, ed. *Edmonton '78: The Official Pictorial Record of the XI Commonwealth Games*. Edmonton: Executive Sport Publications Ltd., 1978.

Regan, Paulette. *Unsettling the Settler Within: Indian Residential Schools, Truth Telling, and Reconciliation in Canada*. Vancouver: UBC Press, 2010.

Robidoux, Michael A. "Imagining a Canadian Identity through Sport: A Historical Interpretation of Lacrosse and Hockey." *Journal of American Folklore* 115, no. 456 (2002): 209–25.

Roche, Maurice. *Mega-Events and Modernity: Olympics and Expos in the Growth of Global Culture*. London and New York: Routledge, 2000.

Rosenberg, Sharon, Amber Dean, and Kara Granzow. "Centennial Hauntings: Reckoning with the 2005 Celebration of Alberta's History." *Memory Studies* 3, no. 4 (2010): 395–412.

Rossiter, David, and Patricia K. Wood. "Fantastic Topographies: Neo-Liberal Responses to Aboriginal Land Claims in British Columbia." *Canadian Geographe/ Le Géographe canadien* 49, no. 4 (2005): 352–66.

Ruhl, Jeff. "Iconification and the Nationalized Inukshuk." Master's thesis, Carleton University, 2008.

Silk, Michael, and David L. Andrews. "The Spatial Logics of Global Sponsorship: Corporate Capital, Cola Wars and Cricket." In *Global Sport Sponsorship*, edited by John Amis and T. Betinna Cornwell, 67–88. Oxford: Berg, 2005.

Simpson, Audra. *Mohawk Interruptus: Political Life across the Borders of Settler States*. Durham: Duke University Press, 2014.

Somers, Margaret. *Genealogies of Citizenship: Markets, Statelessness, and the Right to Have Rights*. Cambridge: Cambridge University Press, 2008.

Stole, Inger L. "Philanthropy as Public Relations: A Critical Perspective on Cause Marketing." *Journal of Communication* (2008): 20–40.

Sykes, Heather. *The Sexual and Gender Politics of Sport Mega-Events: Roving Colonialism*. London and New York: Routledge, 2017.

Tanner, A. "Kleewyck." In *Dictionary of Minor Planet Names*, 6th ed., vol. 2, edited by Lutz Schmadel. Berlin: Springer Publishing Company, 2003.

Tippett, Maria. *Emily Carr, a Biography*. Harmondsworth: Penguin Books, 1982.

Tomlinson, Alan. "The Commercialisation of the Olympics: Cities, Corporations, and the Olympic Commodity." In *Global Olympics: Historical and Sociological Studies of the Modern Games*, edited by Kevin Young and Kevin B. Wamsley, 179–200. Amsterdam: Elsevier JAI, 2005.

TRC. *Honouring the Truth, Reconciling for the Future: Summary of the Final Report of the Truth and Reconciliation Commission of Canada*. Winnipeg, 2015.

– *The Survivors Speak: A Report of the Truth and Reconciliation Commission of Canada*. Winnipeg, 2015.

Trunnell, Eugene E., and William E. Holt. "The Concept of Denial or Disavowal." *Journal of the American Psychoanalytic Association* 22, no. 4 (1974): 769–84.

VANOC. *Vancouver 2010: Bid Report*, Vancouver, 2009.

– *Vancouver 2010: Staging the Olympic Winter Games Knowledge Report*. Vancouver, 2010.

– *Vancouver 2010: Sustainability Report 2009–10*. Vancouver, 2010.

VBC. *The Sea to Sky Games: Vancouver 2010 Candidate City/Ville Candidate Bid Book*. Vol. 1. Vancouver, 2003.

VCGS. *Official Souvenir Magazine of the XV Commonwealth Games*, 1994.

Vernon, Caitlyn. "What New Relationship? Taking Responsibility for Justice and Sustainability in British Columbia." In *Alliances: Re/Envisioning Indigenous-non-Indigenous Relationships*, edited by Lynne Davis, 276–94. Toronto: University of Toronto Press, 2010.

Voyageur, Cora J., David R. Newhouse, and Dan Beavon. "Introduction." In *Hidden in Plain Sight: Contributions of Aboriginal Peoples to Canadian*

Identity and Culture, 2nd ed., vol. 2, edited by Cora J. Voyageur, David R. Newhouse, and Dan Beavon, 3–14. Toronto, 2011.

Wagman, Ira. "Wheat, Barley, Hops, Citizenship: Molson's 'I Am [Canadian]' Campaign and the Defense of Canadian National Identity through Advertising." *Velvet Light Trap* (Fall 2002): 77–89.

Wamsley, Kevin B., and Michael Heine. "'Don't Mess With the Relay – It's Bad Medicine': Aboriginal Culture and the 1988 Winter Olympics." In *Olympic Perspectives: Third International Symposium for Olympic Research*, edited by Robert K. Barney, 173–8. London: International Centre for Olympic Studies, 1996.

– "Tradition, Modernity, and the Construction of Civic Identity: The Calgary Olympics." OLYMPIKA: *The International Journal of Olympic Studies* 5 (1996): 81–90.

Whitson, David. "Olympic Hosting in Canada: Promotional Ambitions, Political Changes." OLYMPIKA: *The International Journal of Olympic Studies* 14 (2005): 29–46.

Wolfe, Patrick. "Settler Colonialism and the Elimination of the Native." *Journal of Genocide Research* 8, no. 4 (2006): 387–409.

Wong, Vicki, and Michael Murphy. *Miga, Quatchi and/et Sumi: The Story of the Vancouver 2010 Mascots/L'Histoire des Mascottes de Vancouver*. Vancouver: Whitecap Books, 2008.

Wood, David G. *The Lougheed Legacy*. Toronto: Key Porter Books, 1985.

Woolford, Andrew. "Negotiating Affirmative Repair: Symbolic Violence in the British Columbia Treaty Process." *Canadian Journal of Sociology/ Cahiers canadiens de sociologie* 29, no. 1 (2004): 111–44.

Worrall, James. *My Olympic Journey: Sixty Years with Canadian Sport and the Olympic Games*. Toronto: Canadian Olympic Association, 2000.

Wright, Jan. "Biopower, Biopedagogies and the Obesity Epidemic." In *Biopolitics and the "Obesity Epidemic": Governing Bodies*, edited by Jan Wright and Valerie Harwood, 1–14. London and New York: Routledge, 2009.

Wright, John, Gregory Millard, and Sarah Riegel. "Here's Where We Get Canadian: English-Canadian Nationalism and Popular Culture." *American Review of Canadian Studies* 32, no. 1 (2002): 11–34.

Younging, Gregory. *Elements of Indigenous Style: A Guide for Writing by and about Indigenous Peoples*. Edmonton: Brush Education, 2018.

Index

Page numbers in *italics* denote figures.

www.ingramcontent.com/pod-product-compliance
Lightning Source LLC
LaVergne TN
LVHW041403090826
845264LV00023B/241
* 9 7 8 0 2 2 8 0 1 4 1 7 1 *